# Group Counseling for the Resistant Client

# Group Counseling
# for the Resistant Client

*A Practical Guide to Group Process*

Jerry Edelwich, MSW
Archie Brodsky

**Lexington Books**
*An Imprint of Macmillan, Inc.*
New York
Maxwell Macmillan Canada
Toronto
Maxwell Macmillan International
New York   Oxford   Singapore   Sydney

For information concerning workshops and training sessions in group counseling, please contact:

Jerry Edelwich, MSW
61 Sunny Slope Dr.
Middletown, CT 06457
203-347-3836

*Library of Congress Cataloging-in-Publication Data*
Edelwich, Jerry.
    Group counseling for the resistant client : a practical guide to
group process / Jerry Edelwich, Archie Brodsky.
        p.   cm.
    Includes bibliographical references.
    ISBN 0-669-21542-2
    1. Group counseling.   I. Brodsky, Archie.   II. Title.
BF637.C6E33   1992
158'.35—dc20                                                    91-19821
                                                                    CIP

Lexington Books
An Imprint of Macmillan, Inc.
866 Third Avenue, New York, N.Y. 10022

Maxwell Macmillan Canada, Inc.
1200 Eglinton Avenue East
Suite 200
Don Mills, Ontario M3C 3N1

Macmillan, Inc. is part of the Maxwell Communication
Group of Companies.

Printed in the United States of America

printing number
1   2   3   4   5   6   7   8   9   10

# Contents

# Acknowledgments

Whatever success we have had in realizing the potential of this book we owe in great measure to the constant support of three loyal colleagues: David Powell of ETP, Inc., Windsor, Connecticut; Kathy Jayne; and John Woods. We also wish to acknowledge the vital assistance of Ernest Bayer, Jr., Jordan Burrill, Donald Coombs, Mark Fonda, Joe Kelley, Kathleen Lomatoski, Maria Morales, Leslie Rupp, and Alfred F. Sancho. Finally, we feel a special debt of gratitude to two early mentors in group work, Al Alissi and Robert Green, and to our editor, Margaret Zusky, for the confidence she has shown in our unconventional approach to the subject.

# Introduction

The practice of counseling and therapy is undergoing revolutionary change as a result of the pressure of social and economic developments. One-to-one, long-term insight therapy in private office practice is becoming a luxury available to fewer people. Moreover, its effectiveness is no longer taken for granted. In a society preoccupied with cost-effectiveness and demonstrable results, psychological counseling is taking place increasingly in groups. Simultaneously, there is a growing emphasis on populations whose needs are as urgent as they are straightforward: substance abusers, people who have run afoul of the law, people who feel victimized or disempowered, people inadequately equipped with basic living skills. It is evident that society cannot afford to provide individual therapy for all these individuals, nor is individual therapy necessarily the best modality to meet their needs. Indeed, the content and process of group counseling are evolving in response to the challenge of rehabilitating the many individuals referred by the courts and employee assistance programs (EAPs). For these individuals, as a rule, short-term, practical counseling is called for.

Unfortunately, neither training programs for counselors nor the literature in the field has kept up with the demand for more effective, economical remediation of common social deviances such as driving while intoxicated and spouse or child abuse. In many programs, instructors and students must make do with one of the two excellent texts—Yalom (1985) and Corey and Corey (1987)—that dominate the field of in-depth group psychotherapy. Although these books serve their intended purpose admirably, a different approach is required for the growing proportion of group practice that deals with criminal misconduct, drug and alcohol abuse, disruptive family or employment problems, victimization, interpersonal relationships and codependency, and physical or mental disability. For training in this type of group work, the Yalom and Corey and Corey texts represent a kind of theoretical overload, bringing to bear detailed psychodynamic analysis that exceeds both the needs of the typical client and the interests and capabilities of the typical counselor. The fact that texts such as these continue to be used to train group counselors attests to the lack of a suitable text specifically addressed to group counseling in problem-solving and decision-making skills. This book is designed to remedy that deficiency.

As anyone who works regularly in this field must be aware, the training of group leaders is uneven and unsystematic, ranging from little or no training at all to the irrelevant psychodynamic background just described. This haphazard exposure is then reflected, damagingly, in the experience of group members. Groups today are a grab bag of ambitious psychoanalyzing, thinly disguised individual therapy, "touchy-feely" self-expression, endless ventilation and acting out, nasty confrontation, didactic education, rap sessions, and/or simply passing the time. This drift, however, is by no means inevitable. Based on the senior author's two decades of experience as a group leader, clinical supervisor, college-level faculty member, staff trainer, curriculum planner, and agency consultant, we have found a reliably effective way of leading groups with the aim of empowering members to take effective control of their lives. Far from being an expedient substitute for individual psychotherapy, this group process has its own logic and its own dynamics. Moreover, it is better suited to the clientele in question than individual therapy because the group setting allows for the modeling of responsibility and social skills needed to function outside the group.

*Group counseling,* as taught in this book, differs from both *group psychotherapy* and *group education* in that it is action and task oriented. As distinct from group psychotherapy, it emphasizes problem solving and decision making rather than insight per se. Its focus is not on the past, but on the present and immediate future. Its goal is not a thorough resolution of prior traumas and inner conflicts, but (as necessary) a pragmatic resolution that allows the individual to go on with his or her life. As distinct from substantive education in a group setting, group counseling has as its primary objectives behavior change and skill acquisition, not content learning. In keeping with these objectives, its form is experiential, not didactic. Group counseling is interactive, with an adherence to group process that is, in its less highly elaborate way, as rigorous as that of group psychotherapy.

In the chapters that follow, the approach outlined here is distilled into practical guidelines for use in the practice of group counseling in a wide range of settings (from groups for drunk-driving offenders to "people who love too much" groups) as well as in counselor education, supervision, and administration. For some group leaders and students, this book will supplement and reinforce relevant aspects of their training and apprenticeship. For others, it will constitute virtually the only guidance they receive. In either case, the group leader who learns to tap fully the rehabilitative potential of group process can expect to achieve a higher level of professionalism and improved effectiveness on behalf of group members.

But what type of group member and leader can benefit most from this approach? Let us sketch the typical situation that calls for process-oriented group counseling.

## Who Is the Group Member?

In the contemporary counseling environment for which this book is written, group members are assumed to have acted so as not to meet their needs in an acceptable and appropriate manner. Heterogeneous in age, gender, and background (racial, ethnic, and educational), they have one thing in common: they have not taken effective control of their lives. Indeed, they may not have learned how to do so, and they may feel themselves to be unable to do so. Drug abuse, violence, romantic or marital conflicts, educational or career problems, and a lack of personal fulfillment reflect self-defeating strategies for getting along in life. Such maladaptive coping styles are associated with an unproductive way of living. Instead of a person's taking control of events, things happen to the person. Issues come up, crises arise, but nothing is resolved, and the person drifts from one external happening to the next. What the person brings to the group is disorganization and instability; what the group should impart is organization and stability.

To do this, the group process must actively challenge the very habits and dynamics that have brought the person to the group. More often than not, the group member is present involuntarily, unmotivated, hostile, coerced, and resistant to intervention. Given this mind-set, the group member is likely to continue in group the same ineffective, disruptive patterns of behavior that got him or her into trouble on the outside. These patterns are likely to involve some form of manipulation or "gaming," such as domination, provocation, attention seeking, seduction, or flight.

Far from seeing the group as a positive opportunity to reorient their lives, members typically do not want to be in the group at all. Brought to the group by a court mandate or EAP referral, they are coerced clients for whom attendance at group is a lesser evil than prison, job loss, or other external sanctions. They are not there to change dysfunctional life-styles; they are there to stay out of trouble by meeting the minimum requirements imposed on them. They may perceive themselves as victims of abuse or injustice, have no idea of what the group is intended to accomplish, and feel no identification or involvement with the group. Under these circumstances, they can be expected to be unmotivated and resistant. They may treat the group as a playground where they can do whatever they please. When they are not actively hostile, their involvement often is limited to providing a "warm body" and having their attendance documented. They will disclose enough to appear to be cooperating with the group leader but not enough to appear deviant to their peers.

It is the leader's job to provide an atmosphere in which these resistant individuals can be motivated to involve themselves more positively in life issues. By using group process creatively, the leader can help members break through their own resistance and reach a more open, questioning posture. Underneath the group member's belligerent or withdrawn posture is a person who is fundamentally uncertain about how to proceed. "What's the game? What are the rules? How do I play?" they want to ask. The group experience, reinforced by problem-solving efforts outside the group, can begin to answer those questions.

## Who Is the Group Leader?

Group leaders who enter into this treacherous terrain generally do not have professional degrees or a background in psychodynamic theory. More to the point, unless they have a master's degree in group work (and perhaps even then), they have had no professional exposure to group process. They may be agency staff members who run groups in conjunction with other duties, or they may be recovering alcoholics or addicts who have made the transition from client to counselor with little or no professional training (Edelwich and Brodsky 1980; Peele 1989). They may have a bachelor's or master's degree in an unrelated field (such as alcoholism counseling), and they may have good interpersonal skills. Such experiences and credentials, while contributing to general counseling skills, do not substitute for training in group process.

Too often untrained group leaders find themselves unarmed in a lion's den of resistance and hostility. Standard group therapy training simply does not prepare counselors for the harassment and manipulation they face. It is like going to war without ammunition. Inadequately prepared leaders face numerous pitfalls and make understandable, but costly, errors. They may be too directive, not directive enough, or both. They may be too self-disclosing to maintain respect and discipline or insufficiently self-disclosing to model constructive behavior and resolution of issues. They may talk to each member in turn (in effect, performing individual therapy) instead of involving group members in interchange and feedback. They may lecture to a passive, uninvolved audience. They may allow themselves or the group to be dominated by an articulate, aggressive member. They may unwittingly abuse group members or expose them to abuse from other members. They may make blaming or exculpatory statements rather than let value judgments emerge from the person's own experience. They may elicit expressions of feeling on cue, as a kind of performance.

When the untrained counselor meets a group of resistant members, the following scenario often can be observed at the first session: Half a dozen people sit sullenly in a circle, nursing their grievances, thinking about how they would rather not be in that room at all. The uncomfortable silence is broken only by the sound of shuffling feet and the leader's ineffectual attempts to induce people to talk about how they are feeling, which serve only to put successive individuals on the spot and drive them further into their alienation. A member who tests limits (by lighting a cigarette, for example) is scolded by the leader. The group drifts into acrimonious bickering.

This atmosphere testifies to a lack of climate setting on the part of the group leader. If the leader does not establish or reestablish focus, responsibility, and discipline, the negative climate observed at the group's first meeting will persist right through to the last. Members will have missed the opportunity to benefit from the group. Indeed, they will leave the group as cynical as they came, and the leader will have taken another step toward job burnout (Edelwich and Brodsky 1980).

Fortunately, this outcome is by no means inevitable. We have written this book to give group leaders (whatever their prior training or lack of it) a road map for this unfamiliar terrain. Our aim is to provide a practical understanding of group dynamics and group leadership, together with a language with which to address a difficult clientele. Of course, one cannot learn the requisite skills and master the delicate process of leading groups simply by reading a book. It takes time and experience (preferably supervised experience) to learn to anticipate patterns of interaction as they arise and to develop the necessary sensitivity, speed, and appropriateness of response. A book can, however, supply concept and structure, precept and example—a workable, hands-on approach to the many challenges of group work.

## Range of Applications

Process-oriented group counseling, while ideally suited to engage members whose attendance is compelled by external sanctions, is not limited in its usefulness to that type of milieu. On the contrary, the skills and techniques taught in the chapters that follow are applicable to a variety of group settings in which people struggle to take effective control of their lives. These include public and private agencies with the following functions and missions:

- Inpatient and outpatient care (intermediate care and aftercare) for drug and alcohol abusers
- Residential treatment centers
- Therapeutic communities
- Halfway houses

- Counseling programs in the armed services
- Group homes for displaced adolescents, the mentally retarded, and the mentally ill
- Groups for young people, including deviance prevention and Outward Bound groups
- Treatment of sex offenders
- Support groups for victims of physical or emotional abuse
- Groups dealing with intimate relationships and experiences of separation, loss, and grief, such as marriage and divorce groups or groups for "people who love too much"
- Codependency groups
- Support groups for the elderly or disabled in convalescent homes and skilled nursing facilities
- Hospital-based or community-based support groups for people with chronic illness

These applications represent an enormous and largely unfulfilled potential for the use of relatively straightforward, cost-effective techniques to help people achieve a higher level of functioning and greater independence and fulfillment. This potential has been least explored in the medical realm, where group process can be of vital benefit to people facing the physical and emotional constraints attendant upon diabetes, cardiac conditions, cancer, multiple sclerosis, Alzheimer's disease, acquired immunodeficiency syndrome (AIDS), and other chronic illnesses. For example, a close look at the emotional, problem-solving, and decision-making concomitants of one of these conditions, diabetes, reveals a complex interweaving of medical realities with issues of violation, autonomy, and life competence (Edelwich and Brodsky 1986).

How can a process developed with involuntary group members in mind be used with voluntary members as well? Let us take the recent phenomenon of groups for love and sex addicts (Peele and Brodsky 1976; The Augustine Fellowship 1986; Carnes 1986), "women who love too much" (Norwood 1985), and codependents (Beattie 1987). Unlike the drunk driver, illicit-drug user, or spouse or child abuser, the typical member of these groups is willing and eager to participate, if for no other reason than to meet people, gain attention, and ventilate. Like the coerced group member, however, this eager participant comes from a perspective of victimization and derives status and power from the role of victim. This underlying commonality matters more than the differences between the two types of groups. Whereas the coerced group member may not acknowledge the existence of any problem or source of discontent—except that of having to be in the group—the uncoerced member may be no more disposed to look at the true nature of the acknowledged problem. Thus, although people come to marriage and divorce groups voluntarily, the group leader cannot assume that they want to change their behavior and improve their lives. When the focus shifts (if it ever does) from ventilation to confrontation of issues, when the mirror is held up and the risks are considered, members may become resistant and act as though they were being coerced. "They [the group] don't understand me either," they may complain.

In fact, the danger of purposeless ventilation and stagnation may be greater in the kinds of groups with no external sanctions and no pressure from authoritative agencies for members to show progress. A participant-observer in a group for "women who love too much" had this reaction:

> The more I think about my group, the sadder and angrier the "therapy" it offers makes me. I see a lot of women here who have real problems they need to conquer. But the group seems to suppress any kind of emotion; instead, it offers up propaganda and a hollow spirit. The women seem to no longer think of themselves as Jane, a pianist, or Tess, a student, but as Jane, a Woman Who Loves Too Much, and Tess, a Woman Who Loves Too Much. They wear the term "love addict" like a tag. And that is sad.
>
> I don't know whether or not these women are truly love addicts. But I know that it's unlikely any of them could ever be remotely changed—not to mention cured—by the experience of being here. And yet they are addicted to this group, or to the idea of needing it; that much seems painfully clear. And that, I feel, is really Too Much. (Schappell 1989, 253)

Self-help and mutual-support groups on the Alcoholics Anonymous (AA) or codependency model are by definition leaderless groups, and both their advantages and disadvantages stem from their having that character. With the rapid growth in the number of groups concerned with love, marriage, separation and divorce, interpersonal addiction, and codependency, however, many of these groups do in fact have leaders, and these individuals typically are unfamiliar with group process. For members who seriously want to benefit from such groups (as with any other groups), the identification, clarification, and resolution of issues is essential. This process requires trained leadership capable of guiding members to take responsibility for bringing about movement in their lives.

## The Content and Organization of This Book

The new perspective we offer group leaders, as well as their teachers and supervisors, is characterized by a systematic reliance on group process. We challenge time-honored bromides such as "Awareness is curative," "Ventilation of emotion is of value in itself," and "Even without participating actively, a person still gets something out of the group." In their place, we assert the following principles:

- Properly run groups are the most economical and productive vehicles for resolving a wide range of human problems.
- The group is a microcosm of the outside world. Group interactions mirror the problems members have in their lives and model solutions for them.
- Virtually everything that comes up in group is to be dealt with through group process, which structures the interactions, keeps the group on track, and serves as a primary support for both leader and members. If the leader ensures that the group stays true to the process, the content will largely take care of itself.
- People learn not what they are told to do, but what is modeled for them by people they respect and what they are reinforced for doing in a setting that matters to them.
- The most important things that happen in group are the things members do outside the group to implement what they learn.

These principles are the basis of the guidelines and illustrative vignettes presented in the chapters that follow.

The first four chapters outline the preparatory steps that set the stage for a productive group. Chapter 1 distinguishes group counseling from other types of groups (psychotherapy groups, program groups, self-help groups, and so on) and defines its distinctive features. It specifies logistical requirements for group counseling and discusses the role and responsibilities of the group leader. Chapter 2 covers the screening and preparation of individual members for the group, including a briefing on group norms. Chapter 3 details the all-important work of climate setting at the beginning of the group (and when needed thereafter), at which the groundwork is laid and the tone set for a successful group. Chapter 4 shows how climate setting is carried out when the group is beginning to raise issues and initial resistance must be overcome. It is here that group process is set in motion.

The next four chapters present the core of group process. Chapter 5 takes the group leader or trainee through the steps involved in identifying and clarifying issues. Chapter 6 continues with confronting and evaluating issues, including modeling appropriate confrontation and overcoming members' resistance to confronting and being confronted. These steps lead to a value judgment on the part of the individual member. Chapter 7 lists, illustrates, and shows how to block various problem behaviors in group (for example, nonparticipation, avoidance of issues, monopolizing, intimidation, scapegoating, red-crossing, seduction, and personal attacks). Chapter 8 continues the process after the value judgment has been made, as the member receives feedback, reviews and consolidates learning, and makes a plan of action and a commitment to act.

The last two chapters address other issues to be considered in completing a successful group. Chapter 9 recommends coleadership as an enhancement of and a check on group process, indicates how the two leaders can most effectively divide their roles, and lists several modes of supervisory observation. Chapter 10 outlines termination procedures and postgroup follow-up, with an emphasis on the implementation of learning outside the group.

In a well-functioning group, the leader models responsibility so that members can take responsibility for themselves and for the group. By assuming collective as well as individual responsibility, members learn to work with one another while making sure that their own needs are met. Group process, enriched by reality therapy (Glasser 1965) and rational-emotive therapy (Ellis and Harper 1975), supports the participation of both the leader(s) and the members in this sensitive enterprise by providing paths out of stagnant, hostile, and otherwise unproductive interactions. For the leader, it relieves emotional pressure by making it possible to maintain or regain control of the group at all times. Group members likewise benefit, for instead of being lectured to, patronized, scapegoated, or put on the spot, they are treated with a respect that fosters their confrontation of difficult issues. If members can learn through group process to express themselves freely and clearly, and if they can take that skill into the larger world, they will be significantly empowered. The group is a living experience, and if the leader maintains the integrity of the process, members will have a model for bringing integrity to their lives.

# Group Counseling for the Resistant Client

# 1

# Group Counseling: Distinctive Purposes and Procedures

I n common usage, terms such as *group, group therapy,* and *group work* have such loose and variable meanings—encompassing everything from rigorous psychotherapy to twelve-step groups to rap sessions—that we must make clear precisely what we mean by *group counseling.* In this chapter, we define process-oriented group counseling both directly and in contrast with other forms of group work. We then discuss the roles, responsibilities, and essential qualities of the group leader in process-oriented group counseling.

## Categories of Groups

Both within and outside an agency, a person may attend groups of various kinds. Listing and briefly differentiating among them serves two purposes. First, it helps define by contrast what process-oriented group counseling is. Therapy, education, and program groups do things that process groups do not; likewise, process groups provide benefits that the others do not. Second, group leaders and agency administrators should know about the range of resources that can be made available to clients, who may need different types of groups under different circumstances. In this way, appropriate placements and referrals can be made, and group assignments within an organization can be properly coordinated. In a human services agency, the term *group* may refer to any of the following categories.

### Group Psychotherapy

Group psychotherapy (Corey and Corey 1987; Yalom 1985) differs from group counseling in several important respects. It places more emphasis on awareness and less on action. It elicits very specific, personal self-revelations aimed at relating an individual's present emotional conflicts to past experiences. It relies on intricate interpretations of transference and countertransference in the group setting. For these reasons, group psychotherapy

1

requires a degree of commitment that only voluntary, outwardly self-motivated clients are likely to make. Notwithstanding the mixed feelings people may have about being in a therapy group and the fact that resistance is a staple of group as well as individual psychotherapy, this level of resistance is of a different, subtler nature than that found in groups with mandated attendance. Group counseling is especially suited to the latter groups (as well as to any groups primarily concerned with practical results) because it bypasses the unfinished business from the past that psychotherapy groups thoroughly explore. In group counseling, members are supported in putting the past in perspective so that they can progress in their lives.

### Self-Help Support Groups

These groups, which began with AA and now include a vast array of groups addressing numerous emotional and personal issues, are voluntary, egalitarian fellowships without professional leadership. As such, they should be viewed not as a part of formal treatment, but as an often valuable adjunct to treatment that individuals may choose or reject at their own discretion. Being voluntary, support groups based on the twelve-step model are free to take on a religious, inspirational character that would be out of place in a professional treatment group. Similarly, they fulfill members' needs for acceptance, companionship, social affiliation, and self-definition, which are not primary purposes of group counseling. At the same time, they lack the disciplined focus on process that a skilled leader can maintain. They also do not have the same concern with problem solving and decision making outside the group. Group members commonly attend meetings of AA or similar groups while they are enrolled in group counseling, but both the group member and the group leader should be careful not to confuse the two.

### Education Groups

The purpose of education groups is to impart information to members on subjects such as substance abuse, impulse control, and interpersonal relationships. This is a legitimate function of groups, albeit a very different one from group counseling. Process-oriented groups are not for everyone at all times. Exposing a person to group process and to the demands of problem solving and decision making without adequate preparation may set the person up for failure. An agency should have the flexibility to meet the needs of all its clients. Thus, an agency that has clients with different informational or developmental needs may offer different kinds of groups, with members attending more than one group at a time or graduating from one type of group to another.

When an education group is called for, it should be structured so as to involve members actively in learning. Films are not the best medium for this purpose because they lend themselves to passivity and time killing. When films are used, they should be chosen for content relevant to members' ethnic, generational, socioeconomic, and educational backgrounds. Films should not be too long and should be shown in a context of group participation. For example, a film might be followed by a discussion based on questions given to the group prior to the showing of the film. Such a discussion gives members an opportunity to make "I" statements that relate the film to what is going on in their lives. It is useful to divide members into subgroups for discussion and processing, as well as to give members homework assignments based on the film. These measures make the film showings more than passive entertainment and facilitate the assumption of personal responsibility by members.

Instead of using canned films, the leader might script vignettes relevant to group members and videotape them. Members might contribute to their own education by presenting cases to their peers—a sharing of responsibility that might help members prepare for process groups. Whatever the mode of instruction, the facilitator should thoroughly research and prepare the topic, specifying the learning objectives for each participant. Learning objectives must be specific and measurable—for example, "to be able to identify . . ." rather than simply "to know. . . ."

The more member participation and interchange are incorporated into the education group, the more closely the group approximates the principles of group process. Not only does this make for more effective learning, but it also puts members in a frame of mind to accept the greater degree of responsibility demanded of them by the process group.

*Program Groups*

Program groups overlap considerably in form and procedure with education groups. In both, the leader comes prepared with an agenda that is presented to the group (as distinct from process groups, which generate a process by group interaction). Active participation is voluntary, and members' privacy is respected. In some agencies, the term *program* is used to mean any group that has these characteristics (that is, is leader- and agenda-driven rather than process-driven), including education groups. In other agencies, it refers more specifically to exercises or procedural learning, not substantive education, that the group undertakes at the leader's direction. This may include familiarization with the agency and its norms, value-clarification exercises, assertiveness training, and even didactic instruction in group process. As a rule, running a program group (where knowledge and authority are assumed to reside in the leader) is a more routine, less stressful task for the group leader than running a process group. Nonetheless, as with education groups, members are likely to benefit more if the program is tailored to the particular group rather than prepackaged—for example, if the leader and group members make up exercises of their own. Again, the leader is responsible for involving members in an elementary version of group process, which is a higher state of functioning to which other groups aspire.

How long a client remains in a program group depends on the length of treatment. The client may participate simultaneously in program and process groups and remain clear about the distinction between the two, provided that this distinction is clear to the leader or leaders as well. Alternatively, an individual or an entire group may progress from program to process. A program group may evolve into a process group if that intention is clearly stated. Even in the most advanced process groups, the leader should retain the prerogative of dictating a reversion to program if the situation warrants. This must be an exception, however, not the norm.

### Rap, Discussion, Community, and Administrative Groups

Groups primarily concerned with social facilitation, ventilation, and living and working arrangements within an agency have little need for the complexities of group process. An exposure to group process may, of course, enable members to express themselves and resolve conflicts more effectively in these groups. Nonetheless, it is inappropriate to introduce group process deliberately into groups whose purpose is, say, to allocate chores among agency residents. This type of group, like those mentioned previously, is not the type with which we are concerned in this book.

### Group Counseling

Group counseling, the modality with which this book is exclusively concerned, has the following distinctive characteristics:

- Its primary purpose is to model, and thereby to empower members to learn, problem-solving and decision-making skills.
- It is task oriented, with an emphasis on what members do outside the group.
- It achieves its objectives by means of a nondidactic, nondirective, but nonetheless disciplined group process.
- The leader's responsibilities are neither to direct the group nor to dispense insight and interpretation, but to facilitate, guide, and monitor group process and to reinforce constructive behavior.
- Group members are collectively responsible for running the group and individually responsible for generating insight and implementing the gains made in group.

Group counseling starts from the assumption that telling people what they *should* do is neither an optimal use of the group setting nor an effective way to influence behavior. Most group members have been told again and again what is good for them, but they have not seen the advice enacted in an atmosphere of mutual responsibility and constructive interchange—an atmosphere they help to create and from which they benefit.

To remedy this deficiency, group counseling offers a structured experience designed to empower group members to take effective control of their lives. It is an economical but powerful technique, very different from individual therapy but equally well suited to its purpose. Group interactions, skillfully facilitated to provide a safe, structured space for learning, both *mirror* the conflicts that have interfered with a person's exercising responsibility in a social environment and *model* what it means to take responsibility for one's statements, intentions, and actions. The group enables members to experience the link between actions and consequences, prompts members to make and implement value judgments, and demonstrates useful living skills that members can take out into the larger world. In this corrective microcosm of life, people whose previous experiences have taught them that irresponsibility is rewarding have a chance to experience more satisfying rewards.

## Characteristics of Counseling Groups

Group counseling proceeds most effectively in groups that have certain structural and procedural characteristics. Allowing for variations in organizational policy and resources, group leaders and administrators should keep the following benchmarks in mind.

### Open-Ended versus Closed-Ended Groups

An ongoing, open-ended group, in which members come and go as their needs dictate, is more clearly a microcosm of life than a closed-ended group with a fixed membership and duration. In an open-ended group, each member steps into the flow of the group experience, meets people, sees some members leave and new members appear, and eventually steps out of the cycle. Such fluid membership tends to restrain in-group dependencies and unrealistic expectations of linear developmental progress.

Nonetheless, the differences between open- and closed-ended groups should not be overstated. Even in a closed-ended group, where the same individuals meet for the duration, individuals are at different stages of development, with different resources, skills, and agendas. It is difficult, therefore, to trace a clear developmental sequence from the beginning of a group to the end, although the intention is to give all members a chance to air their issues and develop essential skills. At any stage of the group, as in families and other real-life groupings, some members initiate bursts of energy, while others feed off that energy. Even near the end, members may act out—for example, by attacking the leader's credibility. Thus, the leader cannot expect either an open-ended or a closed-ended group to conform to a scripted life cycle.

## Size of Group

Optimally, a counseling group should contain no more than eight members. With nine or ten, the group leader (or, preferably, leaders) must be especially vigilant to keep everyone involved. With more than ten, long experience has shown the futility of attempting to maintain group process. Typically, those with the greatest need for counseling will "hide out" while more assertive members fight for dominance. That is why trained clinicians have been known to say, "With more than ten, it isn't a group; it's a crowd."

Occasionally, hard-pressed agency administrators will assign, say, a dozen people to a group and ask the leader to do process-oriented counseling. The leader, knowing that such a request is equivalent to calling the spirits from the deep, will seek relief from the agency. If the agency's limited resources or priorities rule out a reduction in the size of the group, a strategic retreat on the leader's part is advisable. Instead of group process, a program group is in order. Discussion, education, basic skill training, exercises (for example, value clarification), and assessment of members' progress outside the group can be carried out in a larger group.

## Duration of Sessions

As a rule, a group session lasts from one and a half to two hours. In that time, as many as three people may have a chance to air their concerns. However, the questions that members bring up about their lives are to be conceived of not as one person's issues, but as group issues. Instead of putting each individual in the spotlight, the group process is meant to encourage identification, a recognition of the universal applicability of basic life issues.

## Logistical Norms

A group can function effectively only in an atmosphere of discipline and respect for the purposes of the group. To facilitate concentration and serious application on the part of members, as well as to model the requisite accommodation to a variety of norms in real-life settings, certain behavioral constraints are called for. These norms give the group a coherent structure in which learning can take place. They are discussed specifically in chapter 2 in the context of preparation of prospective members for the group.

### Task Orientation versus Emotive Orientation

Task orientation has been identified previously as a defining attribute of group counseling. This does not mean that the expression of emotion is out of place in group. The group does acknowledge and validate personal feelings but does not dwell on them. Within limits, it respects and safely accommodates a member's need for emotional catharsis, but not to the detriment of the group and its primary purposes. Instead, it encourages the member to move from ventilation to problem solving and decision making. Once a person takes effective control of his or her life, unresolved emotional issues tend to be put in perspective. If such issues remain troubling, the member may be referred for individual therapy, but only at the completion of the group. (See chapter 2 for reasons why simultaneous individual therapy is not recommended.)

### Leadership Styles: Autocratic versus Democratic

Although individuals differ as to their personal leadership styles, the appropriate style for group counseling lies on a continuum between autocratic and permissive. The leader does not run the group, but also does not let the group run out of control. The leader is not there to "please the customer" but to lay the groundwork for members to have certain beneficial experiences. Maintaining group process requires constant attention and sensitive decision making on the part of the leader, with a view toward empowerment, not domination. Empowerment is facilitated sometimes by reasserting norms, limits, and structure and sometimes by allowing members to take risks. For example, a member may go on and on, making appropriate statements but with considerable embellishment. The leader, wanting to legitimize the member's concerns and allow him or her to gain recognition and validation from speaking up in group, must make a sensitive, on-the-spot judgment about whether and when to intervene.

## The Leader's Role and Responsibilities

We have said much about what a group leader does *not* do—the leader does not direct the group, does not dispense insight, and so forth. To define the leader's role in positive terms is a more difficult task, but an understanding of the leader's place in group interactions is essential to a successfully functioning group.

The leader does not preach from a pedestal of superiority. Indeed, any group member may be more attractive, brighter, better educated, more accomplished, or wealthier than the leader. There are, however, two key distinctions between the leader and the members. First, the leader has manifested the capacity to take effective control of his or her life, particularly in the group's identified areas of concern. Second, the leader is trained in group counseling and skilled in group process. The leader's status and prerogatives derive from these differences.

Members are in the group to learn to take control of their lives in a specified area in which some agency of society (in the case of coerced groups) or they themselves (in the case of voluntary groups) have decided they need remedial experience. At the outset, members will invest the leader with externally conferred authority and will act toward the leader as they have toward other authorities—that is, by paying deference, by challenging or resisting authority, or by exhibiting a passive-aggressive form of outward compliance. The member's survival instinct is to say or do anything to please the leader. The leader can use this motivation, however artificial, to good effect by assigning tasks to be performed between sessions, encouraging members to make plans and keep a log, and so forth.

In the course of the group experience, the leader has the opportunity to form a deeper relationship with at least some members, who will then operate on a firmer motivational grounding. As the leader's personal and professional qualities are manifested, as trust develops, and as the benefits of the group are made clear, some members will develop a true respect for the leader and a genuine motivation to change. The leader's authority will then derive not from his or her institutional position and status, but from personal credibility and even (with some leaders) charisma. In this way, a skilled leader can work with people who have come to the group under duress, involve them in the group, and keep them involved. At first it is the probation officer who ensures their presence; later it is the integrity and compelling value of the group experience.

To accomplish this transition, the leader must approach the task deliberately and seriously, with a consciousness of process and a professional mind-set. As noted in the introduction to this book, the requisite awareness and attitude on the part of the group leader cannot be taken for granted. The novice leader, terrified by the prospect of confronting resistant group members, tends to share the coerced member's primary motivation, which is to come out of the experience unscathed. Toward this end, the leader secures the superficial cooperation of group members by "pleasing the customer"—that is, by refraining from challenge or confrontation. As a result, the integrity of the group is compromised (however unwittingly), and members derive little benefit. Similarly, leaders who are not securely focused on the process may act out their personal reactions to group members, favoring some over others on the basis of feelings of attraction or repulsion.

They may find themselves lecturing, arguing, approving or disapproving—in other words, being drawn into the content of the issues presented or the personal dynamics between members. In the professional approach to group counseling we present here, the leader is responsible for going beyond these personal reactions and relating to the group according to the principles of group process.

To be a professional is to possess and use the tools of the profession. These are described and modeled throughout this book. In summary, the group counselor is responsible for meeting the following professional standards:

*To keep one's own needs separate from the group's needs.* Whatever the leader does in group should be for the good of the group. The leader speaks or refrains from speaking, intervenes or refrains from intervening, when (in the leader's judgment) members of the group will benefit or the group process will be enhanced—not when it is gratifying for the leader to do so. People in the helping professions are responsible for meeting their personal needs outside the job; otherwise, they may inadvertently use the job situation to meet those needs—for example, for sexual, financial, or egoaggrandizement (Edelwich and Brodsky 1980, 1991). A leader who acts out a need for dominance, attention, approval, or self-display will only reinforce similar behavior in group members. An example of this negative modeling is the leader who implicitly communicates to the group, "Look at me. I'm the great leader who got so-and-so to talk!"

However strong the leader's wish to be liked and appreciated, the leader has a professional responsibility to endure awkward silences, to be unaffected by flattery and implicit bribes or threats, and to risk opposition and disapproval. A leader can derive a legitimate feeling of satisfaction from group work—the satisfaction of doing a job professionally and well, as well as of making beneficial contact with at least some individuals. Other needs must be met outside the group, with the help, if necessary, of the resources identified in the next section.

*To deal evenhandedly with group members regardless of one's feelings of attraction or repulsion toward them or any bias or personal sensitivity toward particular issues or behaviors.* It is natural for the untrained or unreflective group leader (like the helping professional working in any capacity) to favor attractive members or to be influenced by seductive behavior. Likewise, it is easy to screen out people one does not like or to treat them punitively or with benign neglect. Such rejection may be a reaction to the group member's appearance, manner, hostile presentation, or cultural or ideological affiliations or to the type of behavior that brought the person into the group. For example, in a multifamily group, the leader may be biased against a father who has molested his children. Nonetheless, the leader who aspires to work at a professional level can and must set these reactions aside.

We have written extensively elsewhere about the dynamics of attraction, seduction, and repulsion between clinicians and clients (Edelwich and Brodsky 1991). It is normal and inevitable that a group leader will have personal feelings about group members, sometimes including sexual attraction. Such feelings must be acknowledged and validated, but not acted upon. The same is true for feelings of disapproval, distaste, and dislike. Unconditional positive regard is a desired characteristic of the professional interaction, not of one's personal feelings. One may not like Nazis or child molesters, but one can work with them as with anyone else. Group members may not know that they are capable of choice and control; that is what they are there to learn. The leader, however, is there to model the exercise of choice and control.

Any problems the leader may have in meeting this expectation are to be dealt with outside the group. Group leaders who do not feel securely in possession of their professional tools in this respect may benefit from the analysis, case illustrations, and practical guidelines in Edelwich and Brodsky (1991). As indicated below, the appropriate forums for working through disruptive emotional reactions to group members are supervision, peer support, and professional consultation. Within the group, as discussed in chapter 9, coleadership provides a valuable mechanism for checking unintentional favoritism.

*To prepare members adequately for group participation.* One aspect of preparation is careful consideration of what approaches are best for a particular group. For example, is the group ready for group process right away? Is any educational or program component called for? Another aspect, outlined in chapter 2, is briefing members individually so that they can get the most out of the group. For new members, the group is an unknown—at best inconvenient, at worst menacing. The leader, drawing on skills and experience that the member does not share, opens a window into this uncertain prospect by articulating norms, setting limits, acknowledging and dealing with fears, and specifying the degree of safety that can reasonably be offered. This preparation sets the stage for constructive participation.

*To establish a climate of acceptance, caring, reasonable safety, mutual respect, and serious application.* Ultimately, it is the group as a whole that creates the group experience and the value to be derived from it. If left to themselves, however, group members are likely to create a contentious, unproductive atmosphere that mirrors the circumstances of their lives to date. The leader's role in setting and maintaining a climate favorable to a productive group process (as detailed in chapter 3) is vital to the success of the group.

*To model positive life skills, adaptive strategies, and ways of relating to people.* The group experience teaches not by exhortation, but by the modeling of behavior that enables people to meet their needs appropriately. Little that the leader does is more important than demonstrating—without calling attention to—how a person self-actualizes and gets along with others. Throughout the group interactions, an effective leader models a number of essential qualities. These are listed here without discussion because they are illustrated throughout the book, both in the expository text and in group vignettes.

- Responsibility and preparedness
- Observance of group norms (for example, punctuality)
- Self-actualization and mastery of life skills
- Trust and trustworthiness
- Respect and concern for others
- Ownership of feelings
- Risk-taking self-disclosure
- Positive energy
- Assertiveness without domination
- Communication skills
  1. To be able to express oneself clearly and get one's points across
  2. To be able to listen to others with interest and understanding
- Ability to give and receive feedback
- Gentle confrontation
- Sensitivity
- Awareness of one's own and others' limitations

Seen as God-given personal qualities, these traits are not possessed in equal measure by all individuals. Seen as professional skills, however, they can be taught and learned. As Wolf (1974–75) makes clear in his discussion of the interpersonal skills of effective counselors, one cannot be trained to be warm, empathic, concrete, immediate, or potent, but one can be trained to project these qualities in a professional context.

In some cases, this learning takes considerable time and experience. Developing the needed qualities should be understood as a process, not an all-or-nothing proposition. We are always growing, developing our communication skills, assertiveness, and ability to provide feedback and confront others. Even an otherwise sensitive person may find it a challenge to manifest the kind of sensitivity demanded in group counseling—namely, an ability to discern and react quickly to the defense mechanisms of individual members as well as the dynamics between members. It is difficult to walk into a roomful of strangers and pick up the currents of their interactions. It takes more than instinct; one must work at it and build up an empirical base for interpreting future situations. Thus, a novice leader need not be discouraged if the group environment seems at first overwhelming.

*To keep the group true to process.* Together with climate setting and modeling, this is the most important thing the leader does. It is active, demanding work, all the more so because there is no script. The leader acts as an honest broker, making sure members talk to rather than at each other; intervening if the group does not stay focused; facilitating feedback between members; blocking problem behaviors; and opening paths for the identification, clarification, and resolution of issues. Group members can be expected to raise issues (and nonissues) in irrelevant, distracting, provocative, and hostile ways. At any moment, the group may go off on an unproductive tangent. At least initially (and as needed thereafter), the leader's job is to make statements that bring the issues back to the group process. This, too, is a form of modeling. If it is done effectively, group members themselves learn to make process statements, which the leader reinforces. Members thereby learn to take responsibility for running the group. If the leader and members work together to maintain the integrity of the group process, the content of the sessions will flow naturally from the group interactions.

*Never to ask the group to do anything the leader is unwilling to do.* The integrity of the group process depends in part on the leader's open, truthful participation: owning feelings of fear, concern, or frustration; making personal statements as needed to model self-disclosure; and receiving as well as giving feedback. For example, a member (or coleader) may bring up the leader's seeming favoritism toward one member of the group. This issue, like any other, is then resolved through group process. Given that the leader's role and reason for being in the group are not the same as the group member's, the kind of self-disclosure appropriate for the leader differs somewhat from the kind appropriate for a member. (Chapter 3 provides guidelines for appropriate self-disclosure.) Nonetheless, the respect for privacy that protects the leader from involuntary self-disclosure is no more than that extended to group members.

## Resources for Group Leaders

Group counseling requires a variety of skills in which there is always room for improvement. No one can feel completely adequate in all these skills at all times. Fortunately, resources are available to bolster one's skills. This book is one such resource. As in any other profession, the group counselor is expected to keep up with the field: to read extensively, to subscribe to journals in group work, and to attend relevant workshops. Formal training programs, where available, can enhance a group leader's competence and confidence. But overconfidence is never justified. After all the reading and courses, the moment of truth comes in the application. It is similar to the difference between spring training and the regular baseball season.

For the group leader facing the many demands and uncertainties of the job, good supervision is invaluable. Even though groups often are held in the evening when immediate supervision is unavailable, the leader should make every effort to obtain adequate supervisory support from the agency. Failing that, it may be well worth the expense to pay for supervision out of pocket. An experienced group leader acting as a supervisor can observe or colead a group, review audiotapes or videotapes, or even trace and analyze the group process on paper. Further discussion of supervision can be found in chapter 9.

In the absence of an experienced supervisor, peer support may be obtained from colleagues, informal contacts, or professional support groups. When supervision is unavailable through normal channels, the group leader may wish to make cosupervision arrangements with colleagues, who take turns supervising one another.

If neither supervision nor peer support meets the group leader's needs, professional consultation is advised, particularly in cases where personal feelings threaten to spill over into the group interactions or where the stress of group work becomes a personal problem for the leader. As we have said elsewhere, "Helping professionals, whose job is to provide such services or make referrals to those who do, ought not to feel compromised if they sometimes need to avail themselves of the same services" (Edelwich and Brodsky 1991, 126–127).

An added source of support—one that should be part of every group leader's background—is to be found in the perspectives of reality therapy (Glasser 1965) and rational-emotive therapy (Ellis and Harper 1975). Group counseling lends itself to the use of these straightforward, practical therapies. Both are firm but liberating: they challenge the self-serving or self-defeating constructions people put on their experience and help people identify the real choices open to them. In group counseling, rational-emotive therapy is used to dispute irrational ideas, while reality therapy gives the group member a basis for making value judgments and taking responsibility for one's life. These two orientations underlie every phase of group process presented in the chapters that follow.

An experienced group leader once remarked, "This is the hardest work I do." He was referring not only to the resistance of coerced group members but also to the leader's being denied the authority ordinarily conferred by an agenda or lesson plan. "I'm left standing naked before the group," he explained. "All I have going for me is my wits, quickness on my feet, and my knowledge of group process." But the reliance on group process, while it takes away the usual tokens of the leader's status, gives the leader some powerful weapons in exchange. Some of these are offensive weapons, useful in dealing with group members and their issues. Others are defensive weapons, to be brought out when the leader feels vulnerable, frustrated, stymied, or under attack. With experience, a leader who is well versed in group process finds that there is no such thing as not knowing what to expect or what to do; there is always the security of bringing the issues back to the group, thereby getting the group back on track. In the end, group process is the leader's greatest resource.

# 2
# Pregroup Preparation

C limate setting begins before the group has its first session. In the leader's one-to-one preparatory meetings with prospective members, expectations are articulated, norms are established, and a tone is set for the conduct of the group. The care taken at this stage has a significant impact on whether the group will work productively and reach closure on issues.

Preparation for the group has three main dimensions: the leader's own preparation, the screening of members for the group, and the briefing of members individually about the group. In this chapter, we review the leader's responsibilities in each of these areas.

## Preparation of the Leader

As part of the leader's modeling responsibility, he or she is expected to come to the group prepared. In addition to a general background in group process, enriched by reality therapy and rational-emotive therapy, the leader is responsible for knowing as much as is necessary about the subject of the group to keep the group on focus and to identify and clarify relevant issues. For example, to lead a driving while intoxicated (DWI) group, one should be familiar with the distinctions among different types of drinking (social drinking, drinking under stress, and out-of-control drinking). In dealing with alcoholism and other addictions, it is useful to have an overview of what is generally agreed on about the nature, course, and treatment of addictions and what issues are in dispute (Hester and Miller 1989; Monti et al. 1989; Peele 1989; Peele et al. 1991). The same is true for family violence (Gelles and Straus 1988; Shupe et al. 1987). Finally, as outlined in chapter 10, a practical knowledge of local resources for postgroup referrals (for example, halfway houses, treatment centers, support groups, health clinics, social-welfare agencies, and educational institutions) is obligatory. The leader does not need to know, for example, the mechanics of sexual dysfunction counseling, but the leader should have access to appropriate refer-

15

ral paths in this and other areas. By the time the group ends, the leader may be called upon to make referrals to Parents Without Partners, the Consumer Credit Counseling Service, nutritional counseling, AIDS testing, and college extension courses.

While conversant in general terms with the issues of concern to group members, the leader does not need to know every nuance of every human problem. A variety of personal dilemmas and crises will come up in any group, and no leader can be expected to have an in-depth knowledge of them all. The group is about process, not content, and a knowledge of group process will carry the leader—and the group—a long way.

Indeed, it is more important that the leader know about the individual histories of group members than about subjects such as alcoholism or child abuse. Group process deals with the concrete and specific. Therefore, the leader should glean all available information from records and interviews so as to assist members in identifying and clarifying issues. Armed with this information, the leader can better perceive when a group member is evading the most sensitive issues in his or her life by putting up a smoke screen of nonessential concerns. The leader can gently refocus the member on areas where he or she has the greatest need to take effective control. This background knowledge also assists the leader in linking one issue with another in a person's life, as well as in linking one person's issues with another's in order to foster identification and insight (techniques described and illustrated in chapter 5).

If the leader is away from the agency or otherwise out of contact with group members' conduct and progress between sessions, it is the leader's responsibility to find out, before coming to group, whether there is any relevant new information pertaining to any member. In groups where coleadership is used (as discussed in chapter 9), the coleaders meet before group sessions to review members' progress, to attend to any unresolved interpersonal dynamics between leaders and members, to highlight unfinished issues from the previous session, and to coordinate leadership styles and divide leadership responsibilities for the next session. It is critical that the coleaders set aside this time to get together, regardless of the many pressures that might lead them to omit such a meeting.

## Screening Prospective Group Members

By meeting with and reviewing the records of the individuals enrolled in the upcoming group, the group leader evaluates their suitability for participation. The leader must distinguish between legitimate factors that may prevent an individual from participating appropriately or benefiting from the group and vague complaints that cannot be validated. In the former category are the following:

- Documented history of violence
- Evident psychosis or decompensation
- Communication barrier (lack of elementary verbal skills or inability to speak the language in which the group is conducted)
- Medication in dosages that interfere with alertness and cannot safely be reduced
- Inability (due to mental illness or retardation) to sit for the duration of a group session
- Insufficient cognitive skills (abstract thinking) to identify and clarify issues, suggesting some degree of mental retardation

If any of these disabling conditions is present, the leader should report it to the agency responsible for the conduct of the group, which (in consultation with the leader) makes a determination about the individual's suitability for group counseling. If the individual is found unsuitable, the agency initiates remedial therapy or reports the finding to the referring agency.

### The Question of Fragility

Unlike the concrete, measurable factors in the preceding list, the claim or perception that a person is too fragile to withstand the group experience is to be treated skeptically. Fragility (alleged to result from discouraging life circumstances, victimization, or emotional disturbance) is not a medical or psychiatric diagnosis. Because of its imprecision, it is too easy a label to apply or assume, and therefore it is susceptible to abuse. A person who wishes to avoid the confrontations and challenges of group work or to hold out for individual therapy may attempt to do so by giving the appearance of fragility. Moreover, a group member's assumed fragility is often a projection of the leader's lack of confidence. People who come to groups are not as vulnerable as they appear. Therefore, a leader who is frequently confronted with the issue of fragility might seek supervision or consultation to assess his or her perceptions and judgment.

Some people do come to group very vulnerable emotionally, bereft of coping mechanisms, or in a state of profound resignation or despair. The leader, assessing a prospective member's fitness to handle the range of interactions to be anticipated in group, may decide to schedule one or two preparatory counseling sessions on an individual basis before admitting the person to the group. The purpose of these sessions is to prepare the person for the group, not to substitute individual for group counseling. As a rule, it is possible to have a mandated client temporarily excused from the group, provided that the preparatory counseling is brief and does not exceed its purpose. The leader reports to the agency, "This person has a good reason not to be in group just yet. I expect the difficulty to be resolved shortly—say within two weeks." The agency can then explain the circumstances of the postponement to the referring agency. A person should not, however, be excluded from the group for an extended period for appearing to be fragile.

### Negotiating Simultaneous Medical Treatment

Group work does not occur in a vacuum, and the group leader is responsible for being aware of the context in which the group takes place. In particular, the group leader, as a treating clinician, has a legitimate interest in knowing what medical treatment a group member is receiving and, if necessary, in having some input into treatment decisions. For one thing, it defeats the purpose of the group when a member can dismiss issues by saying, "Oh, I'm talking about that with my doctor." Second, group members should be as free of mood-altering drugs (such as antidepressants and antipsychotics) as possible. A person taking psychotropic medication may be too sedated to work effectively in group. If a person is too heavily medicated to participate in the group process and respond to feedback, the leader has reason to intervene.

We recommend that (whenever possible) the group leader be in communication with the prescribing physician. Some physicians, raising the issue of confidentiality, will refuse to share this information, in effect denying the group leader the status of a treating professional with a need to know. In that case, the group leader should appeal to the agency to support the leader's request by making clear to the physician that group counseling is an integral part of treatment. Anything that impedes a person's performance in group is of concern to the leader and the agency.

If the physician does not cooperate, the group member can resolve the conflict by waiving confidentiality so as to allow the physician to share information with the group leader. Sometimes, of course, neither the physician nor the group member will cooperate. In that event, a leader who has the support of his or her agency can reply, "Doctor, it is your privilege to withhold this information, but it is our responsibility to regulate the atmosphere of the group. Unless you cooperate with us, this person is not going to be in this group with this agency at this time."

If agency administrators are captives of political or economic necessity, expediency, or an elitist medical mentality, they may not support the leader's claim to be able to work collegially with a physician. Group leaders routinely face less than optimal working conditions. If an agency accepts group members under any circumstances, without insisting that standards conducive to high-quality group work be maintained, the agency is setting the group up for failure. If members can carry into the group an unchallenged sense of being special (by virtue of having problems so serious as to require medication), they are likely to remain impervious to the beneficial effects of group process.

*No Simultaneous Individual Counseling*

In therapeutic communities, intermediate-care programs, and even outpatient programs, individual counseling or therapy is contraindicated for a person currently enrolled in group counseling. Any individual caseload involving group members is to be limited to practical social-work functions: finding an apartment, setting up job interviews, getting a driver's license, taking care of health needs (for example, medical and dental appointments or contraception), and referrals to community resources such as AA. Counseling with regard to these and other life issues should be limited to the group setting for the duration of the group.

This prohibition is commonly resisted, not only by group members but also by clinicians who have not been trained in group work. Yet it follows from the relatively simple, economical, and productive dynamics of group counseling. The effectiveness of the group depends on there being no alternative to processing issues in group. Individual therapy, by supplying such an alternative, gives the group member a ready-made pretext for resistance. A member who becomes uncomfortable with the confrontation in group need only say, "Excuse me, that's something I'm discussing with my individual therapist," or "Don't worry, I've got that handled. That's not for us in here." Why talk about an issue in group if one can save it for individual therapy? Allowing such an escape route downgrades the group experience and undermines its efficacy. *Not* allowing it drives home the point that there is no issue so sensitive that it cannot be brought up in group. Relying on the group is a well-founded expression of faith in group process.

The prospective member who requests simultaneous individual therapy is to be assured of the safety and potency of group process (examples of suitable wording are given in the next section). The leader might add:

> "Right here and now, individual therapy is a luxury you can ill afford. You have more basic things to attend to, and—trust my experience—the group is the best vehicle for doing that. When you are taking effective control of your life, when you are getting your needs met satisfactorily, then, if you think you can afford the luxury of psychotherapy, maybe we can make a referral at the completion of the group."

## Orienting the New Member: What to Expect

The typical group member comes to the initial interview fearful, suspicious, and not knowing what to expect. He or she is in a state of anomie, or normlessness, with respect to this new experience. The leader begins to reduce this uncertainty with generalized word pictures:

"We're going to sit in chairs in a circle and talk about ourselves, about here-and-now issues we face. You'll be talking to and about others, and others will talk to and about you. One of the things I'm here to do is to see that certain things don't happen. If people try to attack you, to gang up on you, to scapegoat you, or to gossip about you, those behaviors will be blocked."

In the course of outlining the group's objectives and procedures and answering the prospective member's questions, the leader must be sure to cover certain themes.

### Assurance of Reasonable Safety

Nowhere can there be an absolute assurance of safety. Group members do have a right, however, to know that every reasonable effort will be made to protect them from both physical and verbal violence. The leader's mention of blocked behaviors serves this end, as does the discussion of confidentiality (described later in this chapter). The leader may need to disarm stereotypes of encounter groups, with their rough, invasive style of confrontation. A person who fears being hurt, demeaned, or violated in group is to be briefed on the more respectful type of confrontation practiced in group counseling.

### Ownership of One's Presence

The coerced group member's resistance to process, and to learning, begins with a resistance to being in the group at all. Openness to change and productive work on issues are made possible when this sense of being coerced and manipulated is transformed into an acknowledgement of personal responsibility for being in the group. Starting in the pregroup session, the leader must emphasize that the member is in the group not by compulsion, but by choice. The leader explains:

"This agency did not refer you here, nor did I. You came here under your own power. So if you have any questions about whether you should be here, please don't take them to the group. Now maybe you don't *want* to be here—that's different. Wanting to be here is not a requirement for enrollment. Maybe you saw you had two bad choices, and you took the lesser evil. You knew you faced consequences elsewhere for not being here, and you decided not to face those consequences. That's a deal you made with the court or your boss or your spouse or your parents, not with us. For us you're here by choice. And if you choose to come here, you agree not to complain about whether or not you should be here."

This is a key point in climate setting; on it (in great part) rides the integrity and effectiveness of the group. Complaining must be blocked from the start because it so easily generates more of the same. Similarly, the fact that the member has chosen to be in the group underlies the member's presumed acceptance of all group norms.

### Group Process Is Hard Work

Members need to know that the group is not for idle discussion, undisciplined ventilation of grievances, or "touchy-feely" emoting. There will be hard work to do both in and out of group: identifying and confronting issues, followed by making and carrying out a plan of action.

### Expectations versus Limitations: Keeping the Group in Perspective

At the other extreme from fear or cynicism about the group is the magical belief that being "good" in group will by itself cause one's life to change dramatically. It is important to counter such unrealistic expectations at the outset (as well as throughout the process and at termination) so as to avoid disillusionment and to channel members' energy in productive directions. Using the "I" statement locution that is a mainstay of group process, the leader might say:

> "I know that when I go into an experience that is supposed to be educational or therapeutic, I get to thinking it's automatically going to change my life. But I've learned from experience that that's not going to happen. The group provides an opportunity, but what really counts is how I apply it in my life outside the group."

The leader also might say, in the more directive language appropriate for the pregroup interview:

> "Don't get hooked on the euphoria of the group. The group can be a seductive experience. It can be very nurturing and give you a false sense of security. Keep in mind that the rest of the world isn't necessarily going to be like that. The group by itself is not going to be an answer to your needs. It will give you a model for making other situations in your life more positively rewarding for you, but you have to go out and work to make that happen. While you're in group, you may feel as if the group is meeting all your needs for companionship, intimacy, recognition, and status, but that won't last. You have to go out and create the intimacy, the recognition. And you'll have to take risks to do it. The group will help you learn

to take those risks. But the most important thing that happens in group is what you do to make it happen outside of group. That's where you have a chance to fulfill your expectations."

This message must be reemphasized throughout the group experience.

## Briefing Members about Group Norms

It is the agency's responsibility to establish clearly defined group norms. Some of these are uniform for all groups; others allow the leader some flexibility in setting norms for particular groups. The leader, in turn, may make some norms negotiable for each group, provided that there is complete clarity about what is negotiable and what is not. All members, by choosing to be in the group, agree to abide by the norms of the group. A member who violates these norms (especially in a flagrant or persistent way) is choosing not to remain in the group and must suffer the consequences of disenrollment.

Group norms are presented to members individually in the pregroup interview and to the group as a whole at the beginning of the first session. At the pregroup stage, the leader's presentation should be neither long and labored nor terse and authoritative. The leader might begin, "There are certain expectations that we need to clarify to get our job done. I'd like to share some of those expectations with you." While stating the norms, the leader periodically might check out the member's response by asking, "Does this seem reasonable to you?"

What if it does not seem reasonable? An exchange such as the following might occur:

*Member:* I drink coffee at my desk when I work in my office, and it makes me more productive there. What's disruptive about drinking coffee?
*Leader:* It's not disruptive; it's distracting. Our primary goal is to have group members take more effective control of their lives. As in the rest of the world, there are some norms here, some things we agree to do or not to do, and this just happens to be one of them. And I would ask you to respect that—not necessarily to agree, but to respect it.

Choosing to be in a group means choosing to work within the group's norms. The leader may, as needed, use analogies such as the following from common life experiences:

"If you agree to come to this group, these norms are what you agree to. It's just like school, work, the rest of the world. There are some places where, if I agree to work there, I agree not to smoke on the job. If I come to work here in this agency, I agree to work as efficiently as possible. The result of not doing so, of shirking my responsibilities, might be dismissal. You're coming to group to work. That, too, involves commitments and responsibilities.

"Every organization has this kind of control system built into it, whether it be a church, a business, a public-service group, a professional society, or a social club. If you want to avail yourself of its benefits, you agree to its rules. When you buy a ticket to the ball game, don't you agree not to bring in alcoholic beverages or go out onto the playing field? You don't have to agree to wear the home team's hat or cheer when they score. But you do agree to the rules printed on the ticket.

"When you buy a ticket to this group, you agree that you're not going to come in high on drugs, that you're not going to threaten or assault people, that you're not going to smoke, and so forth. There's no prohibition against being obnoxious or disagreeable. At the ball game, I can make people mad by rooting for the visiting team. It's *how* you're obnoxious or disagreeable that matters. If you bring in a bottle or start a fight at the ball game, you'll be thrown out. Here, too, it's your choice whether to accept the conditions of the group or the consequences of not being in the group."

Although the content of the governing norms may vary somewhat for different group leaders, agencies, and populations, the following norms are recommended on the basis of long experience in group counseling.

*Attendance and Punctuality.* Mandatory attendance and punctuality are structural requirements that contribute to an atmosphere of organization and security. Legitimate excuses will be accepted, but the nature of the emergency must be documented. Otherwise, a member who arrives late once is denied admittance to that session. A second lateness is grounds for disenrollment.

For purposes of modeling, the group should always start on time. However, the scheduled starting time can be negotiated at the beginning of the group. If work schedules and commuting distances make it a hardship for some members to get there by 7:00 P.M., the group can agree to begin each session at 7:15 or 7:30. But whatever time is agreed on must be strictly observed.

*No Intoxication.* Members may not come to group intoxicated on drugs or alcohol. A member who is found to be intoxicated will be asked to leave. A second infraction is grounds for disenrollment.

*No Violence.* Members may not engage in violence or threats of violence. Violation of this norm—a serious breach of both the decorum of the group and the safe environment the group seeks to provide for all members—may result in immediate disenrollment.

*No Distractions.* Smoking, eating, and drinking (including coffee, tea, and soda) are not permitted. These diversions, inconsequential as they may seem, interfere with concentration and may be used at tense moments to subvert confrontation of issues.

*No Breaks.* There are no breaks during a group session. A break dissipates concentration for a significant portion of the session and turns the group into a social gathering. Asking members to sit one and a half to two hours at a time is not onerous. On the contrary, like other group norms, it is good practice for adapting to the outside world.

No one may leave and reenter the room. A person who gets up and goes to the bathroom has left the session for good.

*Extracurricular Social Relationships.* Members are told that the group is not a dating service and that its purpose is not to provide social contacts. Members' freedom of association outside the group is respected, but if an extracurricular relationship between group members appears to be affecting the group adversely, it is made into a group issue.

*Dress.* Leaders and agencies vary as to the strictness of their dress codes. A group leader may consider motorcycle outfits or sexually or ideologically provocative clothing (for example, Nazi symbolism) unacceptable in group. The leader may, however, negotiate a more relaxed standard of dress if all concerned are comfortable with it.

*Etiquette.* Also negotiable are points of group etiquette, such as whether members are permitted to interrupt one another. There are, however, norms of courtesy and fundamental personal regard that apply to all groups: to show respect for the person who is speaking; to refrain from attacking, demeaning, intimidating, or gossiping about one another; and to confront gently and straightforwardly. In addition, the characteristic locutions of group process (such as "I" statements and process statements) themselves constitute a specially tailored etiquette, a set of customs for using language appropriately in the group setting. Examples of these appear throughout the chapters that follow.

*Confidentiality.* Members agree to maintain the confidentiality of all disclosures made in group. As with any other violation of norms, a member who gossips about another member outside the group is, if discovered, subject to disenrollment. The protection of confidentiality is vital if members are to feel safe to make disclosures and confront issues. There are limits to confidentiality, however, and these must be explained fully and carefully to prospective members so that they can knowingly assume the risks of disclosure.

The leader cannot give each member an ironclad guarantee that other members will maintain confidentiality outside the group. No environment is entirely free of threats to one's personal security. As with other potential dangers in group (such as physical or verbal violence), the assurance to be given is of reasonable, not absolute, safety.

In addition, the leader is required to make certain types of disclosures outside the group. The agency, not the leader, has jurisdiction over the group and maintains the members' individual records. Clinical information is available to those in the agency who have a need to know, and the leader may present the more detailed (and otherwise confidential) group notes in supervision. The leader might explain these administrative realities in these words: "Confidentiality does not mean that no one outside this group will know what goes on here. The group doesn't work in a vacuum. I am accountable for what goes on in group, just as I am accountable for what I do in individual counseling. So I include material from the group as appropriate when I present cases in supervision to authorized personnel. And your record belongs to the agency, not to me."

Each incoming group member also signs a consent form that allows the treating agency to notify the referring agency (such as the court, probation department, or motor vehicle bureau) of the member's attendance and progress in group. An individual who does not sign the form becomes ineligible for group counseling and must return to the referring agency.

Finally, the leader, like other counselors and therapists, is obligated to report certain categories of dangerous, criminal, or threatening behavior to the authorities. These requirements are established by statute (or, in some cases, by case law and judicial interpretation) in each state. Group leaders and administrators should know the law in their own state and consult the detailed guidelines pertaining to confidentiality and disclosure in Corey and Corey (1987). In general, any admission or revelation of child abuse in group must be reported. So must any statement of intention or feeling of compulsion to commit a crime or to harm oneself or others in the future. Suicidal or homicidal threats must be reported. If a member speaks of being in the midst of committing a crime or series of crimes, the leader is obligated to intervene so that the authorities can act to prevent further criminal activity. If a member reports having committed a crime for which he or she has not been apprehended, the leader as a rule does not report this information except in supervision. However, the leader may be required to testify about the member's revelation in court if a judge rules that a group counselor does not enjoy the same privileged relationship with a client as does a physician, attorney, or minister.

This kind of disclosure represents an exception to the dictum "There is no issue that cannot be talked about in group." In practice, whether an unsolved past crime is to be reported outside the agency depends on the nature of the crime (for example, whether there is an identified victim) and whether there is continuity between past and present behavior. If a member were currently selling drugs to schoolchildren, the agency would report it expeditiously. If, however, this heinous conduct were clearly in the past, the agency would likely treat it as an issue in the person's life to be dealt with in group rather than as a matter for the police. (There would, in any case, be no specific unsolved crime on the books.) An unsolved murder would be another matter. The leader cannot give the new member a definite protocol for every contingency that might come up in group. The leader can, however, say, "I can assure you that I'd never go and communicate with any agency without first checking it out with my supervisors. I'd get as much input as possible to weigh our responsibilities to you against our responsibilities to society."

Concerns about confidentiality, both genuine and as a mask for other issues, are a primary focus of resistance at the beginning of a group. These concerns must be confronted in the pregroup interview and in the initial climate setting in group, when the heightened wariness members feel about the group experience increases the likelihood of acting out. The following exchange illustrates this part of the one-to-one interview:

*Member:* Why should I talk about these personal matters with a group of strangers? I'd rather talk to an individual therapist.

*Leader:* There's nothing you can say to a therapist individually that you can't say in group. Let's say you tell the group that you're homosexual or impotent or that you were abused as a child. The question becomes "Now what do you want to do about it? How can the group help you?" Why can't that be emphasized in group as well as in individual therapy?

*Member:* I feel embarrassed talking about this to a whole bunch of people at once. In a therapist's office, it's private; I can trust the therapist to maintain confidentiality. Here in group, I don't know whether all these people are going to go out into the world and talk about me. I may run into them later, or they may know somebody I know.

*Leader:* That only means that you don't fully accept what happened to you. You're still taking it out on yourself. You're still full of shame.

*Member:* At this point in my life, why shouldn't I be?

*Leader:* Do you want to change your life outside the group?

*Member:* You're saying the group will help me change my life as effectively as individual therapy would?

*Leader:* Probably more so because of the different viewpoints you'll be receiving from members with various backgrounds and the essential support you'll get from some of them. There will be follow-up support and nurturing from group members as well. And it's been my experience that if I make these disclosures you're worried about, I won't die from it. I haven't heard of anyone dying from making disclosures.

*Member:* There are risks in making disclosures, aren't there?

*Leader:* Yes, there are risks. It's up to you to decide if they're worth the benefits. If you're willing to tell me something, what's so different about telling the group? If I was so hung up about that, I'd say that's part of my self-aggrandizement, my own egocentrism, that I think the world revolves around me, so that if I say something, it's really so important. Thousands of people, myself included, have found out that using the group as a vehicle for change has been more effective than individual therapy. And I would strongly urge you to consider participating.

*Member:* Do I have to tell the group a lot of personal things about myself?

*Leader:* If you want to benefit most from the group, it's advisable to participate. However, in a decision-making and problem-solving group, we're not here to do deep-seated therapy, to discover unresolved issues and unearth things you might have done as a child. If you want to use the group for dramatic revelations, that's your choice. But we want to set the stage for what happens in your life from now on. There are appropriate revelations that support that goal. And just as in the larger world out there, any revelation you make may involve some risk. What would happen if you told your neighbor that you committed a crime or abused a child? This isn't diplomatic immunity here. You're still responsible for what you say and do.

*Member:* I'm not worried that I'll tell you something you'll have to report. It's the personal stuff I'm concerned about. I want to know if I can get a commitment from the other people in the group to respect my confidentiality. It might be very painful for me to talk about my sexual functions in this group. What are the rules about respecting one another's privacy?

*Leader:* We do set some norms of personal respect—for example, that the feedback we give one another be solicited, not imposed, and that it be descriptive, not evaluative. Those are some of the safeguards we have. This is group counseling, not a rap group. There's a reason for everything we do here. As for taking this information outside the group, we emphasize that it be kept in group as emphatically as we can. If you're looking for a guarantee of that, I can't give it. But I would pose something else, as I said before: what is so special, so supersensitive about your concerns? If others have a need to talk out of school, that says more about them than about you. If you're concerned about appearances, you'd look better than they would. But anyway, you're here for you; you're here to gain effective control of your life. Remember, you're not a victim anymore. You might have been a victim, but now you're a person. We're going to show you how to do better, and we'll support you in doing it.

\*     \*     \*

By laying out in advance the group norms and expectations, the leader prepares the way for climate setting in group. This is not to say that members' resistance is at an end. But members will perceive (even if they do not say so) the consistency between what the leader has told them and what actually happens in group. The norms spelled out at the beginning are maintained and reinforced throughout the life of the group. That consistency gives group members an experience of integrity and order.

# 3
# Climate Setting

The successful functioning of a group depends on the climate initially established by the leader and maintained by both the leader and the group as a whole. Climate setting does not happen all at once. It begins in the pregroup interviews, where the groundwork is laid for constructive participation by each member, and it continues for the duration of the group. But the most important moment for climate setting is the group's first session. What occurs then, while not irreversible (for better or worse), sets the tone for the entire group experience.

Group members who see themselves as unwilling participants cannot be left to create a constructive group climate on their own, since the climate they would create would reflect the disorganization of their lives. At least initially, therefore, climate setting is the leader's job. Although individual members and even the group as a whole may regress under the stress of confrontation with vital issues, some members—perhaps a critical mass—will pick up the positive attitude modeled by the leader and work to keep the group functioning effectively. In a productive group, climate setting comes to be a group rather than a leadership responsibility. It is, of course, the leader's ongoing responsibility to monitor the group climate and intervene as necessary.

Groups are a natural setting for people, yet members are likely to resist the group, seeing it as an imposition of control. The leader can do much to overcome this resistance by creating an atmosphere of trust, self-disclosure, mutual respect, and empowerment. The group climate must be one that facilitates serious work. As in life, however, work need not be oppressive; there can always be some levity and recreation when people get together. Groups should be serious, not solemn. The atmosphere should be one in which personal consideration is extended and reciprocated; participation is encouraged but not extorted; issues are confronted voluntarily, truthfully, and firmly; and behavior is seen to be purposeful, meaningful, and yet flexible. It is one in which feelings are expressed, responsibility is assumed, and action is planned and carried out. This is a rewarding environment that prepares the individual to take control of his or her life.

## Reviewing Group Norms

In anticipation of the limit testing that is inevitable in most groups, the group norms listed and discussed in chapter 2 should be posted on a chalkboard or poster as the group begins. These norms are not new information to the group members, who have been briefed on them individually prior to the beginning of the group. To underscore the priority given to group norms, it is best to review them at the beginning of the first session, even before the introduction of group members. This review of norms begins the brief (fifteen- or twenty-minute) preparatory remarks that are a necessary prelude to group process.

Just as in the pregroup interview, the review of norms (referred to as expectations) need not be belabored. To model responsibility from the outset, the leader continually uses "I" statements (described later in this chapter). For example, the leader might begin like this:

> "I've found that there are some things that help me get the most benefit out of this group. We start on time, and everyone is expected to be here. No one will come in high on alcohol or drugs. There will be no violence or threat of violence. Don't bring coffee or anything else to drink, and don't smoke; it's distracting. Stay in your chair; don't get up and leave, even to go to the bathroom. These are some expectations we have."

Especially if there is resistance, it is appropriate to reinforce this message with everyday analogies that anyone can understand. Just as in the prior one-to-one meeting, adherence to group norms is tied to the assumption that all members are there by choice. Without being punitive or condescending, the leader may say:

> "We're going on the premise that people are here by choice, even if you think it's a lousy choice. Nobody made you come here. You may go to jail if you don't come to group, but that's between you and the judge. I'm not going to send you to jail. You may lose your license, but I'm not going to take your license. Your wife may change the lock on you and go to her lawyer, but that's between you and her.
>
> "Once you've chosen to come to group, there is a commitment that you are going to attend regularly and be on time. Yes, things happen, but in the end it comes down to your commitment. Some people call in and say, 'My child is sick' or 'My car isn't working; I'll get in if I can'—meaning that they won't. Others make arrangements, contingency plans, move heaven and earth to get here. If I had tickets to the Super Bowl and there was a snowstorm, I'd find a way to get there.

"Now I don't want any limit testing here. If you miss a group, you're out of it. That's the way it is. I don't mean if you miss just one or if once you're half an hour late. Things do happen. If your car breaks down, I'm not going to penalize you for that. However, please be sure to bring in the towing report. If you have to go to a funeral, we understand that, but please bring in the obituary."

At this time, the leader reemphasizes the group's expectations regarding confidentiality, as outlined in chapter 2, and reaches an agreement with the group on any norms that are negotiable, such as dress and starting time. There is to be no confusion, however, about what is negotiable and what is not.

In addition to the norms that must be observed on pain of dismissal from the group, the leader also highlights behaviors that, while not similarly subject to sanction, are inimical to group process and will be blocked. Although the group does not mandate politeness, it does protect members from abuse, and it does see that the business of the group is carried out. Thus, the leader tells the group:

"We have other kinds of expectations as well. We talk about the here and now, not the there and then. We talk about what 'I feel' or 'I do,' not what 'you feel' or 'one does.' We respect a person when he or she is speaking. We identify; we don't compare. Extended silence is not tolerated. Filibustering—monopolizing the group—is not tolerated. Gossiping, scapegoating, and rescuing or ganging up on someone are not tolerated. I find that it helps me to stop these things when they happen, and as the group gets working, others may do so, too."

Initially, not everyone in the group may understand what these terms mean, but no further explanation is called for at this time. As part of climate setting, the leader simply lets members know, in a general way, what to expect. Merely warning against problem behaviors in group will not stop them from occurring. Only by having these behaviors blocked and the group's energy redirected can members learn more effective ways of interacting. This aspect of group process is illustrated in detail in chapter 7.

## Introductions

After the group norms are set forth, the leader asks the members to introduce themselves and tell what they want to get out of the group. That is not the same as "Tell us who you are and how you are feeling." This is not a "touchy-feely" group; the aim is to get right to the issues.

As in other facets of group process, the leader's choice of words can be critical. The question "Why are you here?" turns the group into a "bitch session," with defocusing and blaming of persons, places, and things. The common belief among clinicians that complaining about being in the group cements trust, which in turn makes possible a real engagement with issues, has no known documentation. On the basis of long observation, it seems more likely that complaining generates more complaining, until the venting of resentment becomes the norm.

A more appropriate opening question, therefore, is "You're here—now what do you expect to get out of being here?" This formulation puts the emphasis on the future rather than the past, on action rather than recrimination. Members can own their intentions, even if these are nothing more than to get through the group and stay out of trouble. Typical responses are "I want my driver's license back"; "I want my wife to take me back"; "I want my employer to rehire me"; "I don't want to go to jail." These responses are useful insofar as they put group members on record as acknowledging that their behavior has consequences. It is legitimate for group members to want to stay out of trouble, but the group will not necessarily keep them out of trouble on their own terms.

The leader cannot assume good faith on the part of members of a coerced group. Even in uncoerced groups, members are not necessarily ready to face the issues that affect their well-being. The leader can expect to find most group members initially comfortable in the victim role and unmotivated to change their lives. The challenge for the leader is to turn the members' expressed desire to get out of trouble into a willingness to take risks in and out of group. Seeing the link between one's behavior in group and its natural consequences is a first step toward taking effective control of one's life.

## Group Process

Group process is the mechanism by which the resistant group member is brought into active engagement with the issues in his or her life. For many such individuals, a rational presentation (expository or directive) is like a foreign language, eliciting reactions of incomprehension, outward compliance, or active resistance. In contrast, group process creates an experience in which positive choices are dramatized and made real.

In process groups, as distinct from program groups, education is active rather than passive. The leader does not come with an agenda; instead, group members take the initiative in raising their own issues. Substantive education is incorporated into the confrontation of issues in group interaction, with members owning their statements, giving and receiving feedback, and so forth. People learn by doing—for example, by reading a book, going to a meeting, or seeing a nutritionist or sex therapist.

To set the tone for this active, task-oriented approach, the leader introduces group process even in the opening discussion of norms and introductions. Although the leader briefly alludes to the group's expectations in this area ("Make 'I' statements"; "Always bring things back to group"), group process is taught more by modeling than by direction or explanation. Group members pick up the forms of speech used by the leader.

### Process Statements and "I" Statements

Two indispensable tools of group process are process statements and "I" statements. Process statements are descriptive, not evaluative. They are used when the group is in danger of going off focus—for example, when members gossip, attack, filibuster, or blame persons, places, or things (such as the courts, the "system," or a spouse). Their purpose is to keep the group on focus, or to bring the group back to focus, so that members own what they are talking about and take responsibility for what they say. Process statements consist of locutions such as the following: "Group, I have a question about something. This is what I see going on. I want to check that out with you." Or, "Could someone share what he or she sees going on right now? What's happening right now?" When to make a process statement and how to say it are matters of sensitivity, communication skills, and experience. But the leader need not be overly worried about saying exactly the right thing. No one can always make the best possible judgment in the heat of battle, but it is essential to bring the issues back to the group and have faith in group process to resolve them.

"I" statements are an expression of personal responsibility. Instead of talking about "you," "one," "we," "people," or "groups like this," the speaker owns his or her feelings, observations, and personal reactions. The leader is careful to make "I" statements and to ask group members to do the same when they go off into other-focus. When the group interaction takes the form of "I" statements, a foundation is laid for members to assume responsibility for their lives. Here is an example of an "I" statement made by the leader: "Group, I have a problem. Max is not contributing. Now I know that when *I* don't contribute, that means I'm uncomfortable about something and I don't have confidence in the group to listen and respond to me in a caring way." Instead of laying the problem on Max (which might elicit a defensive reaction), the leader turns the spotlight on himself or herself and makes the problem his or her own. By owning his or her experience and modeling responsibility, the leader invites Max to do the same. It is up to Max to decide whether or not his experience is the same as the leader's.

Process statements and "I" statements often are used together, as in this example: "I have a problem. I'm uncomfortable, Jane, because I see you being defensive. I want to check it out with you. Can you help me out with that?" Both types of statements are illustrated in many variations throughout this book. Group members are to be reinforced for using these empowering locutions. As members assume responsibility for maintaining group process, the group becomes self-regulating rather than leader driven.

## Identify Rather Than Compare

Much of the value of group process lies in the group members' ability to generalize from one another's experiences to their own. If one dismisses the relevance to oneself of what others say ("Oh, that never happened to me; I'm not like that at all"), one is comparing oneself to others rather than finding common ground with them. Group process is intended to encourage the opposite response, that of identification—the "Aha!" effect. The issues raised are not just one person's issues; others can relate to them as well.

For example, in a group for intoxicated drivers, one member might say, "I used to arrive late for work. My productivity fell off. I was short with my kids. I spent money compulsively. I lost touch with longtime friends. I began experiencing insomnia." Another member thinks, "That's not like me at all; I always come to work on time." A third says to herself, "I don't spend a lot of money. That doesn't have anything to do with me." Each member, selectively hearing one thing to which he or she can feel superior, misses the underlying similarity of experience. They are comparing, not identifying.

In climate setting, the leader may address this by saying, "There are some things that might come up in group because we come from different backgrounds and see things from different perspectives. I'd try to concentrate on what you can relate to in a person rather than compare and contrast the things that make you different." Still, the leader can expect this question to come up again. When it does, make it a group issue. Make a process statement ("Group, what's going on here? What's happening?") and then an "I" statement ("Group, when *I* do what I saw Bill do, I'm comparing rather than identifying"). In one group where a member said that she felt out of place among people who had been in trouble with the law, the leader answered as follows:

> "Sometimes I feel out of place, too. But you know what helps me? Instead of looking at the differences, I try to see if there's anything in common. That's what helps me. And I would ask others to give it a shot, too. Because we're here, and we can make what we want of it. I have seen people really grow in groups. I really feel connected with them when I see them engage in their struggle to discard old ways that aren't working for them and begin to try out new ways. Being part of that is tremendous. That can go on here if we

begin to focus on what we can *do* from this experience, instead of letting differences like that come between us."

## Group Ethics

An important aspect of group climate has to do with the tenor of relationships among group members and between leader and members. In what ways is the leader's position different from that of the members? In what ways do the same rules apply to the leader and members alike? The following are some important components of the ethical atmosphere of groups.

### Caring

Caring is a sine qua non for a group; without it, productive confrontation cannot take place. How confrontation and feedback occur in an atmosphere of caring is demonstrated in chapters 6 and 8. How noncaring behavior is blocked is shown in chapter 7.

### No Blaming or Accusing

There is no blaming or accusing persons, places, or things inside or outside the group. Such externalizing of responsibility can spread through the group in wild contagion, sabotaging any attempt to own and confront issues. In climate setting, the leader says, "In here we don't blame. We're not here to discuss laws. We're not here to evaluate armed services policy, employee assistance program policy, or the actions of the police. We're here to take a look at our own issues."

### Truthfulness

Although honesty is a desired quality in a person or an interaction, the word often is used as a cloak for harsh, wounding, or judgmental statements. One group member may say to another, "I want to be honest with you," and then attack with guns blazing. In groups, therefore, we prefer to speak of being truthful. Truthfulness is essential to group process and to an individual's benefiting from the group.

### Trust

Trust is essential, but not in the way it is typically represented to be in the training of group leaders. The long discourses on trust often seen in groups are as much a matter of flight and other-focus as lectures on depression or alcoholic denial. Just as "money can't buy you love," talk can't buy you trust. Trust is created (when it can be created at all) by deeds, not words. The leader models trust by acting in a trustworthy way—that is, by doing the following:

- Being truthful
- Self-disclosing
- Owning one's feelings
- Not being abusive or condescending
- Respecting the confidentiality of members
- Protecting members from aggression and assault
- Not acting out of one's own power needs
- Valuing the uniqueness of each person
- Maintaining the integrity of the group by monitoring the observance of group norms
- Confronting members in a caring manner
- Transmitting strength through confidence in group process

These behaviors, practiced consistently, are what the leader can do to develop trust (an outcome that cannot, of course, be guaranteed). Often, as a natural consequence, a close and deepening bond will form between the leader and members, allowing the leader to take risks and confront the members in ways that an unfamiliar leader could not. If the leader does not do this elementary work of climate setting, any amount of talk about trust will be seen by the group as pious posturing.

### Confidentiality

Nothing is more destructive of trust than the violation of confidentiality. When the leader, exasperated at a member's resistance, says, "Didn't I read in your case history that you . . . ?" or "Your employer was very specific about . . . ," the member is put on edge and the entire group is intimidated. When a group member is raising issues about her marriage, nothing can be more devaluing than for the leader to change the subject and bring up clinical data ("Let's see, I can't remember whether you're here for drug or alcohol abuse"). Yet such exchanges do take place in groups with poorly trained leaders. In contrast, trained, experienced leaders do not bring in information obtained outside the group. It is the member's prerogative to bring up an issue or to give permission for an issue to be aired.

### Modeling

The integrity of the group process is a model for integrity in living. A leader who uses "I" statements and process statements is modeling not just how to act in groups, but how to live responsibly. Every aspect of the leader's conduct—truthfulness, ownership of feelings, self-disclosure, respectful confrontation, and so forth—has clear analogues outside the group. Taken together, these behaviors make up an image of adequacy and effectiveness that group members can carry with them into their dealings with the outside world. The leader is a person who is serious but not humorless, who acts purposefully but flexibly. While not necessarily a paragon of virtue, the leader is perceived as someone who successfully meets his or her needs outside the group. To do so, the leader must have—and, as needed, disclose—a strategy for dealing with his or her life in relevant areas.

## Ownership of Feelings

When a leader begins the group by saying, "Let's talk about ourselves and our feelings," too often that means, "Let's talk about *your*selves and *your* feelings." The leader, meanwhile, remains safely above the battle. "Why don't you tell us a little more about what you're feeling," the leader probes. "What's that feeling about?" For group members, these vaguely intrusive questions are both confusing and threatening. A group member might respond, "What do you mean—'feel'?" One might imagine the leader trying to calibrate a person's feelings in something resembling an Abbott and Costello routine:

> "How do you feel?"
> "Lousy."
> "How lousy?"
> "*Real* lousy."
> "How lousy?"
> "*Damn* lousy!"

This wallowing in ill-defined feelings is more than just pretentious and unproductive; it usually involves a defensive evasion on the leader's part. Group members do not have to be psychologists to realize that the leader has feelings that he or she is not expressing. People do react emotionally when someone tests limits, walks out, is asked to leave, makes a dramatic revelation, or bursts into tears. But when the leader says, "I'm sensing a lot of emotion—there must be a lot of emotion here," the leader is not acknowledging his or her own emotion. Feeling upset, threatened, and challenged, the leader projects those feelings onto the group members, who "must" be feeling the same things.

The leader is, in effect, asking group members to perform for his or her pleasure. (Not surprisingly, members may check out their performance by asking, "Is that what you want me to say?") Members get a double message: the leader tells them to display their feelings but does not model such expression. Evidently expressing your feelings isn't such a good idea, the members conclude. It's just one more thing that sets people who are in trouble apart from people who are not in trouble. Faced with the leader's emotional withholding, the members likewise withhold. They come to see the leader as an adversary in a zero-sum game—analyzing, controlling, standing aside rather than participating in the risks of interaction. It is a failure of climate setting, a failure to create a climate of self-disclosure, "I" statements, and ownership of feelings.

Such a climate is vital to a working group. It is created by a leader who does not ask the group to do anything he or she will not do and who models what he or she asks the group to do. In the following example, the leader models risk taking by sharing a personal reaction and asking for feedback:

> *Member:* You people are always on my case!
> *Leader:* Jack, do you mean me? It sounds like you're really talking to me. I'd say it sounds like you're pissed off at me. I want to check that out with you. I want some feedback.

Contrast the direct engagement of this exchange with the lack of resolution when the leader cajoles the member to "tell us how you're really feeling." By focusing the issue concretely and risking a statement that may be rejected as wrong, the leader invites clarification by the member.

In the following example, the leader owns what might seem to be an awkward or embarrassing feeling that comes up in the course of the group interaction: "Group, I have a problem with Marvin. I feel he's ridiculing me. That doesn't feel good. I'm trying to do a job here. I may not be doing it as well as someone else might, but I'm trying to do it just the same. I need some help with that." A leader who responded to the perceived ridicule with folded arms and pursed lips would be modeling suppression rather than expression of feelings. A leader who retaliated punitively against the group for the affront would be poisoning the working atmosphere of the group. Instead, by opening up the issue for the group, the leader fosters clear communication and resolution. The leader's statement tells group members that they are on an equal plane with the leader and that everyone in the group is responsible for his or her part in the group interaction. By seeing a potentially inflammatory issue resolved in this way, members learn how they can resolve such issues with one another and, by extension, with other people in their lives.

The leader also models ownership of feelings experienced in everyday life outside the group—feelings of inadequacy, vulnerability, fear of risk and rejection, worry, anxiety, and annoyance. This sharing, which makes the leader a credible human figure and forges a bond between the leader and members, comes under the heading of self-disclosure.

*Self-Disclosure*

Appropriate self-disclosure is one of the primary interpersonal skills of an effective counselor (Wolf 1974–75), and nowhere is it more vital than in group work. But what is appropriate, and what is not? The following guidelines, as summarized by an experienced counselor, apply across the board to most clinical relationships:

> If establishing a relationship with a client means telling him what teams I root for, what movies I like, what food I enjoy, I'll tell him. My sex life, how much money I make—these are no one's business. . . .
>
> When I work for an agency, my qualifications are a matter to be settled between me and my employer. They are not subject to discussion with clients. I am not obligated to justify myself to clients by telling them what degrees I have, how long I have worked in the field, or whether or not I have been an addict. Self-disclosure is a tool of the trade that I employ at my own discretion, not when I am pressured to do so. I speak about my background or my feelings only when my doing so will benefit the client or student. I do not do so to create a "high" for myself or for anyone else. (Edelwich and Brodsky 1980, 68–69)

On the whole, these distinctions apply to group as well as individual counseling, with an emphasis on the insistence that the group leader need not justify his or her qualifications to group members. The members' mandate is to the agency, not the counselor, and the members do not have a say in the agency's employment decisions.

Nonetheless, the application of the guidelines is somewhat more flexible in group counseling than in individual counseling. Status distinctions are somewhat more fluid in group, where the leader is simultaneously a participant and a guide. Thus, the manner and spirit of a given disclosure are as important as its content in assessing its appropriateness. In that regard, the counselor's statement that he uses self-disclosure "at my own discretion, not when I am pressured to do so" is of signal importance for group work.

Appropriate self-disclosures are those that encourage identification without compromising the leader's personal privacy or credibility as a role model. Such disclosures take the leader off the pedestal of hero worship and make the leader's experiences and coping strategies accessible for modeling. Normally, for example, while acting in a professional capacity, one would not speak in clinical terms about one's sexual dysfunctions. One might, however, share sentiments such as the following: "As I get into middle age, I wonder how long I'll be able to go on having erections regularly with my wife. I didn't think about that twenty years ago, but it's a concern now." Or, "One question that occurs to me when I think about getting out of the relationship I'm in is whether I can still be attractive to men." These are universal concerns, not individual pathologies. As a rule, one would not tell horror stories about being physically abused by a spouse, but one would allude to the normal vicissitudes of married life. Of course, the appropriateness of such self-disclosures depends on their relevance to the issues raised in group at any given time.

What if the group leader has something more specific in common with the group members—for example, if the leader of a group concerned with drinking problems is a recovering alcoholic? Any predisclosure of this information is inappropriate, since it makes the leader's personal background of alcoholism a badge of identity. For group members, such labeling confuses the distinction between professional counseling and mutual-support groups; among the staff, it creates a polarity between those who have "the right stuff" and those who do not.

This aspect of the leader's background may be appropriately disclosed in the form of "I" statements as part of the group process, provided that it is kept brief and is relevant to the context. The main criterion for appropriateness is "Whose needs are being met by the disclosure?" Thus, the leader's parallel experience is properly used as an example for modeling as long as there is no grandiose announcement and no extended dramatic monologue about "how tough I had it when I was drinking." The leader may mention, for example, something that happened in a recovery group if that comes up naturally by way of illustration. In this or any other area, the leader's disclosures do not take the form of "Once I was lost, but now I'm found; once I was blind, but now I see." The purpose of disclosure is not to compare and contrast, not to score points, not to show the leader's superiority or to glorify past triumphs, but to enable members to identify with the leader's handling of dilemmas in the here and now.

In a positive sense, the leader's disclosures are meant to open a window for group members into normal life, where people may not have all the answers and may not always be happy but somehow manage to cope. Far from being a superhero, the leader stands in for all those people who are trying to earn a living, do satisfying work and have satisfying relationships with people, have some love and some fun in their lives, and enjoy their days. To gain these gratifications and get past the rough spots, one must sometimes be savvy, sometimes stoical, and often resourceful—qualities that the leader demonstrates.

Typically, then, the most effective disclosures show the leader coping with normal human vulnerabilities, hassles, and upsets. Fear of risk and failure are common themes (as they are in the experience of group members). Who does not fear rejection? Who would not empathize with a person who dreads speaking in public, going to a job interview, or being turned down for a date? Such mundane but poignant experiences are the stuff of self-disclosure in groups. One might talk about how one does not like to attend staff meetings. One might say, "I have my problems with authority figures, too. I don't agree with my boss about everything. Here's how I try to get around that." These are portrayed as issues the leader is grappling with currently, just as members are (as opposed to "I used to be just like you are, but look at me now!"). The leader presents himself or herself as vulnerable but as working toward effective control.

One group leader spoke about the insecurity she felt when she auditioned to become a part-time fashion model. Already an accomplished professional person with a career in social work, she experienced a sense of being exposed to the world—a feeling she thought she had left behind in her teens—when she put herself on the line in this unfamiliar, highly competitive, and ego-involving endeavor. Another leader gave this colorful account of some public embarrassments he put himself through:

> "You know what I do in front of strangers at parties sometimes? I do things I'm not very good at. I sing folk songs. Imagine me singing. I do magic tricks. I'm horrible at it. But to me it's a kind of discipline. Okay, I look foolish. So what?
>
> "You know what really helped me a lot with my sense of self-consciousness? On my forty-fifth birthday, my wife (by prearrangement) took the wig off my head in front of all my friends and family, including some who had never seen me that way before. She called everybody out to the patio, put the wig on the grill, put some lighter fluid on it, and had a ceremony. You want to know something? It worked. It was all my ego stuff that I was wrapped up in, when the overwhelming number of people in the world—in Egypt, in China, and even on my own street—don't care if I have a hair on my head."

Self-disclosures also concern the leader's experience in, and of, the group. For example, an inexperienced (or even not so inexperienced) leader may confess to being nervous at the start of a group. Whether such a disclosure is appropriate is a close call, one that depends on the leader's reading of the group in question. On the one hand, the disclosure of nervousness may be understood by the group as modeling truthful self-expression and ownership of feelings. On the other hand, needy members may dismiss the leader and the group as lacking the potency needed to help them. The leader does need to convey openness and truthfulness, but the leader also needs to convey strength and confidence so that members can put their faith in the group and (following the leader's model) in themselves. Even so, the leader's feelings and experiences inside as well as outside the group should, as a rule, be available for self-disclosure. In particular, the tactical value of candid expressions of displeasure with the group will be demonstrated in the next chapter.

The leader's self-disclosures are voluntary rather than coerced; the same is true for group members'. The leader does not ask group members direct questions about their private lives (in the case of a leader who does, one must ask whose needs are being served). Group members are not necessarily there to explore intimate personal questions. They are there to get help with problem solving and decision making in specified areas, and the leader is there to model effective control and provide a climate conducive to skill development in those areas. Members may raise any issues they wish about their own lives, but it is their choice to do so, just as it is the leader's choice to self-disclose.

Nonetheless, the leader may be confronted by group members who, misunderstanding the nature and purpose of the group, assume that the leader's privacy is protected while theirs is not. A leader who faces such intrusive questions need not and should not resort to dismissive, devaluing responses such as "It's none of your business," "I'm the counselor and you're the client," or "We're here to talk about you, not about me." Rather, the questions can be handled as part of group process, in words such as the following:

> "Group, I'm having a problem here. I don't ask people about their sex lives. I don't ask how much money they make. Those are private matters. I think I've respected your privacy, and I'd like the same consideration in return. And these questions, to me, honestly, are voyeuristic."
>
> "Anything that goes on between me and anyone else is private, and I would respect that in your case as well. The group isn't making you talk about those things. But if you do choose to talk about them, this is the safest place you'll get to do it."

For group members as well as for the leader, the group provides an opportunity for disclosure but does not compel it.

## Empowerment

The group experience is designed to empower members to take effective control of their lives. It accomplishes this goal in a number of ways, but primarily by giving group members the responsibility to do in group the kinds of things they must learn to do outside the group. The more that is asked of group members, the more they can give. The leader transmits strength by expressing, implicitly and explicitly, this faith in both the group members and group process: "I believe in you. I've seen a lot of good things happen to people in groups, and I believe that if you want to do better, you can."

Two themes emphasized for the duration of the group are "There's lots of work to do both in and out of the group" and "The most important thing that happens in group is what happens outside the group." Rather than remaining self-satisfied with their awareness or insight, members are confronted with the question "Now what?" Having received feedback, they make a judgment that there is a better way to go. Then they must decide what they will accomplish and how and when they will accomplish it. In group, they state and plan to carry out an intention: write a letter, call someone for a date, take a résumé to the printer, enroll in a dance class, and so on. The plan means nothing, however, unless it is implemented. In group counseling, to be empowered is to recognize and experience the connections between desires and intentions, intentions and actions, and actions and consequences.

## The Leader's Need for Power

The purpose of the group is to empower group members, not the group leader. If members look up to the leader as an expert, that is fine—provided the leader uses group process to transmit this image of competence and confidence to the members. It is not acceptable for the leader to show off his or her expertise so as to remain one up on the members. The greater the leader's need for ego gratification and control, the less able the leader is to allow the free-flowing dialogue and confrontation through which members build their ego strength. The more the leader needs to be the most successful, the most congruent, the most well-integrated person in the group, the more likely the leader is to discourage or suppress challenges from members. Leaders who allow unresolved power needs to affect their handling of groups are like parents who compete with their children; they are not doing their job.

Inexperience and inadequate training also contribute to overly directive, even manipulative leadership. All too common is the sight of the leader standing, hands flailing in the air, beckoning to each member in turn, while the members look up, ready to respond on cue. Novice leaders readily assume that "running groups" means acting like a conductor coordinating the instruments of an orchestra; like a baseball manager platooning players, bringing in the infield, or calling for a pinch hitter. Those who have displayed this leadership style need not conclude that they have a great need for control; they simply may not have learned any other approach. A leader who has persistent difficulty in sharing control with members may wish to bring the issue to supervision, peer support, or professional consultation.

## Confronting the Leader

Like a family, the group conditions a person's expectations about what behavior is acceptable and what is not acceptable in the outside world.

Children learn to express themselves publicly by speaking their minds respectfully to their parents. Similarly, the group environment is set up to encourage appropriate confrontation of authority—or of other individuals—while discouraging the kinds of confrontation that get people in trouble. In this environment, the leader can expect to be the first to be confronted. Such confrontation is to be encouraged, provided that members present their case responsibly, in keeping with group norms pertaining to concreteness, specificity, and personal respect. The norms for appropriate feedback enumerated in chapters 6 and 8 apply to confrontation of the leader as well as of other members. One presents one's case with descriptive, factual evidence, not with a verbal assault or tirade.

The climate set by the leader either invites or inhibits free expression by members. If the leader is arbitrary and controlling, confrontation of the leader will appear to be out of bounds. If the leader puts members on the defensive, the leader's own defensiveness will be apparent, and the leader will lose credibility. It is preferable for the leader to let the criticism be aired and to check it out by asking for feedback. This sort of input may, however, lead to crosscurrents of attack and defense, with members venting suspicions and frustrations about both the leader and other members. If the group becomes chaotic ("He said. . . , I believe. . . , you think. . . , oh, yeah?"), the leader should slow things down with a process statement, such as the following: "What's going on here? What's really happening? Someone make a process statement about what you see going on." Here the leader shares with the group the responsibility of putting the group back on track.

Members who feel threatened by confrontation of their own issues may try to turn the tables on the leader by saying, "Who are you to tell me all these things I should do? What about you—what side of the bed do you get up on? Don't you ever screw up?" The leader who retorts, "I don't want to talk about that," "That's my business," or "I'm the counselor here!" not only is alienating the group unnecessarily but also is missing the opportunity to model effective behavior. Yes, the leader is a person who sometimes "screws up," but he or she has the emotional and practical resources to minimize the damage and fall back on some area of strength.

If the confrontation of the leader by one or more members becomes persistent, the leader should resort to a process statement:

"Group, I seem to be in the focus of attention here. I want to check that out. Is that what's going on? Sure, I can be confronted like anyone else; there's nothing wrong with that. But I want to check this out with you. Are we spending a disproportionate amount of time on me and my issues? Does anyone else in the group see some disparity there? I need some help with this."

One leader, for example, was accused of putting on airs because he wore a three-piece suit while group members wore work uniforms or casual clothes. He replied as follows:

"Good question. Some of you have uniforms; well, this is my uniform for my daytime job, from which I come directly to group. I wouldn't necessarily put on a suit like this for group, but then I could, and so could you. It doesn't violate any of our expectations here to wear a three-piece suit. Does anyone else feel the same way about it? I'm asking for feedback now. Is this so important? Is my suit the issue here?"

What if one member continues to grill the leader about his suit? The leader might say:

We've been talking about my suit for fifteen minutes. If any of you want to go any further with this, would you tell me where you think it's going? I need some help with this. Charlie, I received some feedback about my suit. Would you want to hear some feedback on how people perceive this—my suit and your issue about it?"

With these words, the leader takes the focus off his suit and puts it back where it belongs—namely, on what Charlie is doing by raising the issue and not letting go of it. Having modeled openness to feedback, the leader asks Charlie if he will open up his preoccupation with the suit to comments by the group. The feedback is not imposed; rather, the member is asked whether he wishes to solicit it. If he does not, the exchange punctuates the matter, and the group can move on to other issues.

### Keeping a Group Journal

A tool for achieving empowerment of a different kind is the group journal that members (depending on the nature and composition of the group) may be encouraged to keep. The journal is not a report to the leader or to the group; indeed, no one need see it unless the member wishes to review it with the leader or to share some of it as feedback for the group as termination approaches. It is, instead, a way to measure one's own growth by monitoring one's reactions to people and to the group process. It is concerned with the emotional climate of the group, issues of control, and what one has learned from the feedback one has received. Questions for the weekly journal include the following: Am I anxious about anything? What am I afraid of? What conflicts do I feel? With whom do I identify?

Members who keep a journal can benefit by seeing how their anxiety is reduced and how comfortable they become as the group progresses. As in real life, new anxieties periodically arise, are dealt with, and subside, only to be replaced by other anxieties. The journal helps members keep track of these ups and downs. One leader who has kept her own group journal tells groups, "I don't expect that I'll ever walk into a group where I have so much control that I don't feel any frustration. My journal gives me a handle on such feelings and how they relate to what happens in group."

The journal is a valuable tool when used properly, but it is not for everyone. Some individuals may learn how to participate by keeping the journal. For others, the task of writing may be so laborious that it detracts from the spontaneity of their participation. The difficulty these individuals have in expressing their thoughts and feelings on paper may carry over into the group. It should be left to each member to decide whether the journal is worth maintaining. The leader might introduce the journal by saying, "I'll make this an assignment to start out with. I'd like you to do it for the first three or four sessions. Then see how well it supports your participation in group. If you don't want to continue it, that's up to you." This approach is consistent with the overall strategy of helping members move from dependence on outside events, influences, and authorities to a more self-determined existence.

# 4
# Getting Started

How does the leader get the group started? This question betrays the misunderstanding that most leaders bring to group work. Even leaders who pay lip service to the notion that the group is responsible for itself fall into the trap of "starting" the group. Once the leader assumes this initial responsibility, a norm is set for the group. From then on, members will wait for the leader to initiate. It makes more sense to think in terms of how the leader facilitates the group's getting started. Up to now, the leader has been leading by deference, but the goal is for the group to begin to take responsibility for itself as quickly as possible.

## Initial Resistance

In keeping with the climate setting the leader has done up to this point, the transition from preliminaries to issues is neither cute nor dramatic. The leader begins by reemphasizing a theme that should not be new to the group: "There is no issue so sensitive that we cannot talk about it in this group." The leader may add, "When *I* don't speak up about something that concerns me, it's because I'm afraid I won't be accepted or may sound stupid or because I'm afraid of expressing myself about issues. That's why I've found I don't speak up in groups."

That having been said, the leader asks, "Are there any issues—and that could include anything at all—that people have? Anything at all that you want to deal with?" The responsibility to get the group going now lies with the members. By and large, however, group members are not used to taking responsibility. Therefore, the leader can expect to see several kinds of obstructive responses in the early stages of a group. These patterned reactions occur in group after group, often repeatedly, and the leader must be prepared to deal with them.

## Silence

The most common response to the opening question "Does anyone have any issues?" is silence. One can expect, as a matter of course, that members will look at the leader as if to say, "Well, come on, get the group started." Although the tension that accompanies this silence may be uncomfortable for all concerned, the experienced leader will tolerate it, for this very discomfort may lead a member to step in to resolve the tension.

This is not to say that the leader must wait passively. There are appropriate interventions on the leader's part that empower members to assume the responsibility of participation rather than reassert the leader's control. As opposed to the leader's directing the group ("Why are *you* here? Why are *you* here? You, say something!"), these interventions set the stage for the way the group actually will run.

First, the leader can *clarify explicitly where the responsibility lies:*

> "Everybody's looking at me as though you think I'm supposed to get the group going. No. I arranged to get the room. Everyone has a chair, a place to put your coat. There's enough light in here. It's not too hot or cold. I've done my job. I know how groups work, and I have access to other resources. That's my job. It's not my job to ask questions and manipulate and orchestrate the group, only to facilitate."

Second, the leader can *use humor* to diffuse the tension: "I see we've just had a full minute of silence. Did somebody die? Are we paying tribute to somebody here?"

Third, the leader can *make a process statement:* "Group, I'm having a little difficulty here. It doesn't seem to be moving along. I don't know you all very well. Maybe someone can give me a hand with that, help me with my problem. Will someone give me a hand about what they see going on here now?"

Fourth, the leader can *make an "I" statement that models the expression of discomfort:* "We've been sitting here for a few minutes now, and nobody has said anything. I know I get uncomfortable when that happens, and I'm feeling uncomfortable right now. Can anyone help me with that? Does anyone have similar feelings?" Note how different this approach is from assuming that members feel uncomfortable, telling them they *should* feel that way, or probing for their feelings ("I sense a lot of discomfort in the room"). When the leader owns the feeling ("*I* feel uncomfortable; it's *my* anxiety"), members can feel safe in expressing their own feelings. Once such expression is accepted as a norm, long silences are less likely to occur.

Fifth, the leader can *make an "I" statement that addresses members' fears:*

"When I first started in groups, and even now, I'd say it's a sensitive thing for me to divulge certain things in group: my relationships with my parents and my intimate partners, my fears for the future. When I hesitate to disclose those things, I find that there are certain fears that keep me from participating: Will I disclose too much? If so, how will I be looked on? Will I be accepted? I don't know about anyone else. Does anyone else feel that way?"

When there is an extended silence early in group, or when a member asks for help by expressing reluctance to make personal disclosures in group, an appropriate self-disclosure on the leader's part may be in order. The point of the disclosure is not what is revealed specifically about the leader's life, but the simple acknowledgment that the leader shares certain common sensitivities. The fears articulated by the leader in the preceding passage— "Will I disclose too much? If so, how will I be looked on? Will I be accepted?"—are major obstacles that inhibit people's participation in group. By bringing those fears out into the open, the leader models stability so that the group can become a point of stability amid the unstable systems that characterize the members' lives.

Sixth, if all else fails, the leader can *ask appropriate questions*. Working through the initial silence may be an extended, repetitive process, with the leader trying several of the interventions listed before members feel safe in raising issues. If no one volunteers even after the leader has made process statements and "I" statements, the leader may direct a leading question to a group member. It is essential that the question be open-ended, since yes-or-no questions shut off group process rather than help it flow. The questions also must be about basic, universal concerns—broadly defined issues that most people can speak to without feeling intruded on or put on the defensive.

Questions such as the following are suitable for this purpose: Who are the important people in your life? How intimate are these relationships? What does intimacy mean to you? As shown in chapter 5, it is with questions such as these that the four basic needs outlined in reality therapy are introduced. Such questions are not meant to be asked and answered in a reactive way, with each member giving a "correct" or "satisfactory" answer so that the spotlight will move on to the next member. The purpose is not to fill time or open wounds; rather, it is to identify issues with a view toward clarification and resolution.

### "I Don't Want to Be Here"

The various manifestations of a desire not to be in group—doubts about the benefits of group counseling, a reluctance to share personal information, worries about whether other members will maintain confidentiality, and a preference for individual therapy—will be familiar to the leader from the pregroup interviews. Nonetheless, the fact that these issues were dealt with one on one will not prevent them from coming up again, disruptively, in group. Together they constitute one of the main defenses members use, consciously or unconsciously, to avoid confronting issues.

Inexperienced leaders make a number of common errors in their attempts to counter this obstructionist tactic. One is to *probe for feelings:*

*Member:* This is not for me. I knew I shouldn't have gotten into this. I don't understand it. I don't know these people. I feel uncomfortable here. I think I'd be better off in individual counseling.

*Leader:* Why don't you tell us a little more about what you're feeling. You say you're uncomfortable. What's that feeling about?

*Member:* I don't know. I just feel uncomfortable. I don't know any of these people.

Here, instead of expressing his or her own feelings, or instead of involving the group, the leader goes one on one with the member, as if in individual therapy. The member has already expressed his or her feelings. Why ask again? The leader's probe elicits only a restatement of what the member has already said.

A second error is to *try to justify the group by explaining its benefits.* There is no reason for the leader to take such a defensive position. It is not the leader's responsibility to keep the member in group or to keep the member contented in group. The member is there by choice. If the member does not want to continue in group, that is between the member and the referring agency.

A third error is to *manipulate the member into compliance by inducing guilt:*

*Member:* What good will it do me to sit here listening to all these people? How am I going to get help for my problems that way?

*Leader:* Don't you care about anybody else? Are you only concerned about yourself?

*Member:* I know what my problems are, and I just want to get on with doing what I need to do. Listening to them and all their denials—how's that going to help me?

The wrongheadedness of the leader's judgmental response is apparent. This coercive reaction, with its implication that the member *should* care about others, puts everyone in the group on the defensive. From here on, they will be on guard in what they recognize to be an unaccepting atmosphere.

A fourth error is to *generalize the member's reaction to the group as a whole:* "I sense that a lot of people don't want to be here. Does anyone else feel that way, too?" Such a weak response can act as a self-fulfilling prophecy, accelerating the momentum of a deteriorating situation. If other members don't already feel that they would rather be somewhere else, they may well feel that way now. This is the opposite of empowerment, of conveying strength. A member with some presence of mind would be justified in replying, "That's because of the way you're leading the group. You're allowing that to happen because you're not setting the proper climate." Most group members, of course, are neither so sophisticated nor so disinterested as to put it that way. In reality, this leader's demoralized reaction is more likely to elicit this sort of comeback:

> "Don't take it personally. It's uncomfortable for all of us to sit here like this, putting ourselves on display before a bunch of strangers. Maybe if you could just lighten it up and let us smoke or something, we could feel more comfortable. Maybe if we just talked about who we are and the kinds of things we're interested in, things would go a lot easier, and we could get into our issues more gradually."

In the anarchic atmosphere created by the leader's inadequate climate setting, a member steps in to revise the group norms. She wants to make it easier for everyone—for the leader not to feel bad, for members to smoke, for everyone to talk about whatever they wish. Playing on the leader's discomfort, she says, in effect, "It's your job to make us comfortable. Then it will be more comfortable for you, too." The more the leader buys into this, the more the group is undermined. Lack of leadership perpetuates in group the negative patterns (bickering, wheedling, and manipulating) that pervade members' lives, as members rightly perceive that the group has little benefit for them.

In contrast to these unproductive responses, the leader can deal with members' resistance to being in group in ways that reinforce positive climate setting. First and foremost, the leader must *reassert the group norm that members are there by choice:* "Granted, you may not *want* to be here, but we've already established that you're here by choice." This reminder can be bolstered by two other messages: first, that *making the choice not to be in group has negative consequences;* second, that *the member has the power to make additional choices that have positive consequences:*

> "Group, I'm having a problem. You don't want to be here? Well, what are we going to do? Help me out with this. If you don't want to be here, you don't have to be here. Now, I don't want to be neutral about it. I don't want to say I don't care if you stay or leave. I do care. I don't want to get into a power struggle with you. I'd rather you stayed. But if it's *that* uncomfortable for you, you can

take it up with the agency that sent you. Those are the consequences.

"Meanwhile, you're here, and we can't make you disappear. What are we going to do? My job is to use this time effectively. As for you, you made a choice to be here, and while you're here, you can make a choice to use this time for your benefit. How do you think you can use this group? Think about it. Think about some issues in your life. Let's see what we can do."

All or part of this statement may be appropriate in different circumstances. Note how the leader weaves together a reminder of the reasons people chose to be in group (that is, the consequences of leaving) with an expression of the leader's positive involvement with group members. The leader transmits strength by expressing confidence in the group process to further the members' well-being. Finally, instead of exploring or trying to rebut members' arguments against participation (a common trap that leads to stagnation and demoralization), the leader decisively shifts the ground to the group's legitimate agenda—that of identifying, clarifying, and resolving issues in people's lives.

Other rejoinders may be called for as well. If there seems to be a need to underline the consequences of choosing not to be in group, the leader can use a technique called *backing up the hearse,* which is described in more detail in chapter 6. Here the leader asks, "What would have happened if you hadn't come to group?" Further questions ("And what would have happened next?") take the member step by step, concretely and experientially, through the consequences of nonparticipation (for example, being confronted by the probation officer or being taken to prison). It is the member, not the leader or other members asking the questions, who acknowledges these consequences. In this way, the member experiences that he or she did and does have a choice—a difficult choice, perhaps, but a choice nonetheless.

The leader also may *express personal feelings* about members' resistance to the group—for example, "I'm getting bored listening to people say they don't want to be here." The leader may *challenge the presumed greater benefits of individual therapy,* as with this serious quip:

"People think individual therapy means that while you're talking to your therapist, a light will go on in your head and all of a sudden you'll understand. Well, I'm not a maintenance man; I'm not taking the responsibility to turn on any lights. And you know what? Neither does an individual therapist. You have to work there, too, to get the benefit. Just as in group, the most important things happen outside of therapy when you take effective control of your life."

In response to the complaint that "this is no fun," the leader can deliver a timely reminder: "This isn't a social club, a recreational group, or a dating service. You chose to be here, and you're here for a purpose, which is to think about and take steps to resolve some issues in your life."

A member's request that the group be allowed to smoke and converse about whatever they wish falls into a category of resistance that might be called "Let's party instead." This is a place where an "I" statement can be effective: "Sometimes, when *I'm* uncomfortable, I want to run away. [Here the leader can give a relevant personal example.] Can you think of any times when you're uncomfortable? Is anything like that going on in your life now?" With one stroke, the leader uses group process to create a bond of identification with the member, to parry the limit-testing request, and to bring the group back to its focus on issues.

The strongest language is reserved for the strongest challenges. During the first session of one group, several members said that they would prefer to be in individual counseling. The leader allowed this stalemate to persist to the point where one member felt emboldened to ask for a show of hands: "How many of you would rather have individual treatment?" The leader replied, "Look, I'd rather do individual therapy, too. Why don't you give this a chance. It's only the first session, and you'll see the value of being in group as it goes on." This response was defensive and, given the severity of the challenge, ineffectual. Faced with a bid to reduce the group to anarchy, a leader needs to set limits with forceful words spoken forcefully:

> "We have a problem over here. The problem is that the tail may be wagging the dog. Individual treatment is not an option. I'm not even going to say it's not an option *at this time*—it's not an option, period. Now, for whatever reason you came here, if you feel that this is not for you, I wouldn't agree with you, but I would respect your decision. And if you insist that the only thing for you is individual counseling, you're not going to get it here. Please, if you're going to sulk and pout, do it somewhere else."

### Limit Testing

The member who asked for a show of hands for individual versus group counseling was testing limits. Group leaders can expect such behavior from people who have been testing limits for much of their lives. In a common scenario, the uneasy silence that follows the opening up of the group to members' issues is broken when a member takes out a pack of cigarettes. "Got a match?" he asks defiantly.

The challenge for the leader is to block this behavior and reassert group norms without sounding like a nagging schoolmarm. In this respect, small differences in wording can make a big difference. Rules are imposed; norms are agreed to. Talking about rules tends to convey an image of arbitrary power, which may lead to sullen, silent compliance or to rebellion—for example, a call for a vote about whether smoking should be allowed. It is better, therefore, to speak in terms of norms, expectations, or agreements. Having the norms prominently posted emphasizes the group's collective responsibility for maintaining them. The leader elaborates on this theme, beginning with an "I" statement, to check the limit-testing behavior: "Group, I'm having a problem. When we agreed to come here, we agreed to certain other things as well. Vince agreed not to smoke, and here he wants to smoke." The norms are not someone else's rules; they are what everyone voluntarily agreed to. If Vince does not agree, then he has decided not to be in group.

If the challenge persists, the leader once again draws the parallel between the group and the larger world:

"If you choose to work in a nonsmoking area, can you decide to light up there? If you choose to take a nonsmoking flight, can you change your mind and smoke? Does the flight attendant say, 'We have no smoking here unless the passengers want to discuss it and change the policy'? There are things any group needs to agree on in order to live and work together."

As in this example, limit testing can provide an occasion to model the agreement on norms that any working unit (family, work, or social) must have.

If the leader does not deal decisively with initial limit testing, the atmosphere of the group is likely to deteriorate. For example, early in the first session, one member gives out his business card to all the other members. The leader lets this inappropriate gesture pass without comment. Minutes later, another member, seeing that limits have not been set, asks to borrow a pen and begins furiously scribbling notes, thereby taking himself out of the group interaction and calling attention to himself in the process. This contagion of limit testing commonly occurs when the leader does not set and maintain a working climate in the group.

This contagion must be stopped before it escalates into anarchy. When the first member passes out business cards, the leader should immediately realize that the member is testing limits. Acting in a way he knows he could not get away with elsewhere, the member is trying to engage the leader in a power struggle. An experienced leader knows this, and the member knows the leader knows it. If the leader does not call the member on it, it sets the tone for a group gone out of control.

This is a time to reassert firm control in language that conveys unmistakably the consequences of limit testing:

"Group, I'm having a problem with this. If *I* were doing this, I'd know I was doing something rude and discourteous. Now maybe you've never been in a group before, but it's hard for me to believe that you don't know you're being rude. Right here we've got a problem. This is not a group for psychotic people. You know why you're here. There's no need for me to tell you why you're here. If you're having a delusion and don't know where you are, maybe we'll send you down to the local mental hospital."

Of course, the leader would not speak this way if he thought that this member was legitimately confused, let alone psychotic. The leader knows, however, on the basis of the member's behavior and background information (clinical records and pregroup interview), that the member is not mentally ill but is "gaming." In such cases, strong language, even sarcasm, is a tool of climate setting. It is needed at times to stake out the essential boundary between disagreement and disrespect.

At the same time, the leader is not to be perceived as a police officer or a disciplinarian who withholds privileges if members act obnoxiously, deviate from group process, or simply displease him or her. A person's freedom or well-being is not to be predicated on toeing the line in group. For members to feel safe in group, the atmosphere must not be punitive or intimidating. Alternatively, outright, pugnacious, or combative resistance may make a person ineligible to continue in group. In that event, the group leader must make a report to the appropriate agencies, and the natural consequences follow.

## Overcoming a Negative Climate

Complaints, blaming, hostility, one-upmanship and limit testing are like a volatile chemical compound contained at high pressure, ready to escape through the slightest opening. There is no need to encourage these behaviors in order to demonstrate and process group members' denial and flight; they will occur spontaneously, especially early in group, and the leader's task is to keep them from overwhelming the group. As the griping and sniping reach a fever pitch, the contagion of resistance sweeps through the group like a fire, and members react with the same disorganization as people trapped in a burning building: one looks for a stairway; another heads for an open window; a third jumps in the bathtub. "Let's not fight!" one member appeals. "Can't we all be friends?" There is mass confusion and a breakdown of process.

Despite the proclivity of coerced group members to resist, when things reach this extreme, it is because group leaders commonly have no idea how much they do not know about running groups. It is not necessarily their fault; they lack rigorous training in climate setting. Under the onslaught of hostile, disruptive behavior, group leaders may give up and let their ship be tossed by the waves until the negative energy subsides. Fortunately, group process provides techniques for regaining control. This remedial climate setting is not accomplished by taking a scolding, schoolmasterish tone ("I don't want to have to ask you again not to interrupt!"). Rather, it is done by acknowledging the state of affairs with "I" statements and process statements:

> "Group, I'm having a problem. Everyone seems to be doing whatever they want to do, and that's not tolerable. I can't work this way. What I might ask people to do—I understand that you're upset right now, and I'll take responsibility for not making things clearer in the beginning—but would you please just observe for a few minutes? Actively observe—don't pout and sulk the way you're doing. Actively observe, because that will help me. I have been in groups before. I have felt coerced into it, and I didn't think being in group would do me any good. But I found out that there is something I can learn from this process."

By assuming responsibility and at the same time shifting to a positive focus, the leader conveys strength in a powerful way.

## Climate Setting in Action

The following example of climate setting in response to resistance is taken from the third session of a teaching group for group leaders. Note the misunderstanding of and resistance to group process that occur even among professionals exposed to two prior sessions of climate setting:

*Bob:* This is how it feels when there is silence in my groups. It's as if they're saying, "Shut your mouth, leave me alone, and let's get out of here!"
*Leader:* Is that how *you* feel *now*?
*Bob:* [doesn't answer question] What happens when this happens in group? What do you do?
*Leader:* If what we're going to do is talk about groups, then let's end this right now and go across the hall to the classroom, where I can lecture about groups. As long as I'm the facilitator, this group will stay on focus in the here and now and not talk *about* groups.
*George:* What's the prime focus of this meeting?
*Leader:* There is no prime focus. The prime focus is you and me. I don't

come in here with an issue, the way you come in thinking, "What's he going to talk about today?" That's not what we're doing here.

*Ann:* My issue is that I want to get more out of these meetings. I learn a lot from this process, and I'm concerned that if we don't get more involved in it, we won't be able to do this sort of thing. I think this is very beneficial. I'm just unsure sometimes about what to say and how to participate. I want to be careful that I don't gloss over issues with a lot of superficial stuff. I just don't know what to do at this point, other than that I find these meetings extremely helpful and that I'd like to see them get off the ground and start to do some good work.

*Leader:* I think they have, up to now. I think we've demonstrated that issues can be raised and resolved and that we can get some closure and move on from there.

I take this silence and irrelevancy as resistance, and I'm slightly annoyed. If this continues, if people just want me to entertain them, if people don't want to bring issues to group and use me as a facilitator and a model for how these issues get resolved, then it's much easier for me, believe me, to do case studies, to talk about therapy, about groups. Believe me, this is the hardest work I do. If you folks in this room don't see this as having value, we can just terminate this. I'll lecture, and you'll raise hands and take notes. But in this group, I'm not a schoolteacher.

*Ann:* I'm struggling with what's appropriate to bring to group. I really don't feel I want to go into any personal psychoanalysis with my peers, so I keep asking myself, "What's something superficial that I can safely talk about?" I really am having a hard time knowing what, how much, and how to bring it to group. There are some things that I need to deal with personally that I really don't care to get into with my peers, and I'm having a hard time knowing where to draw the line.

*Leader:* That's fine. I would treat this as a peer support group, not a therapy group. Bring up any issues you have with one another, anything that's going on with clients or people you work with, anything that has to do with your own experience. Issues about what kind of future you envision for yourselves—socially, professionally, anything along those lines. I respect everyone's privacy, which is why it's not my business to ask anyone what's going on in their lives. I won't do that because that's taking responsibility for the group on myself. It's not my responsibility to draw people out. George put the responsibility on me to define the focus of the group, but I'm not going to do that. So go ahead and raise whatever issues you want, knowing that there is some risk involved.

*Ann:* But only to the point where I'm willing to take the risk. If it gets off into a vein that I'm not comfortable with, I still have some responsibility to take control of that, do I not?

*Leader:* For me, from my years both as a group member and a group leader, there is one overriding reason for the kind of resistance we're experiencing here. And that is "Will I look foolish? Will I say too much? Will I expose too much? Will I be accepted? Will I be okay?" That's the major resistance in this room now.

*Ann:* One thing that's stopped me from speaking up is my fear that others will gang up on me and overpower me. I think I've gotten past that because I've learned that group process has built-in safety mechanisms to control that sort of thing. The group is responsible for what goes on here, and I am part of the group, so *I* am responsible. But what I feel I still need to work out is—may I just talk to the group?

*Leader:* Of course. That's what the group is for.

*Ann:* I'm just a little unclear about . . . perhaps we need to clarify with one another what we can bring to group. I'm not real sure how to open up without asking to be psychoanalyzed. Does anybody else feel that way besides me?

*[Silence]*

*Michelle:* I assume this is a pause for people to think.

*Leader:* Is that what it is for *you?*

*Richard:* I'll tell you what's bothering *me*. My wife [looks at leader]— may I?

*Leader:* Anything at all.

*Richard:* I'm having a problem with my wife.

In this example, considerable time and effort had to be spent on climate setting before any member would bring up a sensitive personal issue. The group members repeatedly looked to the leader to teach, to define the issues, to give answers, to grant permission, and to run the group. Even people in training as group leaders habitually fall back into a member-leader dyad rather than a full group interchange. Note the way Ann asked the leader if she could address the group and Richard asked if he could raise an issue concerning his wife, as if that were inappropriate for the group. The leader worked through this resistance by modeling the expression of frustration, validating members' concern for privacy, voicing common fears, and continually putting the responsibility back on the group. Ann, picking up the leader's exasperation, was mobilized to reaffirm the group process and to take positive initiatives to get the group moving. The leader transmitted strength to her, and her contributions in turn contributed to climate setting. Although Ann's issue about personal reticence was not fully resolved, her willingness to risk even as much as she did opened things up for Richard's hesitant raising of an issue. The work of identifying, clarifying, and resolving issues could then begin. The leader was well aware, however, that climate setting is ongoing and would need to be renewed in subsequent sessions.

This training empowered Ann to lead her own groups effectively. Now an experienced leader, she describes her own approach to climate setting under the stress of resistance:

"When a group starts to break down, I turn things around with a process statement: 'Stop for a second. Something is breaking down here. What's going on? Look around and tell me what you see going on here.' I ask, 'What are we doing? Why is everything being directed at me? Is this your group? Are you having trouble saying what you want to say? I'm strictly a facilitator; the responsibility is yours. Now what are we here for?' I make them accountable for their behavior—it's a group problem.

"Once, when my group had been lethargic and unresponsive for weeks, I did just the opposite of what they expected me to do. I came into the group in an extremely good mood. I greeted the group with some self-disclosure. I told them that I was doing an assessment of the group for my supervisor and that I didn't like what I was assessing. I said, 'I have this problem. I'm going to have to tell the truth, and right now this group's a real embarrassment to me. I'm feeling angry because I know the quality of work you can do. Group, what are we going to do about the assessment I have to make tonight? How do you feel about my saying you're part of a group that isn't working and just doesn't give a damn? I'm feeling frustrated; what can we do about my frustration?'

"Then I made known my expectations and got a commitment from the group to live up to them. I asked, 'If I made a deal with you that you could get out of group in forty-five minutes if you paid attention and gave me your best efforts, could you do that? Would you be willing to do it?' The whole group sat up and took a deep breath. I continued, 'These are my expectations of you: I want participation, positive feedback, and so forth.' Then I confronted them: 'You have the skills to do it. Why aren't you doing it? Am I asking too much of you?' Since the group told me they had the skills to do it, they were saying they were choosing not to do it. So I charged them with the responsibility: 'If we can play "let's make a deal," why can't you do this without all the games?' I tried to make the group accountable for doing what they were capable of doing. Then they couldn't hide behind 'I don't know what's going on; I don't know how to do this.' It was up front.

"For some time after that, the group took on new responsibility and new life. Of course, they started slipping and got lazy again—we all do—so I kept stoking the fires. But instead of coming in and chewing the group out ('Hey, you guys aren't doing any work; you're really bad; you're going to be written up'), I tried to spark some enthusiasm. I tried to make the group fun.

"Instead of coming in with a bunch of heavy rules and regs, I usually say to a group, 'I know this is going to be a good group today.' Sometimes if they're expecting discipline, I give them an incentive to pick things up. I give them a little encouragement, saying, 'I know all of you, and I know you can do good work.'

"If a group knows I'm waiting to analyze them and have the final word on everything, they tighten up; it stifles them. The more I can charge my groups with their own responsibility, tell them what's expected of them, and let them go, the more they can flourish."

Ann's account summarizes much of the material in this chapter and the previous one. Implicit throughout is an underlying principle of climate setting: increased expectations elicit increased performance.

# 5
# Identifying and Clarifying Issues

During each group session, issues are raised and brought to some form of resolution. This is the primary work of the group. It is carried out in the climate described in the previous chapters and is guided by the norms established at the outset. The leader's task, therefore, includes climate setting on a weekly basis.

What differentiates this approach from what is typically seen in training and practice is the uncompromising reliance on group process as a self-renewing, self-regulating mechanism, with group members having the responsibility to identify, clarify, confront, and evaluate issues of importance to their lives. Stripped of lecturing, story telling, and venting, group process gives members the wherewithal to exercise problem-solving and decision-making skills in a context of individual and collective responsibility.

The following overview of the process is presented in the language of reality therapy:

*Identifying and Clarifying.* The member is asked, "What do you want?" That is, "What conditions, different from those you experience now, would satisfy your needs?"

*Behavior.* The member is asked, "What are you doing?" Confrontation holds up a mirror to the behavior by which the member currently attempts to satisfy basic needs.

*Evaluation.* The member is asked, "Is what you are doing getting you what you want?" Apparently not, since the member is in group talking about the issue. Faced with the natural consequences of the behavior, the member is asked whether the prospect of greater need satisfaction is worth the risks involved in changing the behavior. The member makes a value judgment whether to stick with the status quo or to risk change.

*Plan.* With the support of the group, the member devises a plan to implement the value judgment outside the group.

Identification and clarification are outlined in this chapter, confrontation (behavior) and evaluation (up to and including the value judgment) are addressed in the next chapter. Chapter 8 continues with the feedback and consolidation of learning that solidify the value judgment, followed by the steps taken to formulate and implement a plan of action.

## How Issues Are *Not* Raised

In a process group of this sort, the group members identify the issues. When the leader identifies the issues, it leads to passivity, as the group continues to wait for him or her to decide what to talk about. Student leaders, reluctant to confront issues, announce topics such as alcoholism, depression, or the problems of parenting in the nineties. Group members are only too happy to talk about, say, denial; any such abstraction has nothing to do with them, of course. Exercises, too, belong for the most part in the realm of program rather than process. An exception is the problem-solving exercise described in chapter 8, which is tailored to the purposes of a process group. Value clarification or planning-board exercises (which we recommend in chapter 10 as an individual postgroup activity) are most useful when members introduce them. Even if an exercise has little value in itself, members who are empowered to take such initiatives in group are more likely to do so outside the group. Gimmicks such as having one member fall backward and be caught by another are to be avoided. This kind of melodrama only undermines the foundation of trust that is built up over time. Group process has no need for cute, staged effects; it is straightforward, practical, and solidly grounded.

There is, however, a place in group counseling for homework assignments and referrals to outside resources. By reading books, attending meetings, and following up on plans made in group, members begin the all-important task of taking what they learn in group out into the community. Such outside activity reinforces group process. In distinguishing between process and programming, the essential consideration is this: what can a group accomplish in eight or ten sessions that has the best chance to make a difference in a person's life? Group members have heard an abundance of lectures. Many also have heard and told numerous "war stories" in self-help groups. What few have had is an active, structured, positively reinforcing experience of problem solving and decision making. People empower themselves by doing, not by endless talk about feelings. The experience of being part of a working group, even if it does no more than plant a seed, is likely to have a longer-term effect than lectures, exercises, or emotional catharsis alone.

A common error arising from both group members' and leaders' expectations is to treat group counseling as a facsimile of mutual-support groups such as AA. Members' resistance to group process often is expressed as irritation at the divergence from the one type of group with which they are familiar: "How is all this going to help me? I'm here because I want to do something about my alcoholism. I want to be with a group of people who have the same problem I do and who *want* to recover. I don't want to be with all these people who are in denial." For their part, group leaders who are themselves experienced in AA and who have not been trained in any other model of professional counseling tend to raise and resolve issues in a manner that closely replicates AA meetings. This duplication of a useful community resource sacrifices the distinctive benefits of group counseling.

It is best to treat group counseling and mutual self-help groups such as AA as separate parts of a comprehensive program for addicted individuals. The two fulfill needs in different ways, and neither takes the place of the other. A person who is actively addicted or is affected by addiction in the family may benefit from a referral to a group such as AA, Al-Anon, Secular Organizations for Sobriety, Rational Recovery, or Methods of Moderation and Abstinence. That group will provide acceptance, a sense of commonality, a social outlet, and a direct, forceful concentration on the issues of addiction and recovery. Meanwhile, group counseling will support the person's sobriety by enhancing self-esteem, self-efficacy, coping skills, and social adjustment.

Group counseling, while it can be an emotionally satisfying, enlivening experience, does not offer spirituality; it aspires instead to a thorough professionalism. The elusiveness of this distinction for inexperienced group leaders leads to hybrid groups and unclear messages to members. To take one example we have observed, the leader's ending each session with the Lord's Prayer is inappropriate in a professional context (especially in a public agency), even if all the members of the group approve. There is likewise no place in group counseling for the extended story telling that is a staple of AA meetings, since issues are raised in a counseling group in order to bring them to resolution.

Group counseling and AA do have some perspectives and methods in common. For instance, in group counseling, we use the expression "Identify, don't compare," which comes from AA. In group counseling, however, the identification that is sought is not a global affiliation with other group members that sets them apart from those outside the group. Rather, it is a recognition of universal human experiences, foibles, and dilemmas, expressed in terms of specific behaviors, feelings, and choices. Although members may come to group with a label such as "drunk driver," "spouse abuser," "child of an alcoholic," or "person who loves too much," it is not the mission of the group to persuade them to accept that identity. On the contrary, the mission of the group is to empower members to use problem-solving and decision-making skills to identify and satisfy basic needs. Group counseling is concerned not with who you are, but with what you do.

## How Issues Are Raised

Rather than raise issues, the leader conveys that it is the responsibility of group members to do so. In the first session, the leader follows up the initial climate setting by asking whether anyone has any issues he or she wants to raise. At the outset, the leader will likely need to tolerate silence and tension, deal with resistance, and encourage participation in ways that do not take responsibility away from the group. These techniques are explained in chapter 4.

A similar procedure occurs in subsequent sessions, with (perhaps) somewhat less effort required of the leader. Everything that happens in group emerges naturally from group process. The leader does not point fingers and ask, "How are you today, Sam?" or "What's going on with you, Helen?" As members become accustomed to the process, the leader can begin the session simply by saying, "Let's group." In a group that is working well, there should be less resistance as the group progresses. Nonetheless, the leader must be prepared to deal with resistance at any time.

Given that more issues usually are raised than resolved in any one session, some continuity from one session to the next is desirable. Depending on the circumstances, the leader may begin by asking questions such as the following: "Will someone review what went on last time?" "Any homework or tasks that you had?" "Any unfinished business from last time that requires closure?" When closure is reached on matters held over from the previous session, the group moves on to new issues. During this transition, there may again be silence and tension, which are dealt with as before.

The leader also may ask individual members whether they want to continue with an unfinished issue from the previous session, as in this example: "When we last met, Sam, there was an issue about your not knowing whether you would get the same job you had before when you leave here, or whether you would go directly from here to jail. We didn't have time to get complete resolution or closure on that. Would you like to talk about that?"

At the same time, the completion of unfinished issues at the start of the next session should not be rigidly programmed. The agenda for the session is to be the members' agenda, not the leader's. To capitalize on the sense of immediacy associated with current issues, the leader might first ask (just as in the first session), "Does anybody have any issues with which he or she would like some help?" If so, unfinished business would be deferred until issues of immediate salience have been aired.

The leader who works in an agency (for example, an intermediate-care program) may have information about issues in people's lives that comes from outside the group. This information may be used only in ways that do not violate the privacy and autonomy of members, compromise relationships among group members, or undermine the trust required for the group to work. This privileged information comes from the work the leader does between groups to keep up-to-date with the progress members are making. While reviewing records, keeping notes up-to-date, and checking on a member's overall progress, the leader may learn about an issue that the member might beneficially bring up in group. If this issue is common knowledge among group members (as it might be in a residential center), the leader may ask the member in group if he or she wants to talk about it.

If the member has divulged this information to the leader between sessions, or if the leader has read it in the records or heard it from colleagues, it remains privileged information. It should not be dealt with individually outside the group, which would amount to giving the member simultaneous individual and group counseling. Instead, the member should be encouraged—strenuously, if necessary—to make it a group issue. Such a between-sessions dialogue might sound like this:

*Leader:* I understand, Tom, that since the last group, your wife ran away with a deliveryman. We've been given that information here. I think it would be good to raise that in group. Is that something that you might want the group to help you with?

*Tom:* No, it's too personal.

*Leader:* I would encourage you to do it. You're here for treatment, and your treatment is in group. Your wife left you—that doesn't say anything about you. It doesn't mean you aren't adequate; it doesn't mean you aren't doing everything you're supposed to. It means that at this time, you've had a loss. How is that affecting you, and what can you do to gain effective control of your life? That's what the group can help you with.

*Tom:* It's too painful. It's just too soon.

*Leader:* Maybe you'd like to bring it up in a week or two. But if you wait more than a month, it will be too late—the group will be over. Remember, there's no issue too sensitive to be brought up in group. People come to groups and talk about child abuse, homosexuality, and terminal illnesses such as AIDS. We've yet to see an issue that's too sensitive for group process. Surely people can identify with the way you feel when your wife leaves you.

It remains Tom's choice whether to bring the issue to group, and that choice must be respected. However, if Tom's holding back is a problem for the leader, the leader can raise and own that problem in group without divulging the content of Tom's issues: "Group, I'm having a problem. Tom has issues in his life that he isn't bringing to group. It's a problem for me that he isn't participating in a way that will give him the most benefit from the group."

The leader, too, may feel uncomfortable with an issue. Although no issue is too sensitive for group process, an issue such as child abuse, homosexuality, or AIDS may be uncomfortable for a particular group leader at a particular time. With coleadership (discussed in chapter 9), it is less likely that one leader's discomfort will lead to an avoidance of the issue by the group. Meanwhile, the leader can work out the problem with supervision, peer support (including the coleader), or professional consultation.

## Identifying and Clarifying

In a group conducted in an intermediate-care facility for drug abusers, one member, Santiago, responds to another member's request for feedback by saying, "Sometimes I say my opinion and nobody pays any attention, so I feel I might as well keep my mouth shut." So as not to go off track and leave the other member's issue unresolved, the leader says, "That's an issue we'll have plenty of time to go into." Reviewing Santiago's record between sessions, the leader infers that the language barrier Santiago experiences in group (where other members do not seem to take the trouble to understand his heavily accented English) may also be a barrier to his adjustment outside of group, where it may adversely affect his self-esteem and contribute to his drug use and delinquency. It is not, however, the leader's job to psychoanalyze Santiago; his job is to encourage him to bring the issue to the group. Santiago can then draw his own connections and conclusions.

At the start of the next session, the leader asks if anyone has any issues. When no one volunteers, the leader has this exchange with Santiago:

*Leader:* Santiago, I recall something you said last time that we said we would get back to. May I go back to that?
*Santiago:* Yes.
*Leader:* I don't want to give you a problem you don't have, but *I've* been having a problem. I observe that you don't usually initiate issues; you only react when you're asked a question. Now I don't expect everyone to participate at the same level, but I realize that I haven't had high expectations of you—and this is my problem, not yours—because of the language issue. Without intending to slight you, I haven't been directing much interchange toward you. You mentioned last time that you have felt some discomfort about this. If you have any thoughts and feelings about it now, this is a good time and place to talk about them.
*Santiago:* When I say something, people ignore it, so after a while, I don't say anything.

This initial statement is only the beginning of identifying and clarifying an issue. Using Santiago's issue and other pertinent examples, we will present various techniques the leader can use to make sure an issue is precisely identified and fully clarified. These are the first steps toward resolution. If they are not followed through, the issue is, in effect, dropped.

### Refocus Any Issue as the Speaker's

"I" statements are the universal currency of communication in group, both for the person who raises an issue and for others who address that issue (until the person is ready for direct feedback, as described in chapter 8). Often the group member will present an issue as if it were someone else's problem: a spouse is fickle, children are out of control, the boss is unreasonable, working conditions are poor, nobody cooperates. Here the leader (modeling for other group members) refocuses the issue so that the member owns it. The leader does this by asking, "How do *you* feel about it?" or "How does that affect *you*?" or "How is this a problem for *you*?" Granted, others may be acting egregiously and may have their own frustrations and discontents, but those others are not in the group. The group can only help the person who *is* there with the problem that he or she experiences.

For example, in a group concerned with marital problems, Cynthia speaks of her uncertainty about whether her husband intends to leave her:

*Cynthia:* I'd like to know where he stands.
*Leader:* Let's set him aside for a second. Let's get to the point. I'm convinced from what you've said that you want to stay married. Is that right?
*Cynthia:* Yes.
*Leader:* What do you think you can do to make that outcome more likely?
*Cynthia:* Is it my responsibility to confront him, or is it his responsibility to tell me how he feels?
*Leader:* Clear that up for me. Does everyone understand what Cynthia just asked?
*Jane:* It's your responsibility, Cynthia, because you're the one who's concerned.
*Leader:* I agree. Your husband is not here today, and it's impossible for this group to deal with what *he* should or should not do. Let's talk about how *you* feel and what *your* options are.

Another way members distance themselves from their own issues is to speak in impersonal terms, as if some hypothetical person were having the problem. The leader (or, eventually, another group member) then makes clear that the issue isn't about "you," "one," or "somebody." The speaker, as in the case of Cynthia, must own the issue with "I" statements:

*Cynthia:* It's the kind of thing you keep putting off and putting off until the whole relationship unravels for lack of communication.

*Leader:* Who's putting it off? I'm not. If *you're* putting it off, say so.

When another member uses impersonal pronouns in place of "I" statements, what might otherwise be a useful point of identification may come off as disengaged and pompous:

*Linda:* I wonder if you might possibly be avoiding this confrontation, Cynthia. When you do that, it can eat at you until it grows all out of proportion.

*Leader:* Could you relate it to yourself, Linda, to any experiences *you* may have had, instead of to what might be possible for Cynthia, because anything might be possible.

If the leader does not block one member from inquiring and probing, others may join in, and the person who raised the issue will become the object of an inquisition. Nothing could be further from the purposes of the group. It is essential that one be able to listen receptively, which is impossible when one is kept busy defending and justifying oneself.

Even well-intentioned advice giving is to be blocked, as illustrated here:

*Ruth:* Everyone in here can commit to being patient and listening carefully to what you're saying, but that's not enough. Out in the world, in the community, you can't have everybody stop and say, "Well, Santiago, I'll go that extra mile for you." You have to learn to be assertive.

*Leader:* I don't know about you, but I don't like people telling me what to do.

Or, more gently:

*Leader:* Is that what *you* have to do, Ruth? Don't lay that on him.

*Ruth:* Okay, I'll stop preaching. Being assertive really helps *me* get people to pay attention to what I have to say. If I have something to say, it's my own fault if people don't hear it. I have to take that responsibility because if I wait for people to ask for my opinion, they never will. If I assert myself, people won't have to make a point of being sensitive to me because I'll demand their respect and they'll listen to me. That's what I've found in my own life, at least.

## Keep on Track by Deferring Other Issues

While one person's issue is being discussed, "I" statements by others create experiential links showing how others react to similar experiences. Sometimes, however, "I" statements made in response to one issue bring up whole new issues. Even when the statements are appropriately made, the leader must intervene, acknowledge the validity of the new issue, and defer it for later consideration. Otherwise, the group can become chaotic, with a string of issues raised but never resolved. At such moments, the leader may need to make a clarifying statement, such as the following: "Wait, we have two issues here: X and Y. Let's concentrate on these two for now. Let's get some closure on them before we go on to other things."

For example, just as Santiago had to wait after interjecting the issue of his communication problem, so Helen is blocked from interposing an issue of her own in the guise of responding to him:

*Helen:* I have to take responsibility for some of this. I have a very difficult time with foreign accents generally. Maybe it's that I wasn't exposed to them enough when I was a child. When someone starts talking fast in an accent, I feel awkward and embarrassed, and I usually just excuse myself and run away rather than stay and work it out. Can somebody help me with this? What can I do about my problem?

*Leader:* Let's hold that for now. We'll get back to it. Right now, can anyone relate to what Helen is saying about how she experiences Santiago's accent?

Here Helen appropriately takes responsibility and makes "I" statements that identify the problem as her own. These statements, however, go beyond process statements meant to illuminate and clarify Santiago's experience; they raise a new issue that threatens to preempt Santiago's issue. The help Helen asks for is not about her interaction with Santiago, but about this more general problem of hers. To avoid going off track, the leader refocuses the group's attention on the part of what Helen said that relates to Santiago's issue.

When the leader says, "We'll get back to that later," it is important that the group follow through on that commitment, subject to the priority given immediate concerns. It is the leader's responsibility to remember issues raised but not resolved, to record such unfinished business in the group notes after the session, and, at an appropriate time, to ask whether the member who raised an issue still wants to take it up with the group. With this demonstrated concern to fulfill commitments and not leave issues unresolved, the leader models organization and stability and builds trust and confidence in the integrity of the group.

### Block Distracting or Disruptive Behavior

The leader monitors group process so that it continues to flow freely. Inappropriate, off-focus comments can interrupt the identification and clarification of issues and make members reluctant to raise other issues. We have shown how the leader blocks advice giving and defers extraneous matters.

More serious disruptions such as judgmental criticism, personal attacks, intimidation, scapegoating, and gossiping are discussed in chapter 7. As a rule, after some initial modeling of appropriate responses, the leader addresses the group with a process statement: "Hold it, I'm having a problem here. What's really going on now?" After a time, group members learn to identify problem behaviors. If no one else does so, the leader says something on the following order: "If I were in Joe's position right now, I'd feel that I was being attacked. I'd be feeling uncomfortable, and I'd probably be pulling back."

## Insist on Concreteness and Specificity

As part of identifying and clarifying, vague, general statements are to be converted into concrete, specific ones. An issue that is not precisely defined cannot be confronted and evaluated; an amorphously defined problem cannot be met with an effective plan of action. The group cannot do much with global emotional states such as depression, anger, "feeling lousy," and so forth. It is imperative, therefore, that the leader and the group ask for specificity: Who? What? Where? When? At whom? At what? This part of the process may include some verbal byplay in which humor is used to take the edge off difficult subjects—for instance, "You say you want to straighten out your life. What's crooked about it?"

Here is how the leader sought to elicit greater concreteness and specificity from Santiago.

*Santiago:* When I say something, people ignore it, so after a while, I don't say anything.

*Leader:* Could you give an example or two of that?

*Santiago:* I'll say something in a group of people, and everybody just goes on talking, and then some other guy says the same thing, and people say he's the one that said it.

*Leader:* Like what group of people? This group?

*Santiago:* This group? I don't know.

*Leader:* Name one person, one time, one place. This is the time to take risks. What I see happening now, Santiago, is that we're talking around something and not really getting to the specific point. And I would ask you to come up with a time and place where that happened. I'll tell you, if it were me, if I didn't specify what I was talking about, then I would always expect to be ignored and slighted and discounted, and I would expect to feel bad a lot of the time when I was around people. Because if I don't let people know what's on my mind, then I can't expect them to take me seriously. And if there ever was a time and place to say what's on your mind, this is it. We ask people all the time to confront each other in group, just the way you saw Joe confront me last week. That's what we're looking for. Is there any time it's happened here, anyone you want to speak to about this?

*Santiago:* Anyone here? Not that I can think of.

*Leader:* You haven't had this issue with anyone here? It's hard for me to understand that. You brought this issue up in group and said it was a problem for you, and if it's a problem in your life generally, I wouldn't be surprised if it were a problem for you here in group. Someone give me some help with that.

*Ruth:* Santiago, you are saying that nothing like this has happened with one of us?

*Santiago:* Not today.

*Ruth:* But it has happened some other time?

*Leader:* That's what I want to know. Is there anyone here—Ruth, Helen, Lucas, even myself—have you had this problem with me, when I haven't listened to you and I've dismissed what you said?

*Santiago:* I don't know. Maybe I don't understand what's going on because I don't speak the language so well.

*Lucas:* That's what we're trying to find out. Which one of us has been doing this?

*Santiago:* Which one of you?

*Leader:* Whoa, hold it! What I see happening now is defensive. Some of us are busy thinking, "Oh, please, not me, not me." That's how things break down. Each of us is responding to our own particular needs.

This extended exchange illustrates the often subtle, unpredictable turns of group dynamics and the importance of monitoring and reacting swiftly to these changing currents. In asking Santiago to be more concrete and specific, the leader correctly reasoned that the most useful confrontation of the issue would be the one closest to home—in the here and now of the group interaction rather than in Santiago's recollections of some other setting. The leader attempted to overcome Santiago's resistance to confronting fellow group members in the interest of empowering him to stand up to others in his life. It might have been liberating for Santiago, as well as for others in the group, to learn how easily one can survive such confrontations in a supportive environment. Instead, Santiago was threatened by the prospect of naming names within the group. As the leader pushed him perhaps a little too long and hard, other group members began to feel themselves the object of an inquisition. Sensing the growing discomfort in the group, the leader quickly retrieved the situation with a process statement. He might have solicited such a statement from the group, but he elected to move decisively to keep things from getting out of hand. Although it would have been ideal for Santiago to confront his discomfort with people in the group, the leader subsequently retreated to safer ground and, with similar questions (Where?

When? Who?), elicited a concrete, specific example from Santiago concerning his interactions with people outside the group.

In addition to *asking* for specificity, the leader *models* specificity in self-disclosure. An example of such modeling is included in the discussion of identification that follows.

### Encourage Identification

"Identify; don't compare" is a motto that group counseling shares with twelve-step programs. When people discover common areas of experience, they develop empathy for others even as they gain insight into their own lives and see greater possibilities for change. Identification works at a number of levels simultaneously. Explicitly, any group member can help clarify any other member's issues by drawing an analogy with his or her own experience. Implicitly, each group member can see his or her issues mirrored in the issues raised by others in the group. In a properly functioning group, the issues actually discussed are only the tip of the iceberg of work being done silently by group members.

Identification sometimes succeeds in clarifying an issue when direct questioning fails. Although Santiago (in the preceding example) was flustered when the leader questioned him, he finds his voice in response to a sympathetic analogy offered by another member:

*Helen:* I know that for me, sometimes I have something I want to express, but there's something else going on and I can't seem to get enough attention. If I feel it's important enough, I have to start waving flags: "Hold it, folks, wait a minute, this matters. I think you people need to know this."

*Santiago:* I think that's it. I think it really isn't just the language thing. I don't demand the attention. I don't scream. I don't talk loud to get the attention.

*Helen:* I don't know if that's the way it is for you, Santiago, but if I let what I have to say be overlooked, nobody else will pick up on it. If I don't get people's attention, I can't blame them for not listening.

*Santiago:* That's my problem right there. I say something, and somebody else jumps right in and takes over, and I just sit there. I guess I'm just too passive.

Identification is a powerful bond, overcoming differences in background, perspective, and current life situation. Here another group member finds a mutually supportive link between his experience and Santiago's even though the details of their stories are different: "I can relate to that. Not so much the accent or language problem. But sometimes where I work, I make so many jokes and bring in so much humor that when I say something that

I consider important, people don't pay attention, and so someone else gets credit for the idea. I think I know what you're saying."

Learning to identify rather than compare is especially important for the active substance abuser. A person who has not lost his job, is not out on the street, is not beating up his spouse, and is not stealing from his children's piggy bank may listen with detachment to those who tell of such things and shake his head, thinking, "No, that's not me." That is what it means to compare. Comparing insulates a person from a valuable part of the group experience and perpetuates the habit of not facing issues. It obscures the kind of basic insight that true identification opens up—for example, that drinking (however different one's circumstances are from the speaker's) has been associated with undesirable consequences in one's life. For this reason, the leader places great emphasis on identification with other group members and their experiences—modeling it, facilitating it, reinforcing it.

From early on in group, it is essential that the leader model active identification through self-disclosure. As explained in chapter 3, the leader's self-disclosures should be genuine and truthful. While they should not be of the sort that would compromise the leader's privacy or professional role, they should exemplify actual conflicts and dilemmas and their effective resolution. As with other aspects of group process, the leader sometimes has to think quickly to find a personal instance with which a particular group member can identify. The following would be an appropriate self-disclosure to make in response to a member who has a problem with self-esteem:

> "For me, the issue really is self-acceptance. What does it mean when I try to do my job and other people don't respond the way I want? It happens when I make up tests. When I ask questions I really think I covered and 90 percent of the class gets it wrong, my first impulse is to blame myself. I say, 'What could I have done to make them get it right?' What I'm doing then is to let people dictate how I feel. But I have to realize that in most situations in my life, there are going to be some people who will not respond. The issue for me is 'Do I accept myself?' Just because others are not responding as I would like, does that make me stupid, incompetent, inadequate, or unprofessional? Sure, I know there's somebody somewhere who could do the job better than I can. But if I really accept myself and I'm comfortable with my professionalism, I'm not going to worry about it. As long as I do everything within reason, I'm not going to beat myself up over 'What could I have done better?' This carries over to other areas of my life: am I a good enough husband, a good enough father, a good enough friend? I'm projecting now because I've seen this happen to me, but I wonder if that's what's going on for you. Does this have any relevance to your situation?"

Note that the leader qualifies the identification at the end, so as not to present it in a facile, presumptuous manner. It is up to the member to accept the validity of the analogy, not for the leader (or another member) to impose it.

To take a more involved example, in a marriage and divorce group, Joanne has expressed concern that her husband may be about to make an important career change that will affect their family life. She wishes he would take her into his confidence and feels that she should have some say in the decision. To create a safe atmosphere for talking about this delicate issue, the leader models self-disclosing identification with an "I" statement:

*Leader:* I don't yet have a good sense of your particular issue with your husband. But there are sensitive issues between my wife and me, and when I decide to raise an issue, there's a risk involved. I have to decide each time whether the benefits are worth the risks. That's what the issue is for me in communicating with my wife. To stay married, I have to know "when to hold them and when to fold them." When is it bothering me enough to make it worth taking a chance? When am I suppressing and repressing it to the point where it's coming out in other ways? Then again, sometimes I fear that if I raise the issue and take the risk, our relationship may deteriorate. I want to check that out with you.

*Joanne:* No question about it.

*Leader:* I find that it's a matter of perception. As much as I'd like it to be a predictable process, I can't control my wife's reaction. If she perceives it to be a threat, then no amount of reasonableness, no intellectualization will make it okay. If anything, my experience has been that the more I try to talk rationally and logically, the more resistance, the more irrational and illogical responses I get. That's what's been happening for me.

*Joanne:* For me, too.

*Leader:* Do you want to talk a little more about that?

As the group continues to identify and clarify the issue, the leader notices that Joanne is still talking in general terms. Realizing that he, too, has spoken in abstractions and generalizations, he models specificity with another "I" statement:

*Leader:* Let me clarify exactly what I mean. I was speaking in general; let me be specific. My wife and I are sometimes competitive with each other. We try to outdo each other in being successful and looking successful. Sometimes when we're out in public with friends, she says some things—and here's where the perception comes in—that I perceive as a put-down. She may not mean it that way, but that's how I perceive it. What I have to weigh is this: Should I let it slide because I know she didn't really want to hurt me and put me down? Or should I say, "Hon, when we were out with Sandy and Chris last night, you said, 'Blah blah blah,' and it made me look like a fool"? I know that if I say that, she'll put on a helmet and shoulder pads and become very defensive. So I have to weigh what it's like for me. Do I hold them—"Oh, what the hell, we have a lot going for us, this stuff is going to happen, and I'm used to it by now"—or do I fold them—"I really don't like being made to look the fool"? I'm left with a dilemma—two bad choices. To do something is a bad choice, and to do nothing is a bad choice. I have to choose which one is less painful. I wish I had a way to say, "Dear, when you said that the other night, you made me look a little foolish," so that she would reply, "Oh, honey, I really didn't mean to. I'll watch it in the future." If I could have a guarantee that she'd respond that way, then I would say it. But there's no guarantee; there's a risk involved. The risk is bickering, becoming territorial, games of power and prerogatives, and all that goes with that.

*Joanne:* That's just the way it is for me.

The leader has set up an identification, first in general terms and then in specific terms, that makes it more comfortable for Joanne to express and explore her issue with the group. Even then, however, the leader does not take for granted that Joanne's issues are the same as his. He adds this qualification: "I don't know if those questions inevitably arise for Joanne's husband. I know that they seem to be inevitable for my wife, but I don't want to project from my wife onto the whole world." Joanne then has the space to decide how closely the leader's statements apply to her experience.

Identification is useful even when it misses the mark. Empathic and supportive identification by another group member can help one clarify one's own issues, if only by contrast with the other member's mistaken analogy, as in this example:

*Paula:* If this were my problem, if my husband were contemplating a major career change, and if for whatever reasons he didn't really sit down and discuss it with me, I think I would have a lot of feelings about that— feelings of hurt, maybe even of abandonment. I'd have questions about his loyalty. All these feelings and fears would be floating around in my head and my chest. You haven't talked about these things, so I don't know if you have the same kinds of feelings I think I would. But I just want to touch base with you about those things I think I'd feel, to see if you're feeling the same kinds of things and if they're affecting how you're dealing with this.

*Joanne:* Not really. I don't feel hurt or abandoned. I feel I'm still very important to my husband, and I know I don't own this person just because I married him. I respect his individuality as he expresses it in his choice of career. So I don't have that problem you speak of. But I do think I should be more a part of his thinking and planning.

### Ask What the Person Wants from the Group

Identifying and clarifying mean more than just stating a complaint. Group leaders and administrators, especially in noncoerced groups (such as victims' groups and those dealing with love and marital issues), commonly assume that getting the issue out is an end in itself, and group members oblige by displaying an unlimited capacity to do just that. (Coerced group members have their own variation of ventilation—the compliant disclosure.) On the contrary, ventilation is unproductive if it simply confirms and legitimizes an unsatisfactory state of affairs. Getting it out is only the beginning of a process that leads to resolution of an issue.

Instead of letting group members vent indefinitely, the leader asks, "how can the group help you with that?" or "What do you want from the group?" The question transforms the issue at hand from an amorphous complaint to a need to be fulfilled, a problem to be solved, a decision to be made, or a plan to be implemented. By soliciting an explicit request for help, the leader puts the member on record as wanting to do something about the problem. The member, who now must expend energy convincing the group that he or she wants to change the status quo, may thereby convince himself or herself as well.

In the case of Santiago's language problem, a timely request for clarification helped move the issue another step toward resolution:

*Leader:* So how can we help you? What are you asking from the group? What is it you really want?

*Santiago:* I'm kind of sensitive about being set apart, pushed off to the side. Wherever I am, I want to participate like anybody else, to be recognized that I can do the job like anyone else.

*Leader:* Let's start right here, then. I'll take some responsibility here. At times in these meetings, I may have discounted you because I didn't take the time to listen as much as I could have. I want you to help me now. If you have a point that you want to get across to me, I'll make a commitment to you to make more of an effort, and I ask you to make a commitment to me: don't let me go so easily, don't give up so easily, just because I've been giving up too easily when it comes to you. Don't allow me to do that. Now what is it you want from other people here?

With successive clarifications, the group interaction became a model for how Santiago could take responsibility to resolve his problem outside the group.

### Identify Basic Needs

Reality therapy (Glasser 1985) outlines four basic needs that a person must satisfy. These needs, and how a person can better satisfy them, are the "meat" of process-oriented group counseling—what the group works toward by identifying and clarifying issues. To focus attention on each of these needs, the leader may ask certain leading questions. These become questions for members to ask themselves as part of taking effective control of their lives. The four needs and a few questions related to each are as follows:

1. *The need for relationships and belonging*
   - Who are the important people in your life?
   - How intimate are these relationships?
   - What does intimacy mean to you?

2. *The need for self-esteem, power, and control*
   - What do you want that you're not getting?
   - Where do you see yourself losing power?
   - What have you done in the past several days that helps you with your image of yourself?

3. *The need for fun and recreation*
   - When was the last time you had fun?
   - When was the last time you laughed?
   - What does fun mean to you?
   - How has your having fun in the past hurt other people?

4. *The need for freedom and choices*
   - What choices do you have in life?
   - What are you doing for yourself in that area?
   - What future do you envision for yourself?
   - What do you have to look forward to?
   - What would you do if things did get better for you?

These are open-ended questions, intended not to elicit perfunctory yes or no answers, but to give members various starting points for a serious exploration of their lives. As members explain to the group what needs they want to satisfy, they are also convincing themselves.

The role of the leader in this examination is that of a catalyst, not an interviewer. The leader models a concern with these key areas of personal fulfillment so that members can learn to ask the same questions of themselves and one another. In chapter 4, we noted that the leader might use one of the questions as a last resort to break a long silence (usually when the group has just begun to meet). The leader should not, however, make a practice of this. A process group is not "Meet the Press," with the leader as a panel of one directing questions to six or eight special guests. Rather than spring one of these questions on an unsuspecting member, the leader asks the question after the member has raised an issue that pertains to one of the four needs. Over the course of the group, the leader sees that all four sets of questions—all four basic needs—are explored as they come up naturally in connection with the issues members raise. It is not, of course, expected that each member will process each of the four areas out loud.

The four basic needs are as close to explicit content as group process gets, but the categories of content are broad, universal ones that individuals can interpret according to their own circumstances and inclinations. Process groups are not about why people abuse children or about why people drink and drive, but about whether these are realistic ways to satisfy needs and what alternative means of need satisfaction are available. People are in group because they have been fulfilling their needs in ways that are not working for them—for example, at the expense of others. The group offers members a chance to question whether the need-fulfilling strategies they have learned really work and to learn new strategies that work better.

Identifying needs leads to confronting and evaluating behavior in terms of its need satisfaction, as discussed in the following chapter. If what you are doing is not getting you what you want, you experience *need anxiety*. For example, you want to feel that you are in control of your environment, but your spouse is too independent, your children thumb their noses at you, or you don't get to choose the projects you do at work. These are *need deficits*—disparities between what you want and what you are getting. The questions listed under the four basic needs are used to identify a person's need deficits. These deficits become clearer when behavior is confronted and evaluated. It is not feasible to remedy, while in group, all the deficits that a group member identifies, nor is it necessary to remedy the largest single deficit. Realistically, the group looks for each member to show some movement in any area involving need fulfillment outside the group. Any such progress is empowering and builds momentum for further change in the person's life.

### Locate Positive Reference Points

Our emphasis on satisfying basic needs addresses a deficiency in substance abuse groups that assume people want to recover but do not identify and clarify what recovery means for a particular individual. As an antidote to the rote negativism of such groups ("How bad is drinking?" "Bad." "How bad is that?"), our process-oriented groups ask, "How *good* is it when you are taking effective control of your life? Do you know what it means to do that? Do you remember when you did it? What did it feel like?" The purpose is to help the member recreate an image of some positive satisfaction in his or her life that has been obscured by more recent experience.

The leader can model this process by describing a personal experience: "When I ran those four miles this morning, it was a bit of a struggle, because I'm not in the shape I once was in. But you know, I can remember when I could practically sprint those miles—at least that's what it felt like." Members likewise are encouraged to evoke past scenes of fulfillment and contentment, to put themselves into those events or settings and recall what they felt like, and then to relate them to present experiences.

A positive reference point can be a springboard for reconstituting one's life. Peele et al. (1991) present the case of Chet, an alcoholic who had been living on the street:

> Previously, when Chet had entered treatment centers, the staff had always asked him about his drinking problems. Chet would nonchalantly list his arrests, lost jobs, failed marriages, health problems, and numerous prior treatment episodes. Not one of those centers had ever asked Chet what he did well or what his biggest success in life had been. It had never occurred to Chet to tell people he had once been an exceptional athlete, that he knew basketball, and that he thought he could teach kids. (p. 224)

When Chet, who "had almost forgotten that he had been an all-city basketball player in high school" (p. 223), landed in a homeless shelter in a gymnasium, he began shooting baskets. Quickly recruited to teach neighborhood boys the fundamentals of the game, Chet reconstructed a more positive personal identity and social role out of this need-fulfilling experience, which gave him "a chance to work and to gain self-respect and appreciation from other people" (p. 225). Group counseling does not provide a gym, of course, and the positive experiences recalled by members need not be reenacted in life to be beneficial (although they may be). What one *can* do in group, having called up from memory the sensation of having one's needs met, is to devise new strategies for achieving a comparably fulfilled state.

### Link Interrelated Issues

Linking is a more deliberate, directed form of identification. It is a tool for giving people insight into their own basic needs, showing how universal these needs are, and involving members who might not otherwise participate actively. The leader looks for opportunities to do two kinds of linking: first, to highlight the relationship between different issues in a person's life; second, to cast light on one member's issues by way of another's.

Members are encouraged to draw parallels between their experiences in group and key issues in their lives outside the group. This type of linking can make previously unexamined issues accessible to group process. For example, Jack, who has been hostile and unruly in group, is asked to leave after he comes to group intoxicated. As the group reacts to his departure, the leader notices that Mary seems to be having a strong emotional reaction. The leader asks her, "What happened with Jack—is that a problem for you?" Mary replies, "I've had enough angry people in my life." The incident in group has brought to the surface what may be an important issue for Mary. The group can now assist her in specifying the issue (Who are the angry people in her life, especially here and now?) and clarifying how she feels about it, what she wants to have happen, and what she is going to do about it.

Drawing out such issues can be a delicate matter. In one group, when the leader saw a pattern of adversarial exchanges developing between two members, Deb and Phil, she tried to explore why Deb reacted so sharply to Phil's overbearing manner:

*Leader:* What about your relationships with men?

*Deb:* I don't know what you want me to say about my relationships with men. I wouldn't go out with anybody like Phil, if that's what you mean. I guess I haven't had much success with men—is that what you want me to say?

The leader's error was to *assume* the link between Phil and other men in Deb's life rather than to let Deb make the connection. Leaping directly from Phil to "men," the leader overgeneralized. Deb, unable to feel the link in her own experience, reacted defensively, as if she were being given the third degree by an overzealous therapist. The leader is more likely to elicit a productive response by proceeding gently but with greater specificity. The leader might begin by asking Phil's permission: "Deb, is there anyone—Phil, do you mind if I use you as an example?—does Phil remind you of anyone in your life right now?" Or "Is there anyone else in your life who makes you so angry [or afraid or frustrated or whatever the case may be]?" This form of question, used to identify reality therapy's four basic needs as an individual experiences them, can serve as a bridge leading directly from a tense encounter in group to a useful self-exploration.

Group process also offers opportunities to link one member's issues with another's. For example, when one member talked about his feelings of grief after his wife left him, the leader asked a woman who had a similar experience, "Can you understand how he felt?" She replied aptly, "All I know is that's how I felt." Such ownership of feelings and recognition of underlying commonalities of experience should be reinforced. It can transform a silent member into a participant and turn passive identification with other members' issues into active engagement with one's own. As in this example, a great deal of linking is done implicitly or with verbal economy and a light touch; generally it is best not to belabor it.

Beyond the level of specific feelings and experiences, linking can be done around the four basic needs outlined previously: relationships and belonging; self-esteem, power, and control; fun and recreation; and freedom and choices. People may experience the need for power in different circumstances or around different issues, but there is a common feeling of disempowerment (loss of control or "looking stupid") that most people can identify with. In groups for woman-batterers, for example, men may express the feeling of being threatened by women who assert themselves. When one member opens up this area, the leader may ask another to share his experiences in a similar situation and any feelings of frustration he may have. This linking technique may be used in process groups on any subject and in connection with any of the four fundamental needs. It is an efficient device for helping members identify and clarify—and then plan how they intend to satisfy—these needs. As one "sells" oneself a better perspective on one's experience, one sells it to the group as well. Likewise, as one sells it to another member with whom one identifies, one sells oneself on it.

# 6
# Confronting and Evaluating Issues

Once an issue has been identified and clarified, the next step is to talk about specific behavior that interferes with the satisfaction of a person's needs. In this process of questioning, issues are first confronted and then evaluated. The person is then asked to make a value judgment.

The transition from "What do you want?" to "What are you doing to get what you want?" should flow smoothly. Every member, by virtue of being in the group, has some question he or she wants answered about his or her behavior, even if it is only "Why do I have to be here?" A member may come to group denying the consequences and seeking validation ("I don't have a problem; I'm not doing anything wrong"). What he or she will get from the group is gentle but thorough confrontation. The group always questions rather than validates.

## Confronting

In keeping with the concepts of reality therapy (see chapter 5), confrontation is directed toward what the person is doing, not what the person is feeling or thinking. Confrontation takes two forms: questioning ("What are you doing?") and mirroring ("This is what I see you doing"). When you ask a question, you control for a specific kind of response. When you make a mirroring statement, you begin a dialogue in which there is input and output, a two-way exchange. In addition to requesting information, you are giving information. There's a place for both forms of discourse in confrontation, and they typically occur in sequence: you ask a question, and on the basis of the answer, you confront.

### Modeling Confrontation

The leader is not necessarily the one who confronts. Ideally, it is best for group members to confront one another. Initially, however, given the nature of the group, the leader almost always has to model confrontation. After the group has helped a member identify and clarify an issue, the leader asks, "This is what you want. Now tell the group: what are you doing? For example, what did you do yesterday? Yesterday is usually a representative day. What are you doing to get what you want?" In a group concerned with marital issues, for example, the member might be asked to select a recent weekend day spent with his or her spouse:

> "You've identified and clarified what you want. To me, what you want is to stay married and, if possible, to work on your marriage to make it better. What have you being doing to keep your marriage and make it better? Was last Sunday a representative day? How did that day go? Just go through the day, from when you got up."

The group listens politely, attentively, and with interest. The leader then asks, "Would you like to go on with this?" If the member says yes, the leader holds up the mirror, showing the disparity between what the member says he or she is doing and what the leader sees the member doing. In general terms, the confrontation might sound like this: "Okay, this is what I see. I see you doing A, B, and C. You say that you want X, Y, and Z, and you say you've been doing nothing or just thinking about it." An "I" statement is part of the confrontation: "When *I* do that, it means that I'm unsure that I want change or I'm unsure of the risks involved. And I see you doing the same thing I do when I face situations where these things are unclear."

Here is an example of how a specific issue is confronted:

*Leader:* Sam, you say you want a college degree and a steady job. Now tell the group, what are you doing about it? For example, what did you do yesterday to get what you want?

*Sam:* Well, I guess I didn't do much of anything. So far I'm just thinking about it.

*Leader:* Would you like to go on with this?

*Sam:* Yeah, I guess so.

*Leader:* Okay, this is what I see. You say that you want a job and a college degree, and then you say you've been doing nothing or just thinking about it. Now when *I* do that, it usually means I'm unsure whether I really want to change, I'm afraid of the risks involved, or I've got some other issue and I'm letting it hold me back. And now I see you doing the same thing I do when I face a situation that's unclear to me. How about it, group? What do you see Sam doing?

Here the leader, having modeled confrontation, opens up the issue so as to involve the group in the process. As a rule, after the first couple of sessions, the leader should not be doing the confronting at all. Instead, the leader (always after asking the member's permission) hands it over to the group with a process statement, such as "Group, what do you see Sam doing?" or "What's really going on? How does this sound to people over here?" Confrontation generally has greater impact when it comes from another group member, who usually is seen as having similar problems.

## Appropriate Confrontation

The guidelines for appropriate confrontation are the same as those presented in chapter 8 for appropriate feedback. Effective confrontation is

- solicited rather than imposed
- gentle and caring rather than aggressive, accusatory, or punitive
- descriptive rather than evaluative
- specific rather than general
- concrete rather than abstract
- appropriately timed
- presented so that the person can hear it (in an atmosphere of trust)

In modeling confrontation, the leader shows how to confront in a gentle and caring manner. There is no need to model the brutal, dog-eat-dog world that group members already know all too well. It takes little skill or training for the leader to say, "Bill, tell Sam just what you think of that. Okay, Marsha, now you. Steve, Joan, Andy, let's jump on Sam." If the confrontation is imposed on Sam rather than solicited by him, or if he experiences it as an attack, he will shut out in self-defense. Even if those confronting him are "right," what good are they doing? There is never a justification for abuse or personal disrespect in group, for confrontation without caring. On the contrary, both by example, and by prompt blocking of aggressive or judgmental confrontation, the leader disabuses members of crude stereotypes of encounter group–style confrontation.

Appropriate confrontation, as modeled and reinforced by the leader, has three essential components:

1. A descriptive statement
2. An "I" statement
3. A reference to natural consequences

These can be combined economically into a seamless whole, as the following example illustrates:

"You say you want people off your case. From what you say you're doing, you're going to get just the opposite. Even from what you're doing right now, more and more people will be *on* your case. I know that, because when *I* do that, I just get hassled more. That's what happened to me when I thought people were really on my case."

What takes this statement out of the realm of scapegoating, finger pointing, or advice giving is that it has the point of reference in the experience of the person doing the confronting. Instead of lecturing, the confronter establishes an identification, a bond of common experience, with the person confronted. The confrontation invites the person to consider his or her behavior from the point of view of someone who has experienced the natural consequences of similar behavior. Anyone can feel the difference between being put on the spot or held to account from a pedestal of moral superiority and being addressed with respect and equality—with words such as these, for example: "When I do that, if I take the trouble to scrutinize my behavior, it means that I'm taking the line of least resistance; I'm avoiding conflict at all cost. I'm not saying that's what you're doing, but I've come to see that it's what I do."

## Overcoming Resistance

Just as group members resist confronting their own issues, so they may resist confronting one another. For example, a member may say something like "I don't really have a problem. I just happened to be drinking after work, and I didn't eat, and while I was driving home, I happened to be stopped. That's my problem." Although the inexperienced leader's first impulse is to confront the member directly on this denial, it is usually best for the leader to avoid going on a fact-finding mission and being drawn into a contest with the member about how much the member drinks. A more effective approach is to throw the issue out to the group and ask for "I" statements. But what if no one speaks up? Early in group, the members may still be in an adversarial, suspicious frame of mind toward the leader. They may hold back from confronting one another for fear of being confronted themselves.

In that case, the leader can model appropriate confrontation through the use of an "I" statement. As noted in chapter 3, this does not require resorting to "when I was drinking" stories. Instead, the leader might simply recall some instance in his or her own life that illustrates the same general pattern of denial. For example, the leader might say:

"I have rationalized these kinds of things when I stuff myself on holidays. Many times without thinking I've said, 'Next Monday I'm going to start on a program for overeating.' That's what was going on with me. That's how *I* rationalize things. Did anyone in the group ever make that kind of allowance for himself or herself?"

Here the leader is doing two things. The first is to portray rationalization as a common human experience, one that anyone can comfortably own up to, rather than as a damning personal deficiency in the individual being confronted. The second is to incorporate others in the confrontation. Having broken the ice by showing that confrontation does not have to be threatening or violating, the leader then seeks to include as many members as possible in the process.

## The Content of Confrontation

How much must the leader know (about substance abuse, for instance) to confront effectively? As the last example suggests, content knowledge is less crucial than an ability to use group process to bring out issues of concern to group members and to create meaningful points of empathic contact around these issues. As discussed earlier, the leader should be able to recognize when a member can benefit from a referral to other resources (such as detoxification, AA, or education programs). In terms of group process, however, a general working knowledge of the issues at hand will suffice. When working, say, with alcoholics in an intermediate-care facility, the leader should have a mental image—and be able to articulate it—of social drinking behavior, situational (stress-related) drinking behavior, and out-of-control drinking behavior. Group members are confronted on the disparity between their perceptions of their drinking behavior and others' perceptions of it. The confrontation focuses on specific behavior, but the leader has a reference point about the kind of drinking that is going on. As an aid to recognition, it is legitimate (though not obligatory) to have members fill out an alcoholism assessment questionnaire and then confront one another about their answers.

It is not, however, the business of the leader or the group to pressure members to accept a preprogrammed conclusion about themselves. We emphasize again that group counseling is concerned not with what a person *thinks, feels,* or *is,* but with what a person *does.* The business of the group is to support members in acknowledging and modifying specific behavior that has gotten them in trouble. One finds oneself in group because one has acted in such a way (for example, drinking while driving or drinking to the point of being violent or noticeably impaired) as to bring about certain negative consequences for oneself. The group invites the member to consider whether he or she wants to suffer those consequences again or change the behavior. As an approach to changing the behavior, one may choose to declare oneself an alcoholic who cannot ever drink safely again. But that is a conclusion that the person must reach voluntarily; it is not to be imposed by the group.

Many group leaders, administrators, and program planners work from a misunderstanding not only of group counseling but also of addiction.

Standard addiction assessment questionnaires (with questions such as "Do you drink alone?" "Do you drink in the morning?" "Do you drink more than you used to?"), while useful up to a point, address the addictive behavior in a rote, formulaic way, isolating the behavior from its meaning in the person's life. In response to this one-dimensional interrogation, members get into a game of denial and resistance that might be characterized as "Try and find me" or "It's up to you to make me think I'm an alcoholic." The result often is an unproductive standoff.

A more comprehensive model of addiction looks at the drinking, drug use, or other addictive behavior as an alternative means of need satisfaction, resorted to when basic needs are not being met in other ways (Peele and Brodsky 1976). In the absence of personal intimacy, a sense of control and self-esteem, fun and recreation, or freedom and choices, one engages in a repetitive pattern of behavior that is immediately rewarding but limiting and destructive in the long run. Assessment of addiction involves more than just a description of the behavior in clinical terms. It entails determining what needs the person is trying to meet through the addiction, how the addictive behavior increasingly frustrates the satisfaction of these or other needs, how these needs might better be satisfied, and what strengths in a person's life can be a starting point for a more positive adaptation (Peele et al. 1991). Group counseling based on reality therapy is ideally suited to undertaking this assessment in a respectful yet efficient manner.

### Dramatizing Natural Consequences: Backing Up the Hearse

Addictive and other dysfunctional behaviors, having arisen typically in response to need deficits, in turn create further need deficits. An important part of confrontation is to point out these natural consequences, among which is the person's very presence in group. When one is reminded that "No one sent for you here" or "You weren't picked out of a telephone book to be here," one is encouraged to ask oneself, "Is what I'm doing really working for me?"

The natural consequences we refer to are those the person has begun to experience (particularly those that brought the person to group), not the abstract consequences about which the person has already heard too many lectures. In the case of a drunk driver, for example, finger-wagging moralism ("Don't you know you could kill somebody?") has little impact. Inwardly, the person will rationalize, "That's not going to happen to me." Outwardly, he or she will be compliant: "Yeah, yeah, I'll be more careful next time. I won't do it again." To break through this denial, it often helps to have the person relive the experience of getting in trouble. This is done through an intensive form of confrontation called "backing up the hearse and letting them smell the flowers."

A group member who says, "I'm here because I was arrested for driving while intoxicated," is not taking responsibility, not owning his or her actions and their consequences. Instead of making a real "I" statement ("I drove drunk"), the person is putting on a protective shield of abstraction and indirection. The task for the group is to make the experience of the behavior and its consequences—and the link between the two—concrete for the person. Thus, the group asks the person to relive the experience step by step so that he or she can see, hear, feel, smell, and taste the consequences. In the case of a drunk driver, the leader (at the outset) or, preferably, group members might recreate the experience with a series of questions such as the following:

"What was going on with you when you looked in the rearview mirror and saw the police car flashing its lights? What were you thinking? Do you remember? When the policeman pulled you over and asked for your license and registration, do you remember groping in the glove compartment? Evidently you didn't do a very good job because he then said, 'Get out of the car, sir,' and gave you the California test—walking a straight line, closing your eyes, touching your nose with your finger. You obviously didn't do too well because you convinced the policeman that there might be reason to suspect you of driving drunk. Do you remember when he told you to put your hands up against the car and began patting you down to see if you had a weapon? What were you thinking? What was going on in your mind? Do you remember him putting your hands behind your back and taking out his handcuffs? Do you remember listening to the 'click' as you were handcuffed behind your back and led to the police car? Do you remember him leading you to the car and putting you in? He didn't bump your forehead on the roof of the car, did he, saying, 'This way, sir—oh, I'm sorry, sir'? Do you remember him calling in your name and address on the way to the station? What were you thinking? What were your feelings? When you got to the police station, do you remember them taking that picture where they turned your head to the side? Remember those fingerprints they took? Remember the drunk tank they put you in? What did it smell like? Who was in there? A bunch of drunks. Really! Do you remember calling a member of your family or a friend to come and get you? What was going on with you? Did you feel pride? Did you feel shame?

These questions, while delivered rapid-fire, include pauses for "I" statements so that the group members can own that "this is what *I* did," "this is what *I* thought and felt," and "this is what happened to *me*." In this way, the group makes concrete what it means to be "arrested for driving while intoxicated." The member being confronted may find it upsetting to hear all this and to own up to it, but this reality-based confrontation is a legitimate function of the group. It is an example of how the group is not there to make people feel good, to "please the customer."

Backing up the hearse goes one step further to help the person envision future as well as past consequences:

> "If your license is taken away, what will happen to you? How will you get to work? Do you live near a bus stop? Who's going to give you a ride? Are you going to hitchhike in all kinds of weather? How are you going to get the kids back and forth to your ex-wife's place? And what do you think will happen if you get arrested again? In this state, the second time you go to jail for thirty, maybe sixty, days."

These are natural consequences of persisting in the behavior in question. By making them concrete, specific, and vivid, the group spurs the member to make a decision based on self-interest.

As with confrontation generally, backing up the hearse is not a soliloquy by the leader. The leader might give the first example and then ask other group members to fill in the next steps by telling what happened to them, so that everyone can participate. All that is asked of the member being confronted is to sit and listen. "Don't get defensive," the member is told. "This doesn't necessarily relate to you. You can discount it if you want. I just want to hear from others: what happened to *you?*" In other words, being confronted by the group does not mean being ganged up on. Meanwhile, others will begin talking on their own as they realize what the issue means for them. Members who might be defensive if the confrontation were directed at them articulate the consequences spontaneously to someone else when the pressure is off them. As they sell the group member on what they are saying, they are also selling themselves. This added benefit is part of what makes backing up the hearse such a useful technique.

This technique can be adapted to any kind of process group, including those for people who are lonely or have problems with intimate relationships. Here smelling the flowers might focus on the sensations of coming home to an empty house or apartment and finding everything as you left it in the morning. "You cook, do the dishes, save the leftovers, turn on the TV. The next day, the things you put in the refrigerator the night before are still there. You take out the leftovers and heat them up." Future consequences might include specific scenes from middle and old age, without a partner to provide care and companionship when one is ill or injured. The leader does not need to prepare a detailed rundown of such consequences for every type of group, since group members will be only too willing to fill in the specifics. Again, there is no blaming, no right or wrong. The group draws a picture, sets a scene, lays out the consequences, and lets the member decide whether the present state of affairs is satisfactory or whether it is worth taking some risks to change.

## Confronting Irrational Beliefs

A crucial part of confrontation is to challenge the "musts," "shoulds," "oughts," and "if onlys" of wishful or self-punishing thinking that stand in the way of identifying, clarifying, and resolving issues. Much of the upset, anxiety, confusion, and paralysis in people's lives results not from actual events or conditions, but from faulty beliefs and interpretations. Rational-emotive therapy (Ellis and Harper 1975) is an invaluable tool for group process in that it strips away the flawed reasoning that obscures the core issues people face, the real choices that affect people's well-being. From this perspective, some common irrational ideas often lie at the root of emotional disturbances. These irrational ideas include the following (adapted from Ellis and Harper):

- The idea that it is a dire necessity for an adult human being to be loved or approved by virtually every significant other person in his or her environment
- The idea that one should be thoroughly competent, adequate, and achieving in all possible respects if one is to consider oneself worthwhile
- The idea that anyone who does not measure up to one's own standards of "goodness" is therefore "bad" and becomes an opponent to be scorned, rejected, or anathematized
- The idea that it is awful and catastrophic when things are not the way one would very much like them to be
- The idea that one's unhappiness is caused by other people or conditions and that one has little or no ability to control one's sorrows or disturbances
- The idea that if something is or may be dangerous or frightful, one should be terribly concerned about it and should keep dwelling on the possibility of its occurring
- The idea that it is easier to avoid than to face certain difficulties and self-responsibilities
- The idea that one should be dependent on others and that one needs someone stronger than oneself on whom to rely
- The idea that one's past history is an all-important determinant of one's present behavior and that because something once strongly affected one's life, it should have a similar effect indefinitely
- The idea that one should become quite upset over other people's problems and disturbances

- The idea that there is invariably a right, precise, and perfect solution to human problems and that it is catastrophic if that perfect solution is not found
- The idea that the image of a person, institution, or system must be kept unblemished and enhanced at any cost

Using the tenets of rational-emotive therapy, the leader can (when called for) guide members through a step-by-step procedure for reinterpreting their experience, as in this example:

1. *Activating experience.* A group member's husband has started beating her again.

2. *Irrational belief or interpretation.* "It's my fault. If I loved him enough, if I were sensitive enough to his needs, if I were a really good wife to him, he wouldn't be beating me. I'll just have to try harder to satisfy him." And/or, "He is a monster, the most evil person who ever lived. How could I ever have loved him?"

3. *Consequences of irrational belief.* As the beatings continue, the woman feels alternately anxious, helpless, depressed, fearful, and enraged.

4. *Disputing of irrational belief.* "What makes me think that I could stop my husband from beating me just by trying to placate him, when I've been doing that for so long to no avail? Why does his behavior make me inadequate as a wife? Why do I have all the power and all the responsibility to prevent bad things from happening? And does the fact that my husband is doing something very bad mean that he never did anything good or that he never had any attractive qualities?"

5. *Cognitive effect of disputing irrational belief.* "Even if I were the wisest person in the world, I couldn't count on being able to stop my husband from beating me. He has been and is subjected to many influences on his behavior besides myself. Just because he is doing something bad now, that does not mean that he will always do it. It makes him a fallible, not a bad, person. But because he is doing something that is very detrimental to my well-being and threatening to my safety, it is my responsibility to do everything that is reasonably within my power to protect myself."

6. *Behavioral effect of disputing irrational belief.* The woman feels less anxious, fearful, and guilty. She regains a sense of potency, of being able to act to influence her destiny. She decides that she has two choices: to leave her husband or to work with him in counseling to stop the beatings. Both because their relationship has been badly damaged by her husband's behavior and because she has concluded that the available therapeutic resources do not offer sufficient assurance of a favorable outcome, she chooses to leave her husband.

A group leader can anticipate many irrational ideas to which this scheme can be usefully applied. A few examples follow:

- "I can drive drunk and get away with it. It was just a fluke, getting caught that time."
- "This is my last chance at love and marriage. If I blow it this time, I'll never again find someone to care for me."
- "Why doesn't everybody just leave me alone?"
- "There's no problem so big or so small that I can't run away from it."

Rational-emotive therapy provides a framework for confronting such irrational beliefs, reducing the anxiety and upset associated with them, and learning more realistic, need-satisfying behavior.

### Nonjudgmental Confrontation

Backing up the hearse exemplifies the principle that confrontation is to be descriptive rather than evaluative. Like all other confrontation in group, the long, elaborate illustration about drunk driving is keyed to specific behavior and its natural consequences; there is no generalizing about the person's character, identity, moral worthiness, or mental health. Such confrontation is conducted entirely in experiential, not judgmental, terms. It is left to the person being confronted to make the necessary judgments and act accordingly.

Group counseling is nonmoralistic, even as it helps prepare members to meet their needs in a manner consistent with their responsibilities to others. It is not the mission of the group to make moral judgments or even to consider the moral implications of members' behavior. As the leader might put it, in the event that one member lectures to another, "I know that when I'm being sermonized to, I tend to shut it off, and I think others might as well." The relevant moral judgments have been made by the law, by society, and by people and institutions with which members must deal. In the case of the universally taboo behavior of child abuse, the law has imposed an obligation on the group to report any revealed incidence to the authorities. Otherwise, the group simply recreates and dramatizes the sanctions applied elsewhere.

Even when faced with an issue with obvious moral ramifications, such as a member's having extramarital affairs, the group keeps its focus on clarifying the questions the member has about the behavior and exploring with the member what the consequences of the behavior actually are. As with any other issue, the leader asks:

"What is it you want from the group when you bring this up? If you want to continue to go outside your primary relationship for sex, do you want the group's stamp of approval? That's not what we're here for. In saying this, we're not making a moral judgment, for if you want us to tell you to stay faithful to your relationship, we're not here to do that either. Help us help you by telling us what you want, what it is you have questions about."

People come to group because they have some question about what they are doing, but they still often seek the easy out of having the group validate or condemn. For the group to do either of these things is to usurp the member's necessary task of clarification and evaluation. It is entirely appropriate, however, for the group to provide information about the natural consequences. Thus, the leader or another group member might say, "My experience has been that, sooner or later, these affairs can't be kept under wraps. Are you willing to deal with that? If you are, fine."

We have noted elsewhere in the context of individual counseling:

> Although the client may be hoping that the therapist will give her an "okay" to do what she is contemplating, she wouldn't be coming to the therapist if she didn't have doubts. Automatic validation leaves the doubts unresolved and therefore is not therapeutic. Just as it is the client who must decide that it would be wrong to be unfaithful or to leave her husband, so it is the client who must decide that such a move would be right for her.
>
> When it comes to sexual conduct, people spend their lives searching the bookshelves for a guidebook that has never been written. . . . Clients believe that therapists have answers to these questions. A therapist who encourages this blind trust or who rubber-stamps the client's own superficially held "answers" is doing the client a disservice. Whether the issue is homosexuality, adultery, or multiple relationships, it is in the best interest of the client to question without judging. It is, however, relevant to consider how others will judge the client's choices and how the client is likely to react to such judgment. If the client feels bad as a natural consequence of acting out, the bad feelings should be examined, not dismissed. Ultimately, the only meaningful validation is one that the client has worked for. (Edelwich and Brodsky 1991, 176–177)

In groups for "women who love too much," it is not the group leader's job to save a difficult relationship or to decide that the rupture cannot be repaired. Rather, the leader must back up the hearse and let the group member "feel" and "smell" the available choices and what they may entail for her:

> "You can do something or do nothing. Is it better to do something or to do nothing? What does it mean to do something? What would it mean to work on the relationship? What is your minimum standard, the minimum improvement that would satisfy you? Say you do end the relationship. What does it mean for you? What are you

going to do? Who are you going to go out with? What are you going to do Saturday night? What are you going to tell your friends?"

If the member feels reluctant to take the risks to find a new relationship, the group can concretize the alternative of living with the status quo, be it an unsatisfying relationship or no relationship at all: "Is that what you want? Maybe for now it's okay. What other interests do you have that might compensate? Is that an accommodation you can live with for very long? When will you check it out again?" Whichever choice the member makes, it will be a clearer and more informed choice as a result of opening it up to group process.

## Evaluating

The last example leads us to the next step, evaluation: "You've told the group what you want. You've told the group what you're doing now. Evaluate that. Is what you're doing getting you what you want?" Dramatizing the consequences of a person's actions (as described previously) leads naturally to questions with evaluative implications: "Is this what you want?" "For how long?" "Is it better to do something or to do nothing?" "What does it mean to do something?" "What is the smallest improvement that would satisfy you?" These are questions that only the person concerned can answer. Confrontation is done by the group; evaluation is done by one person alone. In confrontation, others in the group point out the contradictions between what one wants and what one is doing. In evaluation, the group asks whether one is ready to own the contradictions.

Evaluation does not mean denouncing oneself or repudiating one's conduct ("I've been bad; I've been wrong"). It simply means opening up one's conduct for questioning ("I'm not very happy with the status quo"). When asked, "Is what you're doing getting you what you want?" a group member may reply, "Not when I'm upset, anxious, lonely, and depressed—I'm not living a fulfilled life," or "Not when I'd rather be with my family [or out bowling, watching a ball game, or sleeping] than have to be here in group so I won't lose my driver's license." Someone in the group then asks, "Is living without intimate relationships [drinking and driving] working for you?"

As with confrontation (and other aspects of group process), evaluation is modeled by the leader and, when possible, carried on as an interchange among group members. At this stage, however, the leader blocks any contribution by the rest of the group except for the kind of respectful questioning indicated here. There is no confrontation, editorializing, feedback, or pressure. The value judgment must be solicited, not imposed. The person must decide that he or she wants to change.

As an example of the kind of exchange that helps one evaluate how need satisfying one's behavior has been, Joanne has said that her husband is not communicating with her about a major career change he is considering. To clarify what Joanne is doing to make her marriage work for her, the leader has asked her to go through a representative day with her husband. The following exchange ensues:

*Leader:* Was this a representative day between you and your husband?
*Joanne:* Yes.
*Leader:* The reason I asked you to go through it was not for us to peek into your window, but for you to evaluate your day. How well did what you did on this day satisfy your needs?
*Joanne:* Very well. Nothing essential was lacking.
*Leader:* So you made the value judgment that you really want to stay married.
*Joanne:* Yes, absolutely.
*Leader:* Good. Now I'm asking you to make another value judgment. At any time during that day did it occur to you to raise the issue you've raised here?
*Joanne:* I thought about raising it when we went out to dinner. Then I thought about the risks. Going out to dinner is always something special between us, and I was looking forward to dessert, and, well, I didn't want to spoil it.
*Leader:* That's what we have to talk about. I surely do not want to give you a problem you do not have. If it's okay with you, it is certainly okay with me. Let me check something out with you.

The leader then uses a technique of reality therapy to help Joanne evaluate her need deficit:

*Leader:* Joanne, you have a picture in your mental album concerning what a marriage is, and this picture is unique to you because it is based on your actual experience. At the same time, you have another picture that you've gotten from books, seminars, and so forth about open communication in marriage, about how you should confront things with your spouse. The real picture of a marriage that you have doesn't measure up to the ideal picture, and so you feel some discontent. It's the disparity between what you want—open communication—and what you perceive you're getting. You want your husband to be completely open with you, and you perceive that he's not. The result, for you, is need anxiety. Do you see what I mean?
*Joanne:* Yes, I think so.
*Leader:* Let's talk about where you can go from there. For me, there's

no great need for you to come to some conclusion today. What I'm putting forth to you and the group is this: up to this point you've done nothing; you've procrastinated. It's my responsibility not to make you see the light, but simply to raise a question: is doing nothing getting you what you want, getting you that ideal marriage in your head? *You* have to answer that; no one else can. Do you want to try to answer that?

*Joanne:* Even doing nothing, life is not bad. I can't say it's created the ideal, but it's made for nothing more than everyday problems, nothing I can't handle.

*Leader:* Given that, is *not* confronting this particular problem working out okay for you, or is it worth the risks to do something about it?

*Joanne:* Taking all things into consideration, I guess I'm content to keep things as they are.

Once the leader has modeled this sort of exchange, group members can be encouraged to assume what is presented here as the leader's role.

As the vignette with Joanne illustrates, evaluation consists of a sequence of questions (not all of which need be asked explicitly or in these exact words) that guide the group member toward a value judgment:

1. Is what you're doing getting you what you want?
2. Then is [this behavior or way of living] working for you?
3. Are you satisfied with things as they are?
4. Do you want to do something to change things?
5. Are you willing to take the risks?
6. How can the group help you?

The last three questions point the way to the active phase of problem solving outlined in chapter 8: feedback, consolidation of learning, planning, and implementation—all with the help of the group. These steps are predicated on a true value judgment, made voluntarily in an atmosphere that permits one to decide *not* to change. The value judgment cannot be taken for granted; it must be affirmed, tested, and reinforced.

What if, like Joanne, the person makes the value judgment that it is not worth the risks to change? That choice must be respected. If the value judgment is to mean anything, both choices must be available. However, the fact that Joanne has decided to stick with the status quo does not mean that the group has accomplished nothing by identifying, clarifying, and confronting her issue. Just by having taken the issue that far, Joanne may be more ready to make a value judgment and receive feedback in a subsequent session or to create some movement in this area of her life outside the group. And other group members, having listened to Joanne process the issue, may be closer to resolution of similar issues in their lives.

## Vulnerabilities

For people who have been involved for years in a dysfunctional mode of living, questions such as "Are you satisfied with your life as it is?" or "Is that what you really want?" may run up against a long-held sense of disempowerment. The concept of "vulnerabilities" (Silverstein et al. 1981) is a useful tool for helping people articulate and reexamine disabling assumptions that inhibit their readiness to change. Silverstein and his colleagues list ten ways in which people make themselves vulnerable to persistent need deficits, leading to progressive self-destruction and/or victimization by others:

1. People engage in magical thinking. They think that they alone can drive drunk without ever getting caught or having an accident, that all the food they eat will not show up on their waistline, that they will stop taking drugs or their partner will stop being abusive tomorrow.

2. People don't learn how to think critically. They believe the hype of cigarette or liquor ads or the "jive" of a partner who isn't good for them.

3. People feel that they do not deserve any better than what they are getting. Those who have this attitude are likely to be heedless of their own well-being.

4. People have trouble identifying those things (including people and experiences) that they love. Just as they have difficulty seeing through people or involvements that are harmful, so they seem unable to pin down what is really important to them in a positive sense.

5. People don't envision a clear future for themselves. The capacity to plan for the future on the basis of anticipated outcomes and consequences (payoffs as well as punishments) is essential to healthy emotional adjustment. People who are deficient in this capacity cannot make and implement choices involving temporary sacrifices.

6. People do not believe they have enough to live for. Without ongoing involvements, goals, hopes, and aspirations, people have little reason to take care of themselves.

7. People do not identify with others as role models. Instead of recognizing that others have similar feelings and cope with comparable difficulties, they assume that "nobody has troubles like I do." With this attitude, they lock themselves into a prison of self-pity and self-defeating compensations. It is to overcome this barrier of alienation that we emphasize positive modeling through self-disclosure in group.

8. People have poor intrapersonal skills. These include poor self-discipline and self-control, little tolerance of frustration, and an inability to delay gratification.

9. People have poor interpersonal skills. Unable to make satisfying emotional connections with others, they substitute destructive relationships or other addictions that are safe, reliable, but deadening.

10. People do not accept responsibility for the consequences of their actions. They blame persons, places, and things such as their spouse, their job, or the court. Group process is, of course, set up as an antidote to this flight from responsibility.

The evaluation stage offers group members an opportunity to confront these vulnerabilities. Asked whether they are satisfied with things as they are (once the latter have been specified), members may discover previously unarticulated beliefs that they do not deserve any better, that they cannot envision their own future, or that they do not have positive relationships or things to live for. Questioning such self-defeating assumptions is a key component of growth.

## Resolving the Value Judgment

Evaluation concludes when one either makes or declines to make a value judgment that one wants to resolve the issue (that is, change the behavior or situation) under consideration. The value judgment must be made by the person concerned, not by other group members, the group leader, or a judge, probation officer, parent, teacher, or minister. It is not for the leader or the group to predetermine the outcome of a member's evaluation of an issue. The group lets the member smell the flowers, but if the value judgment is to mean anything, the member must own it.

Group leaders, understandably eager for good news, tend to hurry over this step, accept the value judgment as made, and go on with plans and tasks for the member. That is an error. Without a solid value judgment, feedback is beside the point and planning useless. Therefore, even an apparent choice in favor of change should not be taken at face value. Rather, it should be *tested* and *solidified*. For example, a group member may finally say, "I'm tired of coming home to an empty house" or "I'm tired of coming home to a person who abuses me." At this point, the group leader might ask the person, "You've said this before; what's so different this time? What's so bad about living alone [living with this abuser]? Tell us." As the member sells the group on the genuineness of the value judgment, the member sells himself or herself on it as well. In this way, the group tests and, if possible, solidifies the value judgment.

If the person begins to vacillate and equivocate, it may be time to move on to another member and another issue. A person may be tired of being lonely, being beaten up, being arrested, or having an unsatisfying job but still be unwilling to take the risks outside the group that are necessary to change. In that case, the value judgment has not been made.

A value judgment is convincing when one spends some time backing up the hearse for oneself. In the case of domestic violence, a perpetrator might reach this conclusion:

> "This is not negotiable anymore. I have to think of other ways to deal with my girlfriend when I get pissed off. Putting my hands on her isn't working for me. That's what got me here. I paid money for lawyers. I lost time from work. I could be home watching TV tonight, but I'm here. That's what this behavior is getting me. What I want is to be left to my own devices—to play with my stamp collection, whatever. What I'm doing has brought me here and made me poorer and less happy. And, actually, not too many women that I would want to be with would put up with it anyway."

This is the kind of commitment to look for in group. Once it is made, there is no further need for confrontation. Instead, the member is asked if he or she is ready to receive direct feedback, as described in chapter 8.

### What If the Value Judgment Is Not Made?

A member may react to confrontation by saying, "I don't want to hear any more of this." Or, like Joanne, a member may choose the status quo, saying, "I guess things are okay the way they are. I don't want to do anything about this right now." There are two therapeutic stances the group can take toward a member's unwillingness to face a critical issue. As a rule, a client-centered approach is followed. Members are free to make and express any choices, including the status quo, without fear of punishment. If, however, a member persistently refuses to hear any confrontation or feedback, the leader may treat that refusal as a form of irresponsibility. The leader may challenge the member: "What are you here for? You don't have to be here. You could leave. You could terminate your group at any time. Of course, that may mean discharge from the program. You're making that choice when you don't participate, and those are the consequences."

Whether such a challenge is called for depends on the nature and climate of the group, and on whether the member's recalcitrance is part of a systematic pattern of resistance to, and even undermining of, the group. It is also a question of timing, of whether the leader has done everything within reason to establish trust so that members can hear difficult communications. The following guidelines are useful for the leader when confrontation and evaluation do not have the desired outcome.

First, *do not let the issue become a point of contention between the member and the leader.* Too often, group leaders put themselves at a disadvantage by assuming that "we have them only for eight weeks, and it's our job to bring them to the bottom in that time." Leaders who become personally invested in the *outcomes* of group process risk a loss of objectivity and focus, unproductive power struggles, and reduced effectiveness. Professional burnout may follow from repeated frustrations of this sort. Keep in mind, therefore, that group process takes the pressure to produce outcomes off the leader and places responsibility back where it belongs—with each individual member. It is not the leader's job to make them see the light but simply to create the proper group atmosphere and to go through the process outlined here. If the leader sets positive norms, group members are more likely to take responsibility for themselves. But the leader cannot guarantee this desired result. We have recommended elsewhere:

> *Focus on the Process, not the Result.* There is a great deal more to helping people than seeing the cures and recoveries at the end of the tunnel. There is the exercise of skills, the human contact, the emotional involvement, the development of a rapport and a dialogue with clients, and the pleasure of doing an important job well. As with any art, the "doing" is as important as the "done." Experienced helpers who continue to gain satisfaction from their work despite all obstacles understand that they cannot depend on results which are beyond their control to justify their efforts. (Edelwich and Brodsky 1980, 217)

For group leaders, this perspective can be liberating and highly satisfying.

Second, *bring the issue back to the group.* What takes the place of heroic rescue by the leader is a calm, secure reliance on group process to resolve all issues insofar as they can be resolved. When a member resists making a value judgment, the leader might say, "Okay, this doesn't seem to be going anywhere. John hasn't made a value judgment. He still isn't sure what he really really really wants." Then the leader might throw it back to the group: "Group, I have a problem. The problem is that I don't see John participating. Group, what's going on here? Maybe someone can help me with this." By soliciting "I" statements, the leader checks out how other members are affected by one member's refusal to confront an issue or to commit to change. Among the other members, one may take a reassuring tone ("If you don't want to hear this, that's okay with me"), while another may be dissatisfied ("Hey, I put something into this process with you—I feel let down").

What about the member to whom they are speaking? For the moment, this person may feel too fragile to look into the mirror of direct confrontation or feedback. No one, however, is too fragile to hear how other members are experiencing the process and what they think about what is going on. No one is too fragile to hear "I" statements, and only "I" statements by other members are permitted (attacks, criticisms, judgments directed at the member are to be blocked). Hearing others express disappointment at one's retreat from an issue critical to one's life is a natural consequence of that retreat. Moreover, the group is concerned with the feelings and experiences of all members, and the leader may allow negative reactions to be aired in order to prevent a contagion of sullen withdrawal.

Third, *test a negative value judgment by making its implications explicit*. When asked to make a value judgment, a member may make one that is not to the group's liking. For example, one may conclude, "All these negative consequences of drinking at the wrong times and places don't mean as much to me as the powerful urge I feel to drink." Once a person makes that decision, all the group can do is to hold up the mirror and make sure the person understands graphically what those consequences are. A negative value judgment is no more to be taken at face value than a positive one. Instead, the group backs up the hearse one more time so that the member can own the choice he or she has made. "But just tell me this," the member is asked, "the next time you get arrested, and it's obvious that you will, what do you think is going to happen?"

With help from the group, if necessary, the member articulates the consequences: "I may kill somebody. Or if I don't, I may assault with a motor vehicle. I may serve time in prison and be bankrupted for damages. If not, I'll at least lose my license. I'm willing to accept those things because drinking is so important to me." At this point, the group has done everything within reason. "What about other group members?" the leader asks. "Is that really what *you* want?" In a group for drunk drivers, not many will say that it is. Indeed, other members' revulsion from the anticipated consequences will give the recalcitrant member one last set of dramatic images to consider. The leader concludes, "Okay, if in spite of all that, drinking is such a need-satisfying behavior for you, there's nothing more we can say. But if you change your mind, will you at least commit to call us or another group member?"

Fourth, *leave the issue explicitly resolved or explicitly unresolved*. If the member is not ready to receive feedback or declines to do anything about the issue, the leader goes back to the group and asks if anyone has any other issues. This is not done, however, without noting explicitly the disposition of the first issue—with wording such as that used earlier: "Okay, this doesn't seem to be going anywhere. John hasn't made a value judgment. He still isn't sure what he really really really wants." No issue is allowed to drop without at least this degree of resolution. In a nonworking group, the discussion is disjointed. Issues are raised, discussed, debated, and then dropped. Such a group models a nonworking family or social unit and a dysfunctional way of life outside the group. Clearly, process-oriented group counseling aims to provide a contrasting model of purposeful, organized, effective behavior.

## Wrapping Up

Even in the first session, when perhaps no issues have been brought to resolution, it is not too soon to begin the weekly review of learning (described in chapter 8) by asking everyone in the group, including the leader, to state what they've learned in that session. The wrap-up of the session also looks to the future, both in and out of group. The leader might add, "There are a lot of issues going on for people. Is there anything anyone can do outside the group to make things a little better?" At the beginning, the leader cannot expect much from the group along these lines. The leader will need to do some teaching and modeling, but in the meantime, a tone of participation and responsibility is being set.

From the first session on, it is essential that the leader review the issues covered in that session and establish continuity with the next session. Thus, the leader might conclude an early session with words such as the following:

> "Not every issue has to be resolved in every group, just as we go from day to day working out our issues in real life with family, friends, and work. We now have two issues for next time, Bob's and Jane's, unless we decide to go with something that comes with a greater sense of immediacy. I would ask you, Bob, and you, Jane, to come to group prepared with your issues, and we'll give those priority if we can. And I would ask all of you to participate more in the process, to talk to one another instead of waiting for me to say something. I would like to work less from here on in. I'll still model, but now why don't you begin to take some risks and make process statements."

This continuity is picked up at the next session, which begins with a review of out-of-group assignments and any unfinished business that requires closure.

# 7
# Problem Behaviors in Group

Confrontation and mirroring of highly sensitive issues typically lead to conflict avoidance. A person who is confronted on such an issue cannot be expected to express appreciation and thanks. When the person is asked whether he or she wants to go further with the issue, the group leader cannot take it for granted that the person will opt for positive movement. On the contrary, group members under stress of confrontation regularly manifest defensive reactions that are easily recognizable to the experienced group leader. Meanwhile, other members may likewise engage in disruptive or distracting behavior in a conscious or unconscious attempt to deflect any confrontation from themselves.

Individuals have their own characteristic self-protective mechanisms. Some pick fights; others sulk. Some intimidate; others gripe or whine. Some talk on and on about irrelevant matters; others distract with humor. Some are seductive, offering more or less subtle bribes; others form alliances against other members or the leader. Whatever diversionary tactics members engage in are the same ones they use outside the group to avoid addressing issues of importance to their lives.

In the absence of a positive group climate, this individual flight from responsibility can degenerate rapidly into collective flight. To head off such contagion, ongoing climate setting as outlined in chapter 3 is a necessity. Norms must be set and maintained throughout the course of the group. In countless small ways, even down to the blocking of outside interruptions (except for bona fide emergencies), the leader reaffirms both the value placed on the group and the seriousness of the group's purpose.

Chapter 4 shows how problem behaviors begin when the group begins—as soon as members are asked if they have any issues to raise—and how the leader can counter these behaviors through a steady reliance on group process. The same limit testing occurs throughout the group and is dealt with in similar ways. A leader who knows group process, along with reality therapy and rational-emotive therapy, will not be stampeded and will not allow members' acting out to take the group off course.

In keeping with the techniques of group process, the leader neither abdicates nor dominates. Although greater assertiveness and directiveness may be needed in response to direct challenges, the leader's consistent stance at moments of stress is, as always, to step back and empower the group with process statements and "I" statements. A group leader who is not hamstrung by a need for control can model the purposefulness, combined with the flexibility, that members are asked to practice. The explicit and implicit message is that human beings are not driven, as other animals are, by instinct, impulse, and rote conditioning. Human beings can learn, reflect, and change, and the group is a place to do it. This chapter describes some common forms of resistance encountered in groups and how group process is used to block them.

## Physical Flight: Absence or Lateness

The most overt form of flight from issues is to remove oneself from the group physically. A member who does not accept the group in the first place or who is blocked from changing the subject and going into other-focus (or from attacking, seducing, complaining, or whatever) may simply walk out when things get unpleasant, not show up for sessions, or act out by coming late. This form of resistance may be dealt with in several ways, depending on the circumstances.

In a voluntary group, absence may be made a group issue, with process statements ("Group, what's going on—somebody help me out") and "I" statements ("You've been coming in late; when *I* do that, my attitude stinks"). If this behavior is persistent or disruptive, it is appropriate to question whether the person really wants to be there. In coerced groups, absence or lateness is treated as a form of limit testing that violates the norms established in climate setting (chapters 2 and 3). Such limit testing is dealt with outside the group process by informing the member that he or she is choosing to be disenrolled.

Allegations of mistreatment by other group members do not give a member the right to stop attending sessions, provided that the leader has acted with integrity. If the leader has tolerated an emotional climate in which the member has been scapegoated, he or she must take responsibility for that climate. But the feeling that one was "picked on" in the course of normal group interchange and confrontation is not a valid excuse for staying away. The group is not there to please the members.

Any question in the leader's mind about his or her responsibility for a negative climate is to be resolved with the help of a coleader or supervisor. It is also a group issue, inasmuch as the leader is accountable to the group for what he or she does in group. If other group members charge that an absent member left because "you let such and such happen to him," it is up to the leader to clear the air: "I didn't want him to leave. I may have made a mistake, and this is how he perceived it, but this is what I was trying to do." By the very nature of what goes on in group, there will be mistakes, and people will be alienated. These are realities that the group must acknowledge, and the leader models the acknowledgment.

Still, the group should not spend much time talking about an absent member. That kind of talk is a form of other-focus, as discussed later in this chapter; it reproduces in microcosm the gossip and backbiting that characterize members' lives outside the group. The leader blocks this unproductive talk with an "I" statement: "I'm uncomfortable talking about somebody who's not here. Why don't we wait till he comes back." If the member (having been disenrolled) is *not* coming back, the group may need to reach some resolution about issues connected with the member's behavior and departure. The focus, however, must remain on the experience of the members who are present.

## Extended Silence (Nonparticipation)

If the most extreme form of withdrawal is not to come to group at all, a more common type of passive resistance is to be present without participating. Group members, collectively or individually, often choose to avoid confronting issues by remaining silent. Group leaders who are content to treat this manifestation of resistance with benign neglect can pass the time with group programming, exercises, and talking *about* issues. In contrast, process-oriented group counseling is not satisfied with such superficial accommodations.

### Collective Silence

There may be times, either when the group first comes together or at a later stage, when no one says anything for an extended period. At the outset, members may be ill at ease and reluctant to take risks. Beyond that stage, the group may include a number of individuals who have decided that they do not want to process their issues actively in group. This "I'm not going to say anything" attitude can harden into a test of wills, in which members think, "Let the leader stew. It's not my group, not my responsibility; I don't want to be here anyway." Such resistance can be highly contagious.

Faced with a stalemate over who is going to break the silence, the leader can use one of several interventions presented in chapter 4. These interventions put the responsibility for participation back on the group, not the leader. There is no prescribed time for the leader to wait before intervening. Rather, when the leader becomes sufficiently uncomfortable enduring the silence, he or she owns the discomfort and makes it a group issue: "Group, I'm having a problem with the silence. It's getting uncomfortable for me.

Can anyone help me out with this?" The leader is advised not to lose the moment by deflecting the tension with a question ("How's your week going?" or "Does anyone have a problem?"). By sidestepping the immediate stalemate, the leader sacrifices a valuable opportunity to deal with the silence as an issue in itself.

## The Silent Member

Typically, a group member has one of three motives for remaining silent: (1) "I don't think I have anything worthwhile to contribute"; (2) "I don't want to reveal myself because of the anxiety it creates"; (3) "I won't cooperate with this group leader." Group process aims to bring these assumptions to the surface, challenge them, and empower the member to participate.

The nonparticipating member speaks only when asked a question and only in a reactive, defensive way: "No, I don't have a problem; things are going fine with me." This bare compliance conveys the implicit message that "you have my warm body, and that's all you're going to get. I'm here, all right? That's the only responsibility I have—to get here. Just sign my form; that's all I want out of this." Sometimes this message is more than implicit. A member may actually tell the leader, "I've answered every question you've asked me, so you can't say I'm not involved. Just so you remember this when you make your report." Members who participate in this minimal, negative way have not internalized the purposes of the group. They are there to get out of trouble. Group process is designed to make inroads into that attitude; it creates bridges by which the group member can progress to confronting issues. But the responsibility to do so remains with the member.

It is not the leader's job to get the member to speak or to ask the member how he or she feels about not speaking. It is the leader's job, in climate setting, to model the truthful expression of feeling and to create as safe an environment as possible for such expression. When faced with a silent member, it takes no special training for the leader to ask, "How are things going?" The trained leader knows that it is more productive to bring the issue back to the group with a process statement: "Group, I'm having a problem. Max, you haven't been contributing. When I don't contribute, it means I'm afraid, I'm anxious, or I don't care. Would someone please help me with my problem?" The process statement is made not to put pressure on the silent member, but to elicit whatever perceptions and concerns are out there in the group. By involving other members in dealing with their issues concerning the member's silence, this use of group process invites the silent member to look at his or her own issues.

The following example shows how process statements and "I" statements are used in confronting the silent member:

*Leader:* Jane, I don't hear you saying anything. Are you having a problem with this?

*Jane:* No, no problem. Everything's fine with me.

*Leader:* Group, I'm having a problem with Jane. She answers my questions, but she never initiates. She never interacts with anyone else. She's not nasty; she's polite. But I want to see if we can understand what this is about. I want to see us identify and clarify issues, give feedback, and get some resolution. Jane, that's not happening with you. So maybe the group can help both of us.

*Phil:* Jane, I'd like to hear what you have to say. None of us wants to be here any more than you do. But people are contributing.

*Ruth:* I think it's *your* problem, Mr. Leader. Jane is okay with me. If she doesn't want to talk, she doesn't have to talk.

*Leader:* Then help me with my problem. Jane, you don't want to be here, but you *are* here, and we can't make you disappear. Does it do you any good to sit there and not get the benefit of the group? It's up to you.

*Jane:* I don't think I have anything to say.

*Leader:* Look, the way I behave in group is the way I behave outside of group. I'm not different here from everywhere else. When I feel threatened, I'm silent. When my self-esteem is low, when I don't think I have anything important to say, I get silent. If an authority figure asks me a question, I get silent. That's how I've seen myself behave in group meetings, work meetings, and so forth.

Jane, the fact that you're here means that there has to be at least some question about what's going on in your life. So while we're here, why not see what we can do?

When we raise these questions, there is no one prescribed answer that we expect the group process to produce. The kinds of groups with which we are dealing cannot be counted on to give textbook responses such as "Yes, Jane, we really care about you." We hope that a group member will say what Phil says to Jane, but members' responses (if they are to mean anything) cannot be manipulated. Indeed, the very unpredictability of the interchange can overwhelm an untrained leader who has not learned to trust group process to overcome all foreseeable difficulties.

The process statement is not intended to lead the member or the group to a predetermined conclusion; rather, it is made so that the member's nonparticipation will not go unexamined. In preceding vignette, the leader uses group process to up the ante on Jane's continued silence by making what she is doing more conscious and challenging her to think about it. As a learning device, the leader makes an "I" statement, drawing the parallel between his own (and, by implication, her) silence in and out of group. Without backing her into a corner, he holds up the implications and consequences of her behavior. This is something you can't run from, she is being told, because it will catch up with you elsewhere.

Silence (passive resistance) on the part of some members often occurs in conjunction with attention seeking and monopolizing (active resistance) on the part of others. The silent members hope to slide through the group, doing their time as passive onlookers while others do the talking. They are only too happy to see the group break down into bickering and recrimination. The acting out by some members fills an important need for others, who can take cover while the brickbats fly. In the terminology of *Games People Play* (Berne 1985), the name of their game is "Let's you and you fight."

In this situation, the leader can deal with both the active and passive resistance in one stroke by asking the less active members to respond to the acting out. The leader does this not by pointing the finger at individuals, but by soliciting process statements: "Group, what do you see going on here right now? Somebody who hasn't been talking, help me out, please." This request takes the stage away from the more demonstrative members and simultaneously hands it over to the nonparticipants. By making process statements, the leader raises the nonparticipants' awareness of what is going on and what needs they may be fulfilling. Silent members have an opportunity to question whether this is their strategy for getting by in life—namely, to let someone else create a drama so that they don't come under scrutiny. As they realize how they are limiting themselves with this negative aspiration to get through life unscathed, they may open themselves to learning other ways to fulfill their needs.

If a member's participation is blocked by anxiety about the risks of self-revelation in a group, the leader may use rational-emotive therapy (chapter 6) to identify the irrational beliefs at the source of the anxiety. Likewise, the behavioral techniques of rehearsal and role-playing (chapter 8) may be useful in helping the member get past the emotional block. These modalities should, however, be used as an adjunct to, not a substitute for, group process.

Challenging a silent member often elicits explicit excuses, such as "You don't really know me" or "My problems are so intense, I couldn't begin to explain them here." This is another defense mechanism to avoid confrontation of issues. The member is telling the group, "I'm damaged goods, just a factory second. Don't have any expectations of me because I can't deliver." There is an implied threat: "The more pressure you put on me, the worse I'll get." In transactional analysis (Berne 1985), this game is called "What do you expect from me?" Group leaders can gain insight into this familiar pattern from the list of "vulnerabilities" in chapter 6. For example, someone who does not envision much of a future for himself or herself is not likely to put much effort into self-improvement. The vulnerabilities scheme, together with rational-emotive therapy, can be used to bring to the surface a member's feelings of hopelessness and to examine and challenge the assumptions underlying it.

Is there a point where participation should be enforced? What is the minimum level of participation required of a member if the member is to remain in group? These questions cannot be answered definitively. As a rule, a group member is permitted to remain silent as long as the leader does everything possible to make that silence a group issue. A person cannot be forced to participate, except in the most grudging, compliant way. A leader who dismisses people from the group and sends them back to the referring agency for not participating actively is at the opposite extreme from the evasive leader who entertains in preference to confronting issues. Neither extreme is recommended.

If someone consistently refuses to listen to feedback, however, there may be grounds for disenrollment. If the leader asks, "John, would you like to hear what the group has to say about this?," John should have the right to say no once or twice without threat of consequences. If, however, John takes a defiant line ("I don't care what any of you has to say at any time"), then he is disavowing any feedback, without which he cannot consolidate learning and come to any resolution of issues. At the point where the leader finds this resistance intolerable (especially if it spreads to other group members), a warning may be in order that a lack of quality participation—owning statements, taking the initiative, giving and receiving feedback—puts the member at risk of disenrollment. When to issue and when to follow through on such a warning are judgment calls that depend on the nature of the group and the circumstances.

## Ventilation

At the other extreme from silence is the endless recitation of griefs and grievances that passes in some quarters for group work. Repetitive complaining is one problem behavior that tends to be more severe in voluntary groups, especially those whose members identify themselves as victims. Members of these groups attach value to the group experience to the extent that the expression of emotion for its own sake is indulged. How often we hear group members say, "Oh, it was a great group. Two people cried." Someone, somewhere, decided that catharsis—getting it out—has great intrinsic value, and this belief has come to be accepted uncritically.

Not only has this belief not been substantiated, but the whole notion of cathartic mourning has been called into question by psychologist Camille Wortman's research, which reveals "how common it is for grief to be borne lightly." Wortman suggests that the absence of major emotional upheaval after a loss "can be a sign of resilience." Her findings "call into question the widespread assumption that a period of severe distress leads to a more balanced adjustment." On the contrary, she concludes:

People who are the most upset by a loss are at greatest risk for emotional difficulties in the long run. And contrary to clinical lore that lack of distress just after the loss leads to "delayed grief," those who have a relatively mild initial reaction seem to stay less distressed. (Goleman 1989, C6)

Nowhere does process-oriented group counseling diverge more from common practice than in this area. In our view, ventilation is legitimate up to a point, after which it has diminishing returns and may lead to stagnation for the individual or the group. Catharsis alone does not define the value of the group experience. Catharsis is productive when it leads to resolution of the grieving process. It is counterproductive when it is used to legitimize the status quo—namely, feelings of victimization and disempowerment. The point is not, as group members sometimes insist, whether they have the right to ventilate. Yes, they do have the right; no one is testing anyone's rights in group. The real issue—and it is a group issue—is what the ventilation accomplishes for the individual or the group.

In process-oriented group counseling, the group does not exist to perpetuate a person's sense of victimization. Rather, the group acknowledges the real wrongs the person has suffered and then supports the person in getting beyond them. "Yes, you *were* a victim," the group tells the person, "but now you're a person, and the group can help you do more than be a perpetual victim. Something very real and very heinous happened to you. It happened there and then, but we're here to deal with the ramifications and impact here and now." The goal is not some great catharsis that magically makes things different, nor is it for the person to be able to forgive the perpetrator. Rather, it is for the ex-victim to gather the emotional resources needed for self-support and to make decisions based on self-interest in the here and now.

In telling group members that there are no rewards in group for being a victim, and that it is their responsibility to give up the power of the victim role, the group is conveying a message radically different from what members may have heard elsewhere. Some will find that message upsetting, even threatening; it is like being asked to give up a badge. As a rule, people are not mandated into groups to deal with victimization issues, although a person dealing with such issues may be mandated into a group for substance abuse, child molestation, or criminal violence. Since it is all too easy to stop attending a voluntary group when uncomfortable issues must be confronted or when the group's approach is not to one's liking, it is useful (where possible) to get a commitment from members to continue to attend.

Let us say that Renee, a victim of incest in childhood, remains preoccupied with this trauma. She experiences sleep disturbances, a distancing of relationships, and generalized mistrust of all men. Dissatisfied with these limitations on her life, she comes to group counseling for help. It is appropriate for her to air her thoughts and feelings as she presents her issue to the group. This ventilation is to be listened to respectfully, acknowledged, and affirmed. Then, as outlined in chapter 5, Renee is asked to identify and clarify how she feels the group can help her.

Unlike leaderless self-help groups, which often perpetuate and reinforce the power of victimization, a professionally led, process-driven group will not sustain perpetual victimization, provided the leader has done the proper climate setting. If Renee gets stuck at the stage of repeated ventilation of feelings, she is told:

> "You really were victimized; there's no denying or diluting what happened to you. You told us about it, and the group validated what you said. So if you just want to talk about it, you've had that opportunity. Now, what are you asking for from the group? What can we support you in doing outside the group?"

If she persists in ventilating, the leader might say, "Renee, I really believe we're past getting it out now. You're telling the group this for some reason. What do you want from us?" Here, as throughout group process, the themes of reality therapy run through the interchange. "How can the group help you?" and "What do you want to *do?*" are constant refrains.

### Modeling Appropriateness

The leader also can bring the issue to group with a process statement: "What do you see happening now?" Although disrespectful or abusive behavior is blocked, the group is not a cocoon or womb of total indulgence where anything goes. Rather, as a microcosm of the real world, the group sets limits on redundant self-expression and self-preoccupation. Members take the risk of making voluntary disclosures to which other members may not take kindly. This is a legitimate form of reality testing as long as other members' reactions are expressed appropriately through "I" statements and process statements. If necessary, the leader makes this clear with an "I" statement:

> "I am responsible for my actions, and if I make a person privy to my thinking and feeling, there are consequences for this. I have neither a right nor a privilege to tell anybody something unsolicited. And even if it is solicited, that doesn't necessarily give me the latitude to say everything I might feel like saying."

Part of learning to live in the world is to learn to repress some of our thoughts and feelings. We cannot go around telling people everything that is on our minds. The group is a safer place than most for such expression, in that the harsh, punitive reactions members may have come up against in their lives are not permitted. But the group would not be doing members a service if it perpetuated the *absence* of limits that members also may have experienced.

### Beyond Victimization

How can a counseling group realistically expect to help a person in Renee's position? The group cannot keep her from thinking about the traumatic events in her past. Nor is it the goal to have her embrace the perpetrator. Rather, the group can help her turn her grief into sadness and some degree of acceptance.

The vulnerabilities scheme presented in chapter 6 is especially useful for group members who are confronting experiences of victimization. It may be valuable for Renee to explore whether she envisions a clear future for herself, whether she feels she deserves better than what she has now, whether she has anything to live for, or whether she can identify positive role models or people or things she loves. These questions open up a practical review of her life that may reveal some sources of her vulnerability to a self-defeating preoccupation with victimhood.

This approach leads, in turn, to action—decision making, problem solving, greater involvement with people and activities—as outlined in chapter 8. If Renee is to see herself as a worthwhile person who deserves more than she is getting, she needs to do more than contemplate. She needs to find opportunities to test that proposition in the world, to get positive feedback, and to demonstrate to herself that past wounds need not be a barrier to present satisfaction.

The group's emphasis is on helping Renee devise substitute behaviors and develop other interests. Peele et al. (1991) show how a range of activities—physical exercise, educational programs, community work, and involvement in public issues—can be used as tools for self-empowerment by individuals who are overcoming addictions as well as by victims of trauma. Through problem-solving exercises and other techniques detailed in chapter 8, the group can help Renee focus on the choices before her and identify what she really wants. The specific choices, however, are hers—not the leader's or the group's—to make.

Gaining positive satisfaction from involvements outside the group makes it easier to keep painful experiences in perspective. By processing painful experiences in group and following through on plans made in group, Renee may find that she can put the abuse she once suffered into an area of her mind called "unpleasant memories" so that she can go on with her life. Everyone has unpleasant memories; what varies is their intensity and depth. Group counseling challenges the fatalistic belief that these memories must preoccupy and control us, that they must prevent us from forming intimate relationships, having fun, or accomplishing useful things. The group aims to move the former victim from disempowerment to empowerment, from "It's too painful" to "It's painful, but the pain will be worse if I do nothing," and from "It's too difficult" to "It's difficult but possible, and the rewards are worth it." For Renee, the purposes of the group will have been fulfilled if she can say:

"This is what happened to me. It was painful, and I'll probably take some residue of it to my grave. But I don't let it control me, and I go on with my life. Men are not inherently evil, and not all men perpetrate incest. Nor did I bring this on myself. I just was in the wrong place at the wrong time."

*Resolution versus Closure*

The statement just quoted is an example of *resolution* of a difficult emotional issue. Resolution occurs when one has enough emotional resources not to let the memories of an injustice adversely affect one's life. Resolution is expressed in attitudes such as "I know I can't do anything about that. That's the way it is. Those are the givens." In contrast, *closure* occurs when, even though one can recall the facts, they no longer have any emotional significance. Closure means being able to say, "I've not only accepted and resolved it, but I've also put it to bed. It's no longer emotionally current. It's something that happened, and now I'm more or less detached about it." For someone like Renee, it would mean that she could see the ex-husband who beat her up or the brother who molested her as a child as though he were a stranger.

Resolution is a realistic goal in group; closure is not. Closure occurs subtly over a longer period of time (if at all) as a person implements decisions made in group. Activity (participating in group) is a form of resolution; accomplishment (dealing with issues outside the group) brings about closure. The group leader should keep this distinction in mind and work toward resolution while encouraging the kind of follow-through that, for some people and some issues, will lead to closure.

# Flight (Other-Focus)

Perhaps the most common defense mechanisms used by group members to avoid confronting issues are those referred to collectively as flight or other-focus. Flight means talking about persons, places, and things other than the sensitive issues in one's life now. It means speaking in generalities, talking about abstractions such as society, marriage, men, or alcoholism—anything to avoid staying focused on the issue at hand.

Flight is a universal characteristic of groups, since there are always personal agendas that take the group off focus. Resistance does not disappear in uncoerced groups; it simply takes more subtle forms than "I don't want to be here." People who would not violate explicit norms by failing to attend or violently disrupting the group find it natural—indeed, irresistible—to talk about there and then rather than here and now. Flight runs rampant in voluntary groups such as those for "women who love too much," which have no external sanctions to restrain members' avoidant behavior in group. Leaders may need to be especially vigilant to block other-focus in these groups.

By going into flight, one expresses an unwillingness to take responsibility for what is going on in one's life. Rambling discourses about topics such as capitalism, the criminal justice system, inefficiency and corruption in the military, the unyielding Church, and addictive denial have nothing to do with why group members are here now. Nonetheless, a group will almost inevitably drift in this direction if the leader does not maintain group process. People would much rather talk about, say, the unfairness of the law and the dishonesty of lawyers than look at how they are coping with the world. Such abstractions are the only issues (aside from those that represent an invasion of someone's privacy) considered inappropriate for group work. They are inappropriate not because of their content, but because they are brought up to avoid confronting issues and making a value judgment.

Flight is highly contagious; it is not just an individual but a group phenomenon. As the tension in group rises, members stop listening and responding to one another. Instead, they talk *at* one another by replying, "Yeah, yeah," and immediately moving on to some statement (usually a complaint) of their own. As the group interaction breaks down, the leader may need to intervene by saying, "Please respond directly to Mary. She brought up an issue; let's hear her out and see how the group can help her."

As with any problem behavior, the leader uses process statements and "I" statements to bring the group back on focus. If no one comes forward with a statement about what's going on, the leader (especially in the early sessions of the group) may need to diagram the group's flight pattern verbally, as in this example:

> "Let's stick with one issue for now, before we get all over the place. Mary came up with an issue. I asked if someone could relate to that. Jack related to it and went just a little dogleg left. Margo answered it and took a little dogleg right. Joe said something, and he took the underpass. To the untrained eye, it may seem as if we're all talking about the same thing, but actually everyone's talking around it, like a conversation at a bar, with each person adding their own embellishments. Even though we're talking about similar issues, Mary's issue is getting lost before we can get back to it."

Flight occurs in a number of common variations, including blaming, gossiping, playing therapist, and using humor as a defense. The leader who can recognize these patterns quickly is better able to block them before the group goes too far off focus.

### Blaming

Blaming is an attempt to identify persons, places, or things outside (or occasionally inside) the group that are allegedly responsible for a group member's needs not being met. Typical examples are the following:

- "That cop had it in for me."
- "My wife always picks on me."
- "The boss dumps his problems on me."
- "Men don't want to commit themselves."
- "I can't hold down a job because they make it so hard to get methadone."
- "If anybody should be here, it's my husband. He's the alcoholic in the family."

Blaming is like a stream of water under high pressure that gushes through the group whenever the leader releases the valve. That is why, for example, the leader is inviting trouble by asking group members, "Why are you here?" They will be only too happy to say why: "I'm here because of my wife." "I'm here because of the court." "I'm here because of persons, places, and things." Because blaming is such a reflex response for group members, we have recommended that the leader instead ask, "Now that you're here, what do you want to get out of the group?" Whining in group is a statement that what one wants from the group is to hear one whine, and that is not appropriate.

Blaming is blocked with a process statement: "Group, what's really going on here now? What do you see happening?" The leader looks for someone to say, "I think they're off focus, into blaming." If group members reinforce one another's blaming, the leader's responsibility is not to police, but to bring the group back to process.

When norms are not established and limits set, or when the leader is inattentive, the group may break down into recrimination and withdrawal. This also may occur while the leader deliberately waits to see if someone in the group will take responsibility to question the bickering. Under these circumstances, when the leader decides to reassert normal limits, a stronger than usual "I" statement or process statement may be required, such as "I'm feeling a little annoyed and bored by this. I'm bored; is anyone else bored?" Another variation might be as follows:

"Group, I've been sitting here for twenty minutes now, and I'll tell you what I hear. I hear a lot of whining and bitching. I do want people to feel they can say what's on their minds; that's what the group is all about. But what's going on here is what we call unproductive, and I want you to help me put this back on track. The responsibility is yours, group."

Under pressure, the leader continues to model the truthful expression of feelings.

### Gossip

An easy way to deflect attention from here and now issues is to talk about a group member who is not present. Here is Betty talking about George, a member who has stopped attending:

"This might not seem like a very nice thing to say, but I didn't feel especially comfortable with him in the group. He was kind of strange. His behavior was distracting. He didn't listen very well. He didn't contribute very much. Maybe it's just as well for the group that he's gone."

As long as Betty is talking about George, she does not have to talk about Betty. If this diversion into other-focus is not blocked, other members will readily chime in. Note as well that Betty is talking about feelings she had during previous sessions, feelings she did not resolve in group while they had some immediacy and while George was there to be confronted.

The leader responds by refocusing the group's energy from finger pointing at the absent member to confronting the experience of those who are present. "If someone's behavior is out of line," the leader might say, "I, too, may feel uncomfortable. But George is not the issue now." The leader might go farther and ask whether Betty's reaction to George links up with any current issues in her life:

*Leader:* Does George remind you of anyone in your life—anyone who has acted out in a way that's made you feel not safe?

*Betty:* His behavior was so unpredictable; it reminded me of my father. I have never felt really safe with anyone because of that.

Betty is beginning to identify and clarify an issue of importance to her. Now she can explore, with the group's support, whether she is taking effective control of her life or letting her reactions be driven by past experience.

Another type of gossip occurs when group members get together outside the group and talk about other members. Although it is impossible to eliminate this behavior completely, proper climate setting ("We don't do that") can minimize it. If the leader becomes aware that outside gossip is going on, it should be made a group issue and treated as a form of other-focus.

### Playing Therapist

Many groups have a "professional group member" who has been in the counseling environment long enough to pick up a sampling of group and psychotherapeutic jargon. Often sitting next to the group leader and adopting a knowing air, this individual offers "helpful" remarks about how the group is to be run and how members can best participate. By assuming the role of the leader's volunteer assistant, this member attempts to head off confrontation of his or her own issues. Editorial comments or lectures such as the following should alert the leader to the presence of this potentially destabilizing force:

- "My experience in various groups is that this awkwardness at the beginning is normal. Don't worry; it takes a while for us to get to know one another."
- "The only way this group is going to work is if we open up and reveal ourselves, show our feelings, talk about the alcoholism in our families, all that stuff. We've got to be able to share whatever's inside us."

This variation of other-focus is most provocative when it takes the form of diagnosing other members' ills:

- "I don't know why this is such a big issue for you. It sounds like something deep-seated in you, some paranoia. I'm sure you're feeling very insecure about this, and that's creating problems for you."

There is also a nurturant/seductive version ("Can't we do something to help him?").

A leader who is sensitized to these familiar patterns blocks them quickly, but not in such a way as to put the member on the defensive. For example, the leader would not say, "Are you sure *you* aren't the one who's paranoid and insecure?" Rather, the leader might say, "Mike, instead of guessing about what Sam is feeling, would you like to talk about what *you're* feeling?" The leader also counters editorializing and lecturing by modeling "I" statements.

In a more subtle variation of pseudo-therapeutic other-focus, one may be sidetracked into trying to solve people's problems or change people's behavior outside the group, to the detriment of the immediate, relevant task of clarifying one's own needs and available options. In a vignette in chapter 5, the group leader encouraged Deb to explore the implications of her hostile exchanges with another group member, Phil. The dialogue continues here:

> *Leader:* Deb, does Phil remind you of anyone in your life right now? Is there anyone else in your life who makes you feel that way?
> *Deb:* I've had enough angry people in my life.
> *Leader:* What would you want to tell them?
> *Deb:* Calm down, get quiet, sit back, relax.

The leader's first question elicits from Deb the useful insight that the group interaction is demonstrating something about her life. The leader then gives Deb an opening to go into other-focus. Deb understandably wants to neutralize a frightening, threatening force in her life. But she does not have the opportunity to influence, let alone provide therapy for, all the people whose anger might hurt her. She needs to focus on how she feels when the angry outbursts occur, what she can do to moderate her own reactions, and how she can realistically change the tone of her interactions with others.

### Humor as Defense

Groups are a natural and appropriate setting for fun and recreation. In group as in life, however, humor can be a defense mechanism that a person resorts to under stress. Such a diversion is readily welcomed by the rest of the group, often (because it does not involve overt hostility or disruption) with the connivance of the group leader. A contagion of humor is more pleasant for all concerned than a contagion of recriminations, but it does not help identify, clarify, and confront issues.

In the following example, a leader who recognizes his own tendency to go into flight through humor makes an "I" statement by way of explaining how the group has just gone off focus:

> *Leader:* What just happened?
> *Maureen:* The group dissolved into joking and laughter.
> *Bill:* We were uncomfortable, and we went into flight.
> *Leader:* Right. This is what I saw happen. Naomi, you're really grappling with this issue, and your discomfort, your anxiety, your frustration here is a contagion. I know I feel uncomfortable, and maybe all of us here are feeling a little uncomfortable now.
> *Naomi:* I'm sorry.
> *Leader:* No, no, it's not your fault. You're making us feel uncomfortable. We're taking it on because we care. That's our responsibility. Making jokes helps us alleviate the tension.

*David:* What's wrong with that—making a joke to cut through the tension when it gets too much for the group?

*Leader:* It doesn't help Naomi with what she's dealing with.

[*The group erupts again into joking and laughter.*]

*Leader:* You see? That's how easily an issue can go off track. There's so much pressure to stick a pin in that anxiety and not let things flow. It happens in families, in the workplace, when you're buying a car. I know because I do the same thing. My tendency is, if I'm uncomfortable, to come up with a witty line. I'm quick with that; I'm good at it. But that doesn't help Naomi.

## Monopolizing

Some individuals exhibit an insatiable need for attention. They feel so needy that they take up too much time in group, which may inhibit other members from bringing up their issues. This neediness may be expressed directly, or it may manifest itself in a defensive bluster intended to preempt confrontation.

Brian, for example, pronounces frequently and emphatically that he is using the group to "get well." Whenever another member admits to any weakness or wrestles openly with a painful dilemma, Brian expresses impatience at having to listen to such irresolute individuals—when, after all, he himself "accepts" his "disease" and is committed to his program for recovery. In Brian's case, there is an incongruence between what he says he wants and what he is doing, which is to obstruct the group. His bullying "honesty" and his manipulative, distancing behavior express an implicit message: "Hands off! You can get close, but not too close." This limit testing is sanctioned in his mind by an image of the group as a playground, a place for self-expression without accountability ("Let it all hang out!").

Someone like Brian may need to be confronted forcefully: "Every time people start to talk to one another, you get back to harping on your issue." He may need to be told that the group is for solving problems, not for telling stories, and that he can take his recitations and pronouncements to AA. In most circumstances, however, group process provides the best tools for disarming even the monopolizing member. One does not need any special training or insight to play traffic cop—by saying, for example, "Jack, shut up; you're talking too much," or even "Jack, why don't you give someone else a chance." Instead, the leader makes a process statement: "Group, what's going on over here? What do you see happening? Help me out." A group member may then observe, "When I do this, even though I might not want to be perceived as monopolizing, nevertheless that's what I'm doing." The leader repeatedly models such "I" statements:

> "Group, I have a problem that Jack is taking up all this time. I find
> I don't have time for my concerns, and if I don't, I'm afraid that

others don't, either. When I monopolize the group, it means I'm afraid, I'm anxious, I need attention. I don't know if that's true for you, Jack, but I find it is for me."

What Jack does in group is probably what he does in his dealings with people outside the group. He may not be aware that this is what he does, so a mirror is held up for him in the hope that he will make the connection between his need to monopolize in group and elsewhere. If the group intervention has the desired effect, Jack will gain insight into his behavior, will use the group to deal with the issues that precipitate the behavior, and as a result will be less driven to this behavior.

## Intimidation

Group members who have learned to get what they want by exercising manipulative skills—whether in criminal environments or just in their families—can be expected to use those skills in group as well. They will intimidate the leader and/or other group members with implicit (and sometimes explicit) messages such as "You lay off me, and I'll lay off you," or "Let me bitch, or I'll give you the silent treatment."

Faced with this emotional blackmail, the leader must maintain integrity for the sake of everyone in the group, starting with the leader and the intimidator. In the following example, the leader uses process statements and "I" statements to hold up the mirror to an intimidating member:

*Leader:* Group, I have a problem. Jill, would you mind if I share some of what I've been seeing? I'd like the group to help me with this.

*Jill:* Hell, what've *I* got to lose?

*Leader:* That is what I'm seeing. You've been doing X, Y, and Z. Now when I do those things, this is what I'm doing: I'm intimidating because I don't want people getting too close to me. Whether in words or through body language, I'm letting it be known that "I know my way around here. I won't get on your case if you don't get on mine. As long as you keep things superficial and distant with me, I won't get into your issues. But talk about my basic needs? Forget it."

*Jill:* And you're saying that's what *I'm* doing?

*Leader:* That's what I used to do when I was in groups. I was pretty aware; I had good social skills; I knew something about how groups went. So I'd subtly give the leader a message: "Hey, I'll be compliant. I won't disrupt things. I'll go along with the program—as long as you keep the focus on somebody else. You know, I'm well liked in this group. I can make your job easy, or I can make it hard. You just tell me which way you want it to be."

That's what I did in groups, and that's what I did outside of groups. Same thing. Group, would you help me with this?

Note that the leader asks Jill's permission to share certain perceptions of her behavior and make them a group issue; even then, the leader communicates as much as possible through "I" statements. Jill is not disturbed by the request because she has no idea of what is to follow. How, then, will she react to the confrontation? Can she be reached by the group leader's integrity? The leader's integrity says two things to Jill: (1) "I'm not going to be bought off by your tactics"; (2) "I'm not attacking you. I'm not making you bad for doing this." By conveying these messages to a resistant group member, the leader plants a seed that may bear fruit somewhere down the road. If Jill has heard feedback such as this before, she may be ready to consider it. If she has not heard anything like it, it may take hold with growth and development. Or she may deal with it by not dealing with it.

What if she decides to go through with her implicit threat and make the leader's job hard? Her ability to do so is limited because the leader uses group process to maintain control. Implicitly if possible (through personal bearing, self-confidence, and indirect statements), explicitly if necessary, the leader replies to intimidation as follows:

> "Remember, you have the problem; I have the job. At worst, you could be a minor inconvenience to me. What can you do to me—as long as I deal with your behavior openly, with integrity, and so as not to hurt you? If you rant and rave and really become disruptive, then you're not for this group. I'll continue to bring this issue to you. Remember, I'm not here to please the customer."

If Jill reacts by seething, sulking, or whining, the leader calmly continues to make her behavior a group issue, in the hope that others will pick it up. "How can I expect others to confront you if I don't do so myself?" the leader asks, thereby modeling both personal integrity and the integrity of group process. Other members, especially those who experience intimidation in their lives, then observe that one can stand up to intimidation without suffering undue consequences. Thus, the benefits of the leader's modeling may be felt by the perpetrator, by others in the group who have acted similarly, and by others who have been on the receiving end of such behavior.

## Seduction

Seductive dynamics are inherent in the closeness, intensity, and vulnerability (one-sided or mutual) of the therapeutic relationship. We have detailed elsewhere the many tactics by which clients attempt to seduce, or seductively influence, clinicians, including edited self-presentation, voyeurism, extracurricular contacts, verbal exhibitionism, body language, and outright invitations (Edelwich and Brodsky 1991). In addition to actually seeking sexual gratification, clients may act seductively for a number of reasons:

- To divert attention from treatment or life issues
- To bribe or manipulate
- To establish an unholy alliance in group
- To compromise the counselor's position
- To gain status among one's peers in group
- To gain strength through bonding with a stronger person
- To gain attention and gratification through the use of accustomed strategies

In group, seduction may be directed at the leader or at other group members and may be overt or covert. Overt, active seduction constitutes bribery by flattery and may have sexual overtones. "I'm here to make friends," a new member announces brightly. "I like everybody here." This may escalate to overt seduction of the leader: "You're such a nice guy." The leader can disarm such blandishments by replying, "If you knew me better, I'd be flattered."

Detailed ethical and practical guidelines for dealing with seductive dynamics in counseling and therapeutic relationships are outlined in Edelwich and Brodsky (1991). Consequences of impropriety may include loss of therapeutic effectiveness and benefits for group members; loss of job, loss of license to practice, civil liability, and criminal prosecution for the group leader; and civil liability for supervisors, administrators, and the agency. If the circumstances of the agency bring about incidental contacts between the leader and group members outside of group, these contacts must be conducted in a thoroughly professional manner. Nothing is to occur between leader and member outside of group that could not properly occur in group. Indeed, the member should be encouraged to bring any personal disclosures or requests for help to group rather than confide in the leader outside of group.

Covert, subtle seduction involves presenting oneself as uncertain, fragile, and helpless. "I get really nervous, really confused about all this," the group member says or implies. "If you were to confront me, I'd probably just melt right here, and you would be responsible." This manipulative dependency often is associated with drug and alcohol addiction, especially among addicts who rely on others to obtain their supply for them. Group members who regularly fall back on learned helplessness (Seligman 1975) to get by in life will reenact this accustomed role to get by in group. They are expert in this role, and it plays well in group—more so than an aggressive, demanding posture. The seductive member speaks in a low voice, going on and on about being a victim until the whole group is paying attention (which might not happen if the member were speaking loudly). The message to the leader and to the group is clear: "What happens to me in life is always somebody else's responsibility. What happens to me here is *your* responsibility. Lay off me, or I'll go to pieces. You don't want that, do you?"

It may take special vigilance to see that seductive behavior is dealt with appropriately as a group issue, since this behavior tends to touch off hostile, defensive mannerisms in other members. For example, a woman who appears to use suggestive language or dress may be subjected to nasty denigration: "What you're doing, bitch, is you're seducing the group. You're doing it here because that's what you always do!" It is the leader's responsibility to block such belittling attacks as well as to model a more constructive style of confrontation ("What's going on, group? What do you see happening over here?").

## Personal Attacks

As in the last example, some group members may think that a counseling group is the same as a confrontational encounter group, in which "honesty," however wounding, is extolled and "frank self-expression" is a pretext for antisocial acting out. This harmful indulgence has no place in group counseling. Confrontation is on issues—specific, concrete issues. Global personal attacks are blocked (as they are, sooner or later, in life). For example, one member screams at another, "If you don't want to be here, why don't you take a f——ing hike!" The issue here is not the profanity, but the personal attack. There need not be a group norm against profanity, which for some people is a natural and appropriate way to express feelings, describe experiences, and address issues. There is, however, a norm against personal attacks. There are consequences, as there would be anywhere else, for behavior intended to denigrate, humiliate, or put someone on the defensive.

## Scapegoating

When confrontation and feedback are not given appropriately according to the checklists in chapters 6 and 8—when, for example, the confrontation is unsolicited, overly general, or disrespectful—there is a strong possibility that the confronting members are scapegoating. That is, they are holding another member responsible for their own uncertain commitment.

Group members may feel threatened in their commitment by two things that other group members do. First, the morale of the group is affected when a person is not participating, is resisting confrontation, or is not making a value judgment. There is a legitimate way of owning and expressing such reactions—namely, by making an "I" statement: "It's a problem for me that Max isn't participating." This brings the negative feelings out in the open and permits the resistant member to see how his or her behavior is affecting others. Second, other members and even the leader may feel threatened when a person makes an honest value judgment that change—that is, doing something about an issue—simply is not worth the effort and risks it entails. The backlash that may ensue is to be tempered in order to prevent a negative spirit from spreading through the group. The group respects honest value judgments and accepts the fact that people do not always do what others would want them to do; those are the limitations of people and of the group.

In the following example, the leader and another member use process statements and "I" statements to block scapegoating and to invite the scapegoating members to consider their own emotional investment:

*Leader:* You say you want to lose weight? Well, then, would you like to go to Weight Watchers?

*Phyllis:* No, I don't think I would.

*Janet:* What do you mean, you don't want to go?

*Marsha:* What's wrong with you?

*Leader:* Group, what's happening?

*Karen:* Janet, Marsha, I see you're attacking Phyllis. I'm upset with Phyllis, too. But if I attack her like that, I know it's my own stuff.

*Leader:* Yes, Janet and Marsha, this is what I see you doing. You're jumping all over Phyllis. When I do that, it means that Phyllis isn't doing something I want her to do, and I'm angry at her—maybe like I'd be angry at myself if I weren't doing that same thing. Are you angry at Phyllis? Are you feeling resentment because she isn't the way you want her to be?

## Red-Crossing

A group member who has little tolerance for anxiety or discomfort may identify with and attempt to rescue another member perceived to be under attack. This identification is especially strong in groups for "women who love too much," survivors of incest or family violence, and others who form bonds based on the experience of victimization. The rescuer may question the confronting members' motives, ask them not to be so hard on the member being confronted, or make excuses for the latter on account of a disadvantaged background, alien cultural tradition, or whatever. This defensive tactic is called red-crossing.

If the group leader sees someone coming to the rescue of a member who is being confronted appropriately (according to the criteria in chapters 6 and 8), the leader should block the rescue attempt so that the group can proceed with the issue at hand. The leader tells the group, "There's a lot going on here. I'm having a problem with that. We'll hold off for a second and continue the confrontation."

Once the original issue is resolved, with consolidation of learning (with which the rescue would have interfered), the leader returns to the member who did the red-crossing:

> "Group, I'm having a problem. Maybe the group can help me with this. Sometimes when I see someone who is getting feedback and they're uncomfortable, it makes me feel uncomfortable, too. After all, who wants to be uncomfortable? Do you want some feedback on this, Herb, what just went on for you?"

Taking into account the needs of the red-crossing member, the leader encourages him to process the issue in order to gain insight into a coping strategy that he probably uses outside the group as well. Members who engage in red-crossing typically have a low tolerance for conflict. "Please, let's not fight" is their refrain. The leader may need to open up the process for normal interchange by saying, "We're a group here, and like any group, we have a number of different opinions. There will always be some disagreements. So let's disagree without being disagreeable."

## Unholy Alliances

Personal attacks (sometimes in the form of scapegoating) occur in conjunction with red-crossing when group members pair off in alliances against one another. An emerging alliance can be observed, for example, when one member regularly nods as another makes critical or rejecting remarks about a third. Some such groupings are inevitable along generational or gender lines or in terms of the kinds of issues that are raised. Group process is undermined, however, when members take the stance "You support me, and I'll support you. If you're attacked, I'll come to your rescue. If I'm attacked, you'll come to mine." Implicit in this compact is the assumption that confrontation and feedback are attacks. Of course, group members may well be responding to attacks if the group has been allowed to degenerate into normlessness, the condition in which unholy alliances most commonly flourish.

## Advice Giving

Advice giving, as distinct from appropriate feedback, fails to take into account the needs of the giver as well as the receiver. When giving feedback, one identifies rather than compares. One puts oneself on the line by disclosing real experience. If one is evaluative at all, it is about oneself, not the other person. Appropriate feedback sounds like this: "I once had some difficulty in school, and what I did was play hooky to avoid it because I didn't have confidence in myself." In contrast, advice giving sounds like this: "Why aren't you going to school? You *should* go—you're just avoiding it." Preaching implies that one can live another person's life better than that person can. That is not an effective way to influence people. As the leader may have cause to say, "Who likes to be told what to do? I don't." The distinction between advice giving and appropriate feedback is discussed in detail in chapter 8. However, advice giving should be treated as a problem behavior at any phase of the group's interaction.

## Intolerance

In counseling groups, as in other communities, intolerance of people who are "different" sometimes manifests itself. When it does, it is a group issue. Although people are entitled to privately held prejudices, the group models a community in which the acting out of prejudice is unacceptable. The intolerant person has a value system that allows him or her to call people names with impunity. The leader, replicating the larger world, projects a value system that does not permit such intolerance. The group will not change the way a person feels in an hour's time. But at least for that hour, the person learns to control his or her behavior.

This problem, which often is awkward for group leaders to deal with, tests the leader's command of group process. In one group for male drug abusers, the leader initially ignored sneering innuendoes directed at members who were thought to be gay (for example, "He's one of *your* people"). The leader rationalized that he felt embarrassed for the gay members and also that the group was going so smoothly that he didn't want to do anything to disrupt it. If the group was functioning smoothly, it could have handled any issue, no matter how sensitive, including the leader's embarrassment.

The leader became uneasy when he realized that something had gone awry and that he had done nothing about it. His values and behavior had clashed. After consulting with his supervisor, he saw that he had feared losing control of the group. In other words, he had not completely trusted group process. His first thought was to use indirection to bring the group back to the issue, but his supervisor reminded him that if he modeled coyness, group members would learn to get through life by being coy. So he confronted the issue directly in group and took responsibility for his flight:

"Group, something has been bothering me. Something came up in
a previous group, and I chose the path of least resistance. Bert,

when you made that remark to Greg, I knew what you were talking about, and I'm embarrassed for myself that I didn't mention it, because if we can't be honest and take risks in this group, where can we? It bothers me because I believe in this group. I believe in open, truthful expression of feelings and thoughts, and yet I ran away from it. I would like some help with that. If the group sees me doing that again, please call it to my attention, because the only way this group is going to work is if I, in particular, own my feelings.

"I have a problem with intolerance of people who are different from others. In this group, I'm going to ask you to help me. Now we're not here to talk about homosexuality, any more than we're here to talk about race, ethnicity, or religion. But if you have a problem with a particular member, this is the place to get it out. I'm not here to keep the lid on. On the other hand, if you have a problem with anyone in this group just because he's different—not because you have an issue with him personally—I would ask you to hold it, sit on it. That's your problem; don't lay it on me, even if he doesn't mind. I don't care if Greg tells you, 'Yeah, you can call me "faggot," "sissy"—I don't care.' It's intolerable to *me,* and in my presence, please help me by controlling your doing behavior."

Here the leader distinguishes between flight issues—abstractions such as homosexuality, alcoholism, or the state of the world—and issues that arise between one member and another, which are the substance of group interaction. The leader also distinguishes between concrete issues that arise out of particular experiences and the mere venting of prejudices. If Bert said of Greg, "I think he's gay, and that threatens me," or "I thought I saw him looking me up and down, and that offends me," he would, by taking responsibility for his perceptions and feelings, be making a disclosure that the group could deal with. Greg could then talk about how it felt to be the object of such perceptions. If a group member said, "I'm afraid of Jews because they're so smart; I'm always afraid they'll get the best of me," that member would be owning his or her feelings. A member of the group who was Jewish could then talk about what it meant in his or her life to be stereotyped in that way. But to announce, "I don't like homos" or "I don't like Jews," is unacceptable in group, as the leader makes clear:

"The more you talk about not liking homos, the more upset you'll get. In any case, it's intolerable here in this facility. You don't have to like anybody. I'm not here to educate you about your attitudes. I may not like everybody, either. But if I want to get along in this world, I'll find an outlet for expressing those attitudes where my doing so won't hurt me or anyone else. I may not like a person, but I'd better learn to respect him."

The leader is not saying that the member's attitudes or values are inferior to anyone else's. The member is free to hold those attitudes and values and to express them among those who share them. The group's concern is with what the leader referred to as "doing behavior." Treating someone disrespectfully is unacceptable in group because it is intolerable to the leader and the agency, which stand in for a world that does not take votes about whom one is permitted to vilify.

None of this is meant to compromise a person's constitutional right to freedom of expression. The group restricts free expression in other ways as well, as part of its mission of teaching basic life skills. In so doing, the group is modeling informal, nongovernmental sanctions against behavior viewed by social consensus as inappropriate.

One way the group can deal with these questions is by having members talk about the feelings they have had when they thought they were being discriminated against for any reason. To model such disclosure, the leader might describe an experience such as the following: "I feel that way when I work at the university. The researchers at the academic center talk in their own jargon, in a way that excludes me. Sometimes it gets to a point where I tell them, 'Guys, I'm feeling stupid.' "

### Second-guessing

Second-guessing (also called Monday-morning quarterbacking) occurs when a group member recalls an earlier moment in the group interaction and attempts to reinterpret or question the appropriateness of what went on. Near the end of a session, often during the weekly review of learning, the Monday-morning quarterback will say, "There was a point back there when I felt so-and-so was lecturing instead of speaking to the issue." An appropriate response on the leader's part is as follows:

> "Wait a minute. It's hard enough doing what I'm doing. I get exasperated when, after it's over, people ask, 'Why didn't you do this or that?' I'm fully involved in monitoring the process as it's happening; I can't keep a transcript in my head, too. Say it when you see it, would you? Just say, 'What's going on here? I see so-and-so lecturing,' or 'When *I* do that, I'm sermonizing.' Can you do that for me?"

### Doorknob Disclosures

Group leaders should be on alert for last-minute bombshells dropped for dramatic effect rather than with the intention of achieving resolution. In a seductive, manipulative gesture, a member raises an issue when it is too late to resolve it. Suddenly serious, with a note of concern in his or her voice, the member announces that he or she has molested a child, burned down the family home, resumed drinking, or whatever. The leader blocks this behavior by saying, "This issue isn't going to be resolved in this session. This is the fourth group session out of ten. We'll meet again." The leader then continues with the weekly review of learning on the part of each member, as described in chapter 8.

In another, more literal variation of the doorknob disclosure, a member waits until the group session has ended and then approaches the leader privately as everyone is leaving the room. This is a bid for individual counseling. The leader's response, as should be clear by now, is "Bring it up in group. There's nothing you can tell me outside of group that you can't tell me in group."

## Breaking Confidentiality

The breaking of another member's confidentiality by disclosures away from the group is an outright violation of group norms. As such, it is to be dealt with outside of group process by disenrollment, although a "one warning" rule may be applied at the discretion of the leader and the agency. Violations of confidentiality are most likely to come to the group's attention in residential centers where group members (and perhaps the leader as well) have considerable contact with one another outside of group.

By the same token, a persistent expression of concern about confidentiality as a justification for not making disclosures in group can be a form of resistance. This behavior is to be dealt with through group process, along the lines recommended in chapter 2.

## Violence

Physical violence is the most serious violation of group norms. It is dealt with outside of group process by disenrollment, normally without further warnings or second chances.

To maintain the integrity of the group and prevent demoralization, we recommend that the group leader bring charges of physical violence to the appropriate authorities or support group members who choose to do so. The agency may not always back this stand on the part of the group leader for several reasons. First, the agency may be concerned about jeopardizing the referrals that are its source of income. Second, administrators may view group members as not responsible for what they do. Third, they may blame the victim ("What did you do to make him mad?"). Nonetheless, the leader is advised to press charges, if necessary seeking the backing of a professional association. By taking this action (even when unsuccessful), one recognizes the reality of the violence, defends one's own authority and safety as group leader, and gives group members moral support as well as confirmation of what they have experienced. Although unable to guarantee the outcome of the proceedings, the leader makes clear to all concerned that violence will not go unaddressed.

## Summary

Resistance by group members takes many forms. It is to be expected as a matter of course and derives from the reasons members are in group in the first place. Group process is the trained leader's armament against this resistance. Counselors who come to group thoroughly grounded in the principles and techniques of group process can go in with confidence, knowing that there is no issue they cannot handle, no territory where they need fear to tread.

Group process is analogous to the organizational procedures by which an organization's policies are implemented. It is self-managing, self-correcting, and self-protecting. As such, its operation transcends the leader's role. An individual who is well organized and follows the guidelines for group process—whether as leader or as member—can contribute to keeping the group on track. This is how the group models responsibility in life. By keeping the group on track, one learns how to keep one's life on track. It is a conception of responsibility that is tremendously liberating.

# 8
# Feedback and Consolidation of Learning

When a member makes a value judgment in favor of change, the leader takes some time to test and solidify the value judgment, as detailed at the end of chapter 6. If possible, the leader involves other members in clarifying, questioning, and evaluating. If the value judgment holds, at least for the moment, the leader asks whether the member is ready to receive feedback. The value judgment creates the opportunity for feedback. Feedback, in turn, leads to a consolidation of learning, after which the group supports the member in making, and committing to, a plan of action.

## Feedback

In making a value judgment, the group member tells the group why it is in his or her best interest to change: to live within the law, to go to school, to practice job skills, to learn to communicate better, to seek help for a medical or family problem, or whatever. As noted in chapter 6, the more the member is encouraged to specify exactly *why* it is in his or her interest, the more the member is publicly committed to change. The leader then asks, "How can the group help you with that?" Specifically, "Do you want some feedback from other members of the group?" or "Do you want to hear what others in the group have to say about that?" The group is looking for an attitude of receptiveness, whereby the member thinks, "I question whether what I'm doing is getting me what I want, so I'm ready to listen to others tell how they handle situations like mine."

### Dealing with Resistance

If the member does not want to receive feedback, it would be counterproductive to say, "We're going to give it to you anyway." If feedback is to have a positive impact, it must be solicited, not imposed. The refusal of feedback must therefore be respected. It does, however, call into question

133

the value judgment the member has articulated. Thus, the member may be confronted: "You raised the issue. Did you do it for some reason? You indicated that you wanted to change. Do you want the group to help you?"

If the member persistently refuses feedback, the leader falls back on the self-managing, self-correcting mechanisms of group process. The leader might make a simple process statement such as the following: "Group, I have a problem. Max is not accepting feedback. Now when I don't accept feedback, it's because I'm afraid, and I don't want to hear what's being said. Maybe some people can help me with that." If the circumstances call for a more elaborate, emphatic response, the exchange might go something like this:

*Leader:* Group, I'm having a problem. Can you help me with this problem? What this group is about, Max, is giving and receiving feedback. If you continue to resist this, it's affecting me, and I don't know how it's affecting other members of the group. You don't have to respond to this feedback, Max, but I want the group to help me on how I might better help you. We're talking about my problem now. Your not wanting to receive feedback is not your problem. It's my problem, and I'm asking the group to help me with it.

*Max:* What's your problem?

*Leader:* That I and the group are not having much effect on you. I'm giving it my best shot. I really believe in this group, but your continually resisting this is affecting cohesion. You're one component of the group that's not contributing. I'm having a problem with this. Whatever you want to do, it's up to you. I'm not prepared to disenroll you, but maybe I could get some help with this. People aren't going to bombard you here, but you'll have to listen to people talk *about* you to me and how it's affecting them.

Then Max and the leader listen as other group members make "I" statements. For example, one member might say, "Max, you look sullen. You have a little-kid expression on your face. And when I'm that way, it means I'd rather be somewhere else. It also means that I'm somewhat fearful." Another might say: "Max, when I'm this way, when I'm resisting what's going on, it's because I don't want to let people see me because I'm afraid they'll reject me." The responsibility to accept or refuse feedback remains with the individual member. However, the member hears from other members that his or her choice has natural consequences. For example, a member who does not want to listen to feedback may be seen as bringing up frivolous issues. Moreover, other members may not want to hear feedback from that member.

*Criteria for Appropriate Feedback*

If the member does accept feedback, the leader (if it is still early in group) orients the member and the group on what it means to receive and give feedback:

> "Max, what I'd ask you to do now is listen. Don't respond. Don't feel you have to defend yourself. Group, I would ask you to use 'I' statements with Max. Don't tell Max where he's at. He knows where he's at. He's sitting in this chair right now in this room. Not everybody has to give feedback. But if there's anything in your experience that relates to what Max is facing, just tell what you see and say, 'This is what works for me. What *I* do is . . . ,' or 'I've found that such and such doesn't work for me.' To give effective feedback, keep to the point; make it concise; be specific and concrete; and don't talk *at* people. And we'll check whether Max is hearing each of you clearly before he gets overloaded."

Note that the group is now beyond confronting Max on the contradictions between what he wants and what he is doing (although those contradictions may reemerge if the feedback is not to his liking). The emphasis now is positive, on "what works," on the "doing" of a plan of action that Max will develop with the help of the group.

The more the group has progressed to the working stage, the less the leader must structure the feedback process. Ideally, the process becomes more free flowing as members become accustomed to it. A member may solicit feedback spontaneously in the course of talking about an issue—by asking, for instance, "Am I taking too much responsibility at work?" Other members can then respond, "What I do when I find myself taking on too much is. . . ."

Even then, the leader must monitor the feedback and be prepared to block that which is inappropriate. Appropriate feedback has the following characteristics:

- Solicited rather than imposed
- Gentle and caring rather than aggressive, accusatory, or punitive
- Descriptive rather than evaluative
- Specific rather than general
- Concrete rather than abstract
- Appropriately timed
- Presented so that the person can hear it (in an atmosphere of trust)

Giving feedback in the form of "I" statements ensures the fulfillment of most of these criteria.

Group leaders must be alert to block feedback that is imposed, judgmental, or prescriptive. Regrettably, untrained leaders themselves sometimes give such feedback. In one group we observed, the leader talked at a silent member: "What do you do when you go home at night? Don't you have anybody to talk to? I'm going to give you an assignment: go home and write a letter to someone." There was no interaction, no group process. Instead, the leader publicly humiliated the member by being so directive in front of the group. This is an extreme example, but if group leaders can make that mistake, it must be expected that group members, who are untrained in counseling or in restraining the expression of their own needs, will exceed the boundaries of appropriate feedback. They may have learned in other kind of groups to tell another member where he's at (for example, "You sound angry"). They may become diagnosticians, as in this example:

*Roberta:* This is beginning to sound like a self-esteem issue, where you're having trouble getting affirmation for feeling good about yourself.
*Max:* I definitely do feel good about myself.

Here Roberta's feedback is evaluative rather than descriptive. Predictably, hearing his problem labeled in this way puts Max on the defensive.

Let us suppose that Roberta, perceiving Max to be insufficiently assertive in group, infers that he must have that problem outside of group as well. She identifies with him because this is an issue she has had to deal with in her own life. If the identification is unconscious, Roberta may express it in a defensively hypercritical way: "You're just too passive, Max. You'll never get anywhere that way. You have to speak up more." That kind of feedback is considered unhelpful in group and is blocked. If, however, Roberta is conscious of the parallel between her experience and Max's, she may be able to phrase her input more sensitively. Were she confronting Max as outlined in chapter 6, she might combine a descriptive observation with an "I" statement:

> "I don't see you speaking up a lot, Max. From what I can see, sometimes you'll make a contribution, but if nobody picks up on it, you'll let it drop. I know that when I do that, I usually end up feeling really frustrated because it seems as though nobody's paying attention to me and to the things that matter to me. And that feeds my perception that I'm not respected. I don't know if it's that way for you, Max, but I mention it because that's how it is for me."

When it comes to giving feedback (by which stage Max has made the value judgment that he wants to do what is necessary to get more attention), Roberta does not need to dwell on her observations of Max. Her "I" statements can be directed toward specific strategies for improvement:

"What I find works for me when I feel I'm not being listened to is to blow a whistle on the discussion and simply insist that what I'm saying is too important to be ignored. I know that may not be the easiest thing for you to do. Frankly, it's out of character for me, too, and I haven't always been comfortable doing it. But I've learned that it's what I sometimes have to do to be listened to, and I've reached the point where I'd rather be listened to than stew about it afterward."

At both the confrontation and feedback stages, Roberta makes it possible for Max to hear her by owning her statements, putting her own experience on the line, and establishing an emotional link with Max over the issue she feels she and he have in common. In fact, she may be mistaken in assuming this link—that is, she may be projecting her needs onto Max—but that can be clarified when he responds to her feedback.

Another example of constructive feedback—one that emphasizes its gentle, caring tone—comes from a group dealing with intimate relationships. Acting on a commitment made in a previous session, Kathleen has taken the initiative to try to form a closer relationship with someone and has been rebuffed. She returns to group disheartened, wondering whether such risks are worth taking after all. Another group member, Ginny, supports her with this feedback:

"I think I can understand what you're feeling. I, too, am very sensitive to rejection. I also crawl out on limbs, only to find out later that I can't get back. But I've found that for me what really works is to say, 'What the hell, I got out there, I tried something, and it didn't work out. So what?' I've been all through what I sense you're doing, which is to take the thing to a biology lab and dissect it with a scalpel. But I remind myself that it was a moment out of my life, and if I humiliated myself, it was in front of one person. The rest of the world doesn't know what happened and wouldn't care if they did know. I know how easy it is to blow this sort of thing out of proportion by processing it over and over again. But I find I do better just to let it go. Nothing ventured, nothing learned. Part of being a worthwhile person and a fulfilled person is to take chances and dare to make mistakes. And this wasn't even a mistake, except from hindsight. This was something that might have turned out all right but didn't. That's how I'm learning to take these rebuffs. And so I hope you won't stop reaching out, taking risks, and trying some different things."

This is a far cry from the feedback people get in confrontational encounter groups.

Whether feedback is appropriately timed and whether the person is ready to hear it are more subtle issues. Is this feedback something the person has heard before? Can the person do anything about it? Does the person giving the feedback care enough to hear an angry response, to be the object of the impulse to "kill the messenger"? In part it comes down to a question of trust, of whether a strong enough relationship has developed over a period of weeks between member and leader, or member and member, to permit certain sensitive things to be said. (Of course, even when the leader does everything within reason to model trust, some individuals will not become trusting.) Readiness also hinges on the level of openness and awareness the recipient of the feedback has reached with respect to the particular issue under consideration—in other words, the strength of the value judgment.

Group members err on both sides of the question of timing and readiness. Members commonly bombard one another with blunt feedback for which the emotional ground has not been prepared. At the other extreme, members shy away from giving feedback because they are afraid of becoming the messenger who gets killed. Typically, one member will try to go through the leader to speak to another member: "Do you think Joe should do such and such?" Rather than give feedback directly, the member asks the "teacher" for permission. This lack of confidence in one's confrontational skills, together with fear of retaliation, likely reflects the way the member acts outside of group. Such indirection, if not blocked, can become an unproductive group norm. An appropriate response on the leader's part is simply to say, "Speak to Joe directly."

### Blocking Advice Giving

Advice giving, discussed in chapter 7 as a problem behavior in group, is a major impediment to effective feedback. As the leader (when necessary) reminds the group, people do not like to be told what to do. Being told that "you should do this; you should do that" only puts a person on the defensive; therefore, this type of feedback is blocked. Similarly, the expression "If I were you" comes across as preachy, since it assumes that I can live your life better than you can; it, too, is blocked. Changing the wording to "If it were me" is not much of an improvement. Although this locution does not portray the giver of feedback as usurping the receiver's autonomy, it involves the giver in a merely hypothetical way. Because the giver's experience is not real and concrete, it carries little benefit for the receiver. Feedback has real impact when the giver owns his or her statements and when those statements convey an investment in actual experience: "When I'm in that position, this is how I feel, and this is what works for me" (in other words, "This is how I've gained effective control of my life"). By putting oneself on the line, by identifying rather than holding oneself superior, one transmits something real that the receiver can hear and apply to his or her needs.

### Considering the Needs of the Giver and the Receiver

Feedback is a two-way process that engages two persons' needs. The leader must monitor the process to see that the two sets of needs interact appropriately and that the expression of one does not block fulfillment of the other. For example, a member who gives feedback in an uncaring, finger-pointing way may have a need to scapegoat. There are many ways in which the giver's needs may blunt the clarity of the message or even distort it. That is why it is so important to check for clarity of communication, as discussed below. If the giver's agenda makes the feedback irrelevant or useless to the receiver, the leader blocks it and suggests that the giver raise his or her own issues separately. There may, however, be a positive synergy between giver and receiver in which one sells oneself—along with the other person—on a way of gaining effective control of one's life. That reciprocal transmission of strength is what the group is about.

As a rule, the giver's needs will mesh with those of the receiver if (1) the feedback is given appropriately (according to the criteria listed previously) and (2) there is a reference point in the giver's experience that generates empathy and relevance. Not every member will have a reference point grounded in similar experience, and not every member need give feedback to a particular person at a particular time. Indeed, overloading a person with feedback is to be avoided.

### Checking for Clarity of Communication

While feedback is being given, the leader frequently checks for clarity of communication with questions such as "What did you hear her say?" or "Before you get overloaded, what do you hear people saying?" Although this is the first step in consolidation of learning (which follows feedback), it is mentioned here because it begins almost as soon as feedback begins. Clarity of communication is to be checked after no more than two or three people have given feedback; otherwise, the person receiving the feedback is unlikely to retain it. "Before we go on," the leader interjects, "I'd ask you to summarize what you heard Peter say, what you heard Ellen say, and what you heard Stan say." Clarification of communication may even occur while one member is giving feedback if the feedback goes on longer than usual. In one such case, the member giving feedback had two things to say. After finishing the first, he asked, "May I go on to part 2?" The leader replied, "First, get clarification on part 1."

### Ongoing Assessment and Maintenance of the Value Judgment

In the evaluation stage (outlined at the end of chapter 6), the leader makes a provisional assessment that a value judgment has been made. Subsequent feedback may challenge this value judgment by revealing discontinuities the group member has not yet confronted between "what I want" and "what I'm doing." One may verbalize a value judgment, but when the risks it entails and the changes one needs to make are specified concretely, one may hedge on the value judgment. One may think, "I really want the supervisor's job, but I don't want to go back to school and get the training for it," or "I wouldn't mind being on the softball team, but I don't want to call the coach because he might tell me they have too many people already." What one is saying is "I want the benefits, but I don't want to take the risks."

Articulating the risks and benefits by means of a problem-solving exercise (as described later in this chapter) may help to resolve this dilemma, but not necessarily in the direction of positive action. One may decide, for example, "I've found out what this entails. Relationships are at best an iffy thing. I've been hurt, and I don't want to be hurt again. I don't even want to risk it. Certainly I would do it if there were a guaranteed outcome, but this group has shown me that there is no guarantee." Other group members who find their own commitments threatened by this frank decision to stand pat may react resentfully by scapegoating the offending member. It is the leader's responsibility to block such behavior and, in anticipation, to establish a climate in which the group can be prepared to respect whatever value judgment a member makes.

Ongoing assessment and maintenance of the value judgment is a practical necessity in the kinds of groups under consideration here. It would be ideal if the group member were to arrive at a value judgment by a smooth, linear progress, listening seriously and taking the confrontation and feedback to heart. This is not to be expected of people who have been mandated into group counseling or who are there to confront issues they have dealt with ineffectively for a long time (such as marital problems). When a person comes into group motivated by fear of consequences or by accumulated frustration with unfulfilling experiences, a period of testing and strengthening—of confrontation, feedback, and consolidation of learning—usually is necessary before he or she can begin to take control of his or her life.

### Consolidation of Learning

When a solid value judgment has been made, the group member can proceed with a plan of action. Before moving on to the plan, however, the group helps the member assimilate the feedback, articulate its impact, and assess whether the value judgment has been strengthened or weakened. In this consolidation of learning, the leader asks the member three questions:

1. What did you hear each person say?
2. What have you learned from this feedback?
3. What are you going to do about it?

### "What I Heard"

After no more than two or three people have given feedback, the leader begins the consolidation by asking the recipient of the feedback, "Okay, before we go on, what did you hear people say to you?" The exchange typically takes this form:

*Leader:* Max, what did you hear Henry say?

*Max:* Henry, I heard you say that when you hesitate to make a decision in a situation like mine, it means you're fearful.

*Leader:* Is that right, Henry?

*Henry:* Right.

*Leader:* What did you hear Irene say?

*Max:* Irene, I heard you say that you think I'm afraid. Is that right?

*Irene:* No, that's not what I meant. I didn't mean you were afraid, just that, going by the way I've felt when I've been in the same spot, you seem to have some questions you don't know how to deal with.

*Max:* Okay.

*Leader:* Now do you know what Irene said?

*Max:* Yes.

The leader checks for clarity of communication not only by asking Max what he heard each person say but also by confirming whether what Max heard them say is what they actually said or thought they were saying. What Max heard Irene say is different from Irene says she meant, and the two of them have a dialogue to clear up the discrepancy. This process sometimes degenerates into fruitless arguments, since the person giving feedback may not always stick to what he or she originally said. That is just one of many contingencies that make the group leader's job challenging. Nonetheless, it is essential to support group members in listening to feedback without becoming defensive and at the same time to make sure that people are not talking at cross-purposes. As the group goes on, the leader should have less need to intervene to direct every step of the process, since members will have learned to initiate the questions and clarifications themselves. In the preceding example, the leader asks Henry if Max heard him correctly, but Max himself asks this question of Irene.

Sometimes this kind of exchange can produce a real breakthrough in communication and understanding, and with it a transmission of strength. In the following example, Max has said that he feels powerless and fears that he is losing control at his job. He says he wants to do something about this. Irene asks permission to give feedback:

*Irene:* Would you like to hear some feedback?

*Max:* Yes, go ahead, Irene.

*Irene:* I've been listening to you, Max, and I think I understand what you're trying to say. When I feel I'm losing power or losing control of a situation and I feel frustrated about it, usually I go back to the basics and ask myself, "Irene, do you need more training in this type of work? Are you feeling, perhaps, that you don't know the rules of the game well enough?" So what I do is look into possible ways to get further training. The kinds of problems you're citing I regard as signs that I don't have my act together on the job. So I look to get my act together by going to a class, reading, whatever. I can deal with the particulars all my life, but I have to look at the bigger picture if I really want to resolve the problem.

*Leader:* Max, what did you hear Irene say?

*Max:* The way I heard it, you're advising me to check out my competence, to make sure I feel competent in what I'm doing.

*Irene:* What I said is simply what works for me, what's in my best interest.

*Max:* And if not, to study up on it, to go for it.

*Irene:* Did you hear the part where I talked about how sometimes the nitpicky things that make me feel I'm losing power are only symptoms of a larger problem? The larger problem is that I may not feel competent and secure in what I do. Did you hear that part?

*Max:* Yeah, but I'm not sure it really applies.

*Leader:* You don't have to answer that. I'm checking whether you heard what she said the way she meant it, not whether you agree. I don't want you to feel you have to say yes to everything. What I want to ascertain now— and I'm modeling this for everyone—is this: are you satisfied, Irene, that Max heard what you meant to say?

*Irene:* Not really. I say that, Max, not to dispute what you said I said, but to acknowledge how I jumped in and tried to clarify what I said to help you with your clarification. I would have done better to be quiet and let you finish your whole statement before deciding that you hadn't understood a part that I was anxious to have you hear, the part about not confusing the symptoms with the larger problem. I would have been happier hearing you give that piece back to me instead of thrusting it at you again. I apologize for my impatience, but it was very important to me that you hear that.

*Leader:* Now, Max, please rephrase what you heard her say. I'm doing this for myself. I have a need for you to be clear about Irene's feedback.

*Max:* What I understand you to be saying, Irene, is that the problems I'm facing at work may be symptoms of a larger issue that I may not feel able to talk about—namely, how well I know my job. Is that right?

*Irene:* In part that's what I said, but only in part. I did not say that that might be your problem. I stated only that that was my problem. Whether you feel that way, I have no idea. I'm owning it: when *I* feel that way, that's what it is for me.

*Max:* That's why I said I'm not sure that's the case for me.

*Irene:* Okay.

This type of interchange often occurs early in group, and the leader can use it to model clarification of communication as well as to set a tone for the conduct of the group. Even so, both members are involved in an authentic way, owning their statements and feelings. Irene's "I" statements enable Max to acknowledge a problem he "may not feel able to talk about," even if he declines (as is his prerogative) to own it as the problem he really has.

### "What I've Learned"

Having checked for clear communication, the leader then asks, "Now you've heard people give you feedback, and you've checked out what you heard. Did you learn anything from this?" If the member answers in the affirmative, the leader goes on: "Maybe you can tell the group what you've learned." The member then generalizes from the feedback and owns it. For example, the member might say, "Yeah, I guess I *have* been reacting to these things out of fear." When one does the work of listening to feedback and putting it together and saying it oneself, the message sinks in more deeply than when it is merely pointed out by someone else.

Ideally, the group would hope to get this kind of response from a member who has received feedback: "I've said I don't have a communication problem, but three people have said they have one with me. When the third person says I have egg on my shirt, I'd better take a look. If it walks like a duck and quacks like a duck, I can't keep saying it's not a duck." Here, feedback and consolidation have reinforced and solidified the value judgment and left the person ready to take steps to change. At the same time, as in the case of Max and Irene, the group member is under no obligation to accept any feedback as gospel. It is up to the member to sort out the implications of the feedback and to decide how much of it to own.

### "What I'm Going to Do"

Awareness is important, but it is not curative. Whether or not it is a necessary condition for change, it surely is not a sufficient one. In group counseling, as in reality therapy, the most important things that happen are those that happen outside the group. That is where change really occurs. To get this point across, the leader might use an illustration such as the following: "A man with secondary impotence may get crucial support in group (as well as referrals to educational resources), but his problem is not that he can't get an erection in group, and it is not in group that he will implement the solution to the problem."

Therefore, the leader asks a third, all-important question: "What are you going to do about this problem? What are you going to do outside this group?" With it, the leader makes a commitment: "We'll support and validate you for doing what you say you're going to do. The group will support you for doing some homework assignment and taking some risks on the outside."

If, in answer to the leader's question, the person volunteers to undertake a particular intervention or solicits the group's help in devising such an intervention, the next step is to move to a plan of action. However, a person may be receptive to feedback and may have a good consolidation process, but may not reach the decision that the group would prefer. Joanne (in chapter 5) has presented to her group her concern about her husband's failure to take her into his confidence about a career change he is planning. She would like to participate in making this important decision with him. Joanne has received relevant feedback from other group members, such as the following from Gloria:

> "Joanne, let me share with you what's been helpful for me and my husband. In fifteen years of marriage, we've gotten to know each other pretty well. He knows what I'm thinking, and I know what he's thinking. We've found that if he feels one way about something and I feel another way, as the days go by, the distance between us grows larger and larger. It gets to the point where one of us will finally say, 'Look, we've got a problem. We've got to sit down and talk about it.' We do this carefully and deliberately. It has to be in the evening when the house is quiet. We put some music on and start talking. I can't remember a time when after fifteen minutes or two hours or whatever, we haven't come to a resolution. I feel that if we didn't do this, the divisions between us might get more and more serious. And who knows what might happen then?"

After Joanne has told the group what she heard each person say, the leader asks her the second and third questions in the consolidation of learning:

*Leader:* Okay, if you could just consolidate: what did you get from this feedback?
*Joanne:* I guess my husband and I have to make an effort to commu-

nicate. I guess we have to set a time to get together and confront the situation directly. But I also have to ask, as at least one person here did, "What about the risk? Do I see the benefits as worth the hassle of stirring things up between us?" I see the situation basically as all of you have put it, but the ultimate decision sits right here.

*Leader:* As you're sitting here right now, what decision have you made?

*Joanne:* None.

*Leader:* Let us know if in the future the group might be able to assist you. (To the group) That's resolution, for now. She knows the natural consequences that were spelled out, and she said no. Let's respect that and move on.

Here the leader anticipates and tries to head off any fallout that might result from other group members (such as Gloria) becoming overinvested in Joanne's decision. "After all that work we did," they might complain, "you're not going to do anything?" But it is Joanne's issue, her life, her decision.

The process of identifying and clarifying an issue, receiving feedback, and consolidating learning generally can be completed in one session. The leader should strive to bring the group up to the working stage as quickly as possible so that these feedback cycles can be completed even in early sessions. As a session nears its end, the leader moves toward resolution (if at all possible) of the issue under consideration. If resolution cannot be reached, the leader announces that the issue will be taken up again and, at the end of group, makes a progress note to this effect.

In the outside world, issues often are left unfinished at the end of a meeting, a workday, or a social engagement. Sometimes these issues are picked up again; sometimes they are not. In group, it is essential that issues not be left unresolved indefinitely. When issues are left dangling, it is a reflection of what goes on in the disorganized, chaotic world from which group members come. Dysfunctional individuals, families, and relationships are characterized by this tendency to let issues fester until they surface again in a combative, vindictive way. In contrast, the group strives toward resolution, even if it is not the full resolution (or closure) a person may desire. The group leader brings a sense of organization and stability to people whose lives have been chaotic and unstable. One way the leader does this is by indicating clearly whether the issues raised during a particular session have been adequately resolved and, if not, bringing up the unresolved issues next time. In this respect, the group is not a true microcosm of life; it is more organized and secure.

All this is to no avail if the group remains the only part of a person's life in which there is organization and accountability. The group models these qualities so that members can learn to actualize them in their own lives. Without this application, what goes on in group is just an exercise. That is why group process includes expectations—plans and commitments—concerning actions to be taken outside the group.

## Plan of Action

The group member's plan of action is developed in response to the question "What are you going to do about it?" The plan is a practical blueprint, broken down into small, concrete, incremental steps and backed by commitments to specific actions on the part of the member as well as commitments of support on the part of others in the group. The plan is programmed for accountability and designed for success.

### A Problem-Solving Exercise

The elements of a workable plan are illustrated by a problem-solving exercise used in many kinds of groups and workshops to help people out of ruts of hopelessness and inaction. This exercise may be used in group counseling if group members want it and if the leader believes that its benefits are worth the investment of time. However, there is no need to go through the entire exercise; rather, the leader may extract from it what will benefit a particular group or individual. The leader may decide to do the exercise once or twice as a demonstration of practical, group-supported problem solving and then address subsequent issues in a more focused, streamlined way.

In this exercise, the leader writes the member's problem on a chalkboard or easel and then solicits suggested solutions from the group. It is essential that everyone brainstorm freely, so as to generate as many solutions as possible. The members and leader must put aside the natural impulse to evaluate, criticize, and reject. Instead, they write down every alternative that anyone comes up with, however impractical it sounds.

When the group has finished brainstorming, the person who has the problem evaluates each proposed solution by putting it into one of five categories. Silverstein illustrates these categories with the example of a person who wants to lose excess weight:

1. *Most Likely:* "The easiest alternative, that is, continue 'as is.' "
2. *Most Desirable:* "I go to sleep tonight, and the Fat Fairy comes and takes the thirty pounds away."
3. *Alternatives with More Than a 50/50 Chance of Success:* "Weight Watchers, any reasonable diet."
4. *Alternatives with Less Than a 50/50 Chance of Success:* "A 'fad' diet to lose ten pounds the first week."
5. *Least Desirable:* "Sew up my jaw for six months so that I can eat only liquids." (adapted from Silverstein, 1977, 82)

For someone who is dealing with a work related problem (for example, "A coworker speaks to me in a high-handed, patronizing way that makes me lose face with others and makes it harder for me to get the cooperation I need"), here are some possible solutions:

1. *Most Likely:* Other things being equal, what do you think will happen? Usually the answer is, "I'll go on complaining, and nothing will change."
2. *Most Desirable:* This is the "magic wand" solution, where you can indulge in any fantasy. For example, "The offending party will disappear from the face of the earth."
3. *Alternatives with More Than a 50/50 Chance of Success:* An example here might be, "I'll write a memorandum to the director documenting my co-worker's unprofessional conduct."
4. *Alternatives with Less Than a 50/50 Chance of Success:* Here you might list some remedies that have been tried previously without success, such as, "I'll have a talk with my errant co-worker about the harm he/she is doing."
5. *Least Desirable:* This might be, "I'll criticize my co-worker publicly, thus causing him/her to retaliate in such a way as to damage my professional reputation." Or "I'll give up on the situation and quit my job." Or it might simply be the same as the "most likely" solution: "I'll do nothing, and things will stay the same." (Edelwich and Brodsky 1980, 227–228)

Having listed and evaluated the alternatives, the person chooses one that appears to be workable and worth the effort, discomfort, and risk:

The next step is to decide on a plan of action by informally weighing the probable costs and benefits of each proposed solution. What is it likely to accomplish? How unpleasant will it be to carry out? Is it likely to have consequences that you want to avoid (e.g., making you lose your job)? This is where the value judgment comes in: "Do I want to do this? Is it worth it? What consequences am I willing to risk to have a chance at solving the problem?" (Edelwich and Brodsky 1980, 228)

Weighing risks and benefits means reconsidering and (it is hoped) reaffirming the value judgment. In the case described in the previous section, Joanne must decide what she has to gain and what she has to lose by raising a sensitive issue with her husband.

With the help of feedback from the group, the person devises a step-by-step plan whose components are readily implemented and monitored. This approach to planning is derived from the principles of reality therapy:

According to [William] Glasser, it is our job as "helpers" to make the plan small enough to be realistic but large enough to be rewarding—in other words, to try to ensure that the plan doesn't fail, because the people we're dealing with sure have been experts in failure. We always make "Do" plans, not "Don't" plans. We need to keep plans in an affirmative, positive context because we need lessons in success, not failure. So we avoid complex plans. We can always increase the complexity as we achieve success. We make small plans so that we can recognize, reward, and support the smallest achievement. We are goal-oriented, but with moderate, progressively rising goals. (Silverstein 1977, 85)

The plan's success is measured not by outcomes that are beyond the person's control, but by the person's having taken each step at the agreed-upon time. In a group dealing with intimate relationships, for instance, a person's overall plan may be to take the risk of asking someone out, but there is no guarantee that a date will result. The immediate plan is first to obtain the phone number and then to make the call by a specified time. Similarly, if a person plans to go downtown to apply for a job, the blueprint worked out with the group contains each step necessary to accomplish this goal: How are you going to get there? What bus will you take? Do you need anyone's help to do it? Is there anything that might stop you? When will you do it? The time set should be as soon as is practically possible. These last steps of formulating the plan and making a commitment to carry it out are the parts of the problem-solving exercise most directly applicable to group counseling.

### Feedback and Modeling of Plans

Here again, feedback of the "what works for me" variety can be useful in helping a member formulate a realistic plan. For one thing, feedback is called for when the member announces an intention to do something unrealistic, as in this exaggerated example: "I really want to play professional basketball, but I'm too short, so I'm going to go out next week and work on getting taller." Ultimately, it is up to the member, not the leader or other group members, to determine that this is not a realistic plan. The leader can, however, ask whether the member would like to hear feedback from the group on that point. If the member still chooses to go ahead with the plan, the leader's and the group's stance is "I might disagree, but I respect your choice."

On the positive side, detailed feedback can provide models of concrete, specific, sequential plans that pertain to the member's area of concern. The member may solicit such feedback by asking the group, "Please help me with this. Tell me some things I can do." For a person who is facing an interpersonal or bureaucratic stalemate on the job, for example, the following "I" statement made by one group leader models an effective plan of action:

"I'll tell you what works for me. If I feel that I'm not getting what I need to do my job, I go to my immediate supervisor with a list of issues. I come prepared with an agenda and present it in an orderly way: 'These are some of my issues, and what I'd like to do is get resolution or closure on one issue before we get to the next.' I don't allow myself to be condescended to (you know, by being told what a wonderful job I'm doing), nor do I allow myself to be intimidated, browbeaten, or threatened. I come in good faith, and it's a reasonable expectation that my issues be dealt with in good faith. My *issues*, not my persona.

"If that doesn't work, I bring it to my peers. How do people who do the same thing I do look at the issue? Is it a problem for them? Am I the only one who has this problem? If someone has had the problem and resolved it, how did they resolve it? If not my peers at work, maybe I'll go to someone who works across town at a similar organization, to a teacher or mentor, or to someone I went to school with—some professional person whom I respect and whose judgment I trust.

"If that doesn't work, the problem becomes a little more serious for me. I have to weigh the entire picture and ask the question 'Is it worth it? Is it more anxiety-producing than I can comfortably bear?' There's a value judgment that comes in here. If I still want to press on, I go to my supervisor's supervisor—again, with my issues, not my persona. In effect I'm saying, 'Don't tell me how much you appreciate me; don't tell me what a great contribution I'm making. I know when I'm being patronized.'

"Then, if *that* doesn't work, I may seek out my own professional help and make some adjustments if necessary. That is, I'll hire a 'mercenary,' a trained, objective person who has no investment in me, doesn't care how I feel about her or him, and doesn't know the other players or the subtleties of the situation. Many times I can't see the forest when I'm in the midst of the trees, and it can be very difficult for me not to bring personalities into it. You know, 'It's *them*.' One thing I will *not* do is go to a close personal friend or family member because they can't be objective. They'll either blame me, saying, 'You know how you are around here,' or take my side uncritically.

"Those are the steps that work for me. In other words, I don't want the chaos, the uncertainty, the instability, and the disorganization to consume me. The system may be in flux, but I want to stay in control of my life. I find this approach incredibly liberating. I'd like your comments on this. Do you think it applies to your situation?"

This particular feedback may be useful in many types of situations for group members who have difficulty with authority figures or who lack experience in dealing effectively with organizations. It also has much general relevance for group counselors and helping professionals generally.

### Planning in Concrete, Nonideological Terms

Although there are risks attached to any action, decision making can be made less intimidating by framing alternatives in terms of concrete choices rather than global self-identification. For example, instead of having to decide whether or not to "be" gay or lesbian, the group member need only ask, "Do I want to act on my attraction to this particular person? What will be the consequences? Do I want to take the risk?" (Edelwich and Brodsky 1991, 177). General questions of identity do not need to be decided in group; they are better left to be resolved over time by a series of choices that the person makes in life.

Likewise, it is not the group's or the leader's job to jump on an ideological bandwagon and promote popular choices, even if that produces a rush of good feeling in the group. Professional group counseling, like individual therapy, does not operate from preconceived notions of what is right and wrong. Rather, it supports the individual in identifying and clarifying particular needs and making focused choices in the individual's best interest. For example, this is the approach a professional counselor or counseling group would take to the emotionally and politically charged issue of coming out as a homosexual:

> The client can get immediate validation and ready-made support for "coming out" from a homophile consciousness group. Knowing this, the client has come to a professional adviser for more objective advice. Facing two risky choices—to "come out" and risk rejection from family, friends, and employers, or to continue to feel the emotional weight of concealment as well as isolation from other homosexuals—the client needs to decide which choice he or she can more easily live with. As therapist for such a client, one can easily gain the applause of homophile groups and satisfy one's own liberal instincts by saying, "Sure, come out!" But it is the client who must walk the lonesome road afterward. A better clinical intervention is to explore the client's relationships with the people who are important in his or her life and to assess the likely consequences in each case. If some of these people are likely to accept the client as a homosexual while others (e.g., parents) are not, one might recommend "coming out" selectively (telling some people but not others), at least as a first step. In any case, there can be no assurance that the world will be fair. (Edelwich and Brodsky 1991, 177)

### Substitute Behaviors

For people who persistently engage in harmful behaviors (perhaps because their experience has taught them that the only way to get attention is to get in trouble), the group can help come up with substitute behaviors to call upon when familiar stimuli might touch off the accustomed response. For example, Bruce was reported to the police after a neighbor heard disturbing noises while Bruce was home alone with his child. Bruce is coming to group in preference to going through a legal process that might result in his losing custody of the child. How can he give reasonable assurance that he will stop the behavior that brought him to group? After Bruce has told the group why he *wants* to stop, group members can give him feedback about substitute behaviors they have used, such as the following:

- "When my kid gets under my skin and I feel like murdering the little SOB, what I do is go out and have a cup of coffee with my friend across the street."
- "That happened to me, and I called Parents Anonymous."
- "What I did was call somebody in a group like this."

Then Bruce can plan his own substitute responses and share them with the group: "If I feel the kid is getting to me, I'll call Parents Anonymous, go out and walk around the block, or call someone in this group."

For substance abusers, common substitute behaviors include leaving the stressful or threatening situation immediately, engaging in a diversionary activity such as physical exercise or chewing gum, or calling one's spouse, therapist, fellow group member, or sponsor in AA. To expand upon this repertoire, group counselors should be aware of recent approaches to addiction treatment and self-help (see, for example, Cox 1987; Hester and Miller 1989; Monti et al. 1989; Shiffman and Wills 1985). Rational Recovery, a self-help program based on rational-emotive therapy, substitutes a different way of thinking for the old addictive habits of thought. By thinking differently at the moment of craving a drink, the drinker can substitute a different behavioral response (Trimpey 1989). This is an application of a technique called *cognitive restructuring,* in which a person learns to replace self-defeating thoughts with constructive, self-enhancing thoughts (Sanchez-Craig et al. 1987). Peele et al. (1991), applying the work of various researchers (for example, DiClemente and Prochaska 1985; Ludwig 1985; Neidigh et al. 1988; Prochaska and DiClemente 1985; Shiffman 1985), present numerous substitution strategies (cognitive, behavioral, and situational) in a self-help format. Relapse-prevention techniques (Marlatt and Gordon 1985) also are relevant to breaking the chain of dysfunctional thinking and behavior in high-risk situations.

### Commitment to Act

No step in the process is more important than making the commitment to carry out the plan of action outside the group. We have explained this step as follows in our outline of the problem-solving exercise described previously:

> When you have chosen a course of action, make a commitment to act within a definite period of time. Ask yourself how soon you can expect to be able to put your plan into effect. If you choose "having a talk with my co-worker," you may not be sure that both of you will have the time open to talk Monday morning. Can you do it by Monday at 2 o'clock, then? Perhaps your co-worker will not come in Monday. Then how about Tuesday? If you choose "writing a critical memo to the director the next time my co-worker acts inappropriately," how soon do you expect that to happen? How about two weeks from now? The idea is to set a realistic time limit that allows for no excuses.
>
> A commitment is really only a commitment if it is avowed publicly. That is why this exercise works especially well in groups. For one thing, another person might come up with a solution for someone who is too close to the situation to see it clearly. The major benefit, though, is the support one can enlist from others in holding oneself to one's commitment. The workshop leader might instruct group members to exchange phone numbers and arrange to call each other at specified times to see if they have followed through on their commitments. Of course, one does not have to be in a formal group or workshop situation to do this; one can do it privately with a co-worker. (Edelwich and Brodsky 1980, 228–229)

To make a commitment, the group member takes the following steps with the help of the group:

1. *Set a definite time to implement the plan.* Make it as soon as is realistically possible.

2. *Anticipate and eliminate excuses.* What might stop you from doing it? What might go wrong? How can those obstacles be removed or circumvented? What contingency plans may be needed? What high-risk situations (for example, a drinking party or a stressful interpersonal encounter) might arise, and how will you plan for these? It is necessary to get these considerations out of the way in advance so that the commitment can be definite, not equivocal or contingent: "I will," not "I'll try" or "I will, if. . . ."

3. *Make it public.* Announce in front of the group, "I'm going to do it on Thursday at six o'clock."

4. *Provide for follow-up.* Arrange to report to the group the following week about whether and how the plan was carried out. Or ask other group members to call after the specified hour.

If the group member wavers or equivocates about making the commitment, it is a sign that the value judgment is not firm. Just as at any other stage of the process, the leader then brings the issue back to the group.

*Rehearsal and Role-playing*

Anxiety about an impending interpersonal interaction (work related or social) often gets in the way of deciding on or committing oneself wholeheartedly to a plan of action. When a person appears to be vacillating for this reason, the group can rehearse the situation realistically with the person, with another member playing the role of the feared antagonist. At this time, the leader may review rational-emotive therapy's twelve irrational beliefs (see chapter 6) to identify which irrational belief is the source of the anxiety. Members might role-play asking someone out on a date, seeking parental consent, asking the boss for a raise, or working out a difficult issue with a spouse or coworker. This exercise has value as long as it really is a rehearsal— that is, as long as it is used to strengthen the person's commitment to take action outside the group. Role-playing must be more than a time-filling game in group; it must be a purposeful, effective component of group process.

*Follow-up on Previous Commitments*

When the leader says, "Let us know next time how things worked out," that promise of continuity is not to be forgotten amid the rush of issues presented to the group. On the contrary, the group models organization and demonstrates caring by checking back on commitments made in previous sessions. In the case of Santiago, who brought his communication problem to the group in chapter 5, here is how the leader might follow through on a commitment he has made to confront Santiago if he sees him not participating fully in the group:

> *Leader:* Now, in light of last week's group, Santiago, I'm going to keep my commitment to you—may I?
> *Santiago:* Sure.
> *Leader:* If I want more recognition, if I want more freedom, there's a responsibility that goes with that. And although I think you're participating, I think you're participating passively, and my expectations are a little higher now after last week's group. So I couldn't let this group pass without sharing that with you. I don't want to get back into the old mode of "Well, there's Santiago—if you ask him a question, he'll answer, and no more than that." Do you want to respond to that?

Note that the leader asks permission, affirms his own commitment to Santiago, and confronts him by making an "I" statement. By picking up the thread of continuity, the leader makes clear that the group is not "finished" with Santiago just because "we did his issue last week." Instead of being allowed to fade into the background once again, Santiago is encouraged by the group to continue to realize his stated intentions—in other words, to achieve and demonstrate personal growth.

Even when a group member declines to make a commitment—that is, a value judgment—the group may follow up to see if there has been any further movement on the issue. In a vignette in this chapter, Joanne decided not to commit herself to speaking to her husband about a career change he was considering. Nonetheless, the leader returns to Joanne's issue during the following session:

*Leader:* I'd like to ask you, Joanne, if you'll share with the group what transpired with your husband this past week.

*Joanne:* Well, we did have a talk about it. We generally go for a walk a couple of times a week, and one night after our group meeting, I was still pondering, "Is it worth the risk?" Finally I said, "What the hell, I'll ask him." So we talked about it, and he said he feels very much committed to his plan. I wish he had talked with me about it earlier, but I still feel I can support him in this. It was good. As we walked, we tried to clarify our respective long-range plans and visions for our lives—how they're similar, how they're different. I always try to hit common bonds in such a situation. It went very well. He's comfortable with what he wants to do, and I have no problem with it as long as he's making a real commitment to it.

*Leader:* Can the group help you any more with this today?

*Joanne:* If anybody feels they have anything to offer, I'm open to it.

*Leader:* Other than what I said last week about risks and benefits, it seems to me you're much less anxious now, so there's no need for me to pursue this.

*Joanne:* I was concerned that he might become defensive, but he wasn't. That indicates to me that he feels more comfortable about what he wants to do.

*Sue:* I really appreciate your sharing that with us last week; it was taking a risk. As I thought about it, I realized something I do, which is to make something into more of a problem than it is.

*Joanne:* Thank you. Thank you all.

*Leader:* Any other concerns that people have?

Sometimes group members do less than they say they will; in this case, Joanne did more. Although (perhaps because) the group did not pressure Joanne to decide on a course of action before she was ready to do so, the group's processing of her issue proved to be a catalyst for movement in her life. With additional time to reflect, Joanne found herself ready to do what she had not been quite willing to promise. As an added benefit, Joanne transmitted strength to Sue as Sue transmitted strength to her—which is the beauty and the power of sharing in group.

When Santiago speaks up more because the leader prods him or Joanne experiences a silent ripening of readiness in which her issue seemingly resolves itself, the potency of group process is demonstrated. Especially for people who have spent their lives doing only what they can get away with, increased expectations elicit increased performance. The member who commits to a course of action may not be making a commitment to the *plan* so much as to the *group*. Even if one is not really sold on the benefits to be derived from taking an English-language course or applying for a driver's license, one follows through on these plans because one sees the group as useful and supportive. The group atmosphere rewards one for taking constructive action before one has a chance to experience the rewards directly in life. A group that holds this kind of positive sway over members can be a powerful motivating force.

## Weekly Review of Learning

Another form of consolidation occurs at the end of every group session, when each person in the group reviews what he or she has learned during that session. As the session nears its end, the leader moves toward resolution of the issue under consideration so as to leave sufficient time for the weekly review. In the absence of such consolidation and ownership of experiences in group, the group sessions would simply mirror the unstable, disorganized patterns of members' lives. Members would be present, but to little purpose and with no clear outcome.

To start the review, the leader asks every group member, "What went on for you today? Make an 'I' statement." The leader models such statements—for instance, "This went on for me today. Joe, I learned that I have something in common with you that I didn't realize before. Sara, I have some of the same fears about growing old alone that you have."

Since this review is just a quick snapshot of each member's experience in the session, it does not involve confrontation or feedback. Indeed, as noted in chapter 7, the leader must be alert to block second-guessing or Monday-morning quarterbacking, as well as the raising of new issues (doorknob disclosures). Each person simply makes a statement, although others may relate to that statement when making their own, as in this example:

*Member:* I learned how easy it is to get caught up in flight and not even realize what's going on, and how we all really need to stay on our toes and keep alert, because these little diversions and offshoots of the issue can lead us farther and farther away from what we're working on.

*Leader:* And when I do that, I'm losing control of the group, and I'm getting frustrated. I find myself looking at my watch when there's nothing going on except moaning and complaining. That's what went on for me at that point today. It was a relearning experience for me, about how important it is to maintain group process and how remiss I am when I let things get out of hand.

These statements are about group process. More typically, members review what they have learned about themselves and about the issues raised in group.

If someone says, "I didn't learn very much at all," that is to be respected. One could not, however, plausibly make this statement after every session. Even members who have been silent are obligated to say what they have learned that day. They might model their responses after the experiences others have related.

Is such vicarious learning a valid model for a person to follow over the entire course of a group? Given that the group cannot give equal time to each member's issues and that not all members are equally disposed to air their issues, can a person learn by "osmosis"? We do not rule out the possibility that one can learn vicariously by hearing others process their issues, provided that one has the opportunity—and takes the responsibility—to identify, consolidate, and implement what one has learned. In other words, the learning process must be more active than the image conveyed by the word *osmosis,* especially at the time of termination.

## Resolution versus Closure

At the end of a session, some issues may be in the process of resolution or the resolution attained may feel incomplete to the person who has raised the issue. Unlike psychodynamic therapy groups, group counseling does not seek complete closure on issues. Indeed, it should be stated explicitly in group that complete closure is not to be expected. Group process is designed to extract the passion from issues, but it is possible to do so only in varying degrees for different individuals and different issues. Therefore, as explained in chapter 7, the group aims for a reasonable resolution and then moves on. The group's provisional, pragmatic goal is to make it possible for a member to say:

> "What happened to me was unjust, and I do have strong feelings about it. While this may still be an issue for me, I've resolved that I have enough resources now not to let it affect my life. Given a magic wand, I would rectify matters, but it's not in my best interest to pursue it, so I'll put it in a compartment of my brain called 'unfinished business' or 'unpleasant memories.' "

More complete closure (when it can be achieved at all) awaits implementation of problem solving and decision making outside the group. It also awaits the passage of time, as when neglectful or rejecting parents come to be seen as too elderly and powerless to be the objects of active resentment.

# 9
# Coleadership and Supervision

For the most part, we have referred to the group leader in the singular. It is preferable, however, for a group to be led by two trained counselors (if staffing levels permit). This chapter presents the benefits and pitfalls of coleadership, some considerations in matching counselors for coleadership, and guidelines for how coleaders can work together. We also outline some methods of supervision of group leaders.

## The Benefits of Coleadership

Coleadership is recommended for several reasons. It enhances the objectivity and integrity of group process; it places a check on transference and countertransference; it increases efficiency and productivity through a division of labor between substance and process; and it offers a model of constructive resolution of differences.

### Objectivity and Integrity

When members see group process as represented by one leader, the process may be obscured by the leader's charismatic persona. Coleadership introduces another dimension of objectivity and professionalism, thus further emphasizing process over personality. The leaders continually check out the process with each other and ask the group to do so as well. Thus, each leader represents the process to the other and, by extension, to the group. Group members, in turn, experience the process as filtered through two different viewpoints, in addition to their own, and through two different personal images or role models. With these additional checks and balances, the group can better serve the needs of members.

For example, a member may confront the leader appropriately, but a person who combines a strong personality with a group leader's authority can easily overpower the member and intimidate the group—if there is no one of equal authority to confront the leader. Likewise, if someone leaves the group and the leader is accused of driving the person away, it is very helpful to have a coleader available to process that issue. On the one hand, the leader may indeed have driven away the member, who may have been a threat or a nuisance to the leader. On the other hand, the member may have been disrupting the group. In this way, each leader checks out and shares the other's responsibility for maintaining group climate.

### Transference and Countertransference

One way in which coleadership strengthens the integrity of group process is sufficiently important to be highlighted on its own. Group dynamics may be affected by personal chemistry, overt or covert seduction, and interpersonal attachments that go beyond the scope of counseling. We have discussed these dynamics briefly in chapter 7 and extensively elsewhere (Edelwich and Brodsky 1991). Whether they originate with the group member or the group leader, coleadership can serve as a valuable restraint.

Transference on the part of group members is to be expected. Some members may favor one leader over the other, just as they may favor one parent over the other. They may sit next to one leader and play up to him or her, acting as "the good sibling," to create an alignment against other members and/or the other leader. It is essential that such dynamics be addressed by someone in the group, and the other leader may be in the best position to do this. This is not to say that the leaders are to play good guy/bad guy in group; quite the contrary. But when the leaders see members playing good guy/bad guy with them, it should be made a group issue. In this way, coleadership helps bring out patterns of favoritism in people's lives.

Coleadership also provides a check against countertransference on the part of a group leader. As a rule, proper training and the cultivation of a professional attitude should minimize the possibility of a leader's finding an issue too sensitive to deal with comfortably. (Such reactions should be processed in group, with the coleader between groups, or with a supervisor, peers, or a professional consultant.) In cases where a leader's effectiveness is temporarily impaired in this manner, coleadership provides an alternate path to resolution of the issue before the group.

As noted in chapter 3, a group leader is responsible for his or her conduct in group and may be confronted just as a group member is confronted. If a member observes that the leader may be favoring a particular member, it is important that the member call it to the group's attention. The norm that the leader can be confronted has more potency when it is modeled than when it is merely stated. Typically, a coleader can model constructive confrontation most effectively, as in the following example:

*Chuck:* Al [Leader 1], I think you're being soft on Melinda.

*Leader 1:* What about that, group? Does anybody else see the same thing?

*Tony:* Chuck, I think you only said that because you have eyes for Melinda yourself.

*Barbara:* No, you're crazy. *You're* the one who . . .

*Leader 1:* Whoa! What's going on here?

*Leader 2:* Group, I have a certain reaction I'd like to share. Al, as my cofacilitator, do you mind if I share this?

*Leader 1:* Not at all. Go ahead.

*Leader 2:* This is what I see happening. When Melinda was being confronted, I noticed twice you came to her defense. I also noticed before group that you were smiling at her; there seemed to be some little byplay going on. When *I* do that, it means I'm developing a special relationship with a group member.

*Leader 1:* I guess you're right. I didn't realize that.

*Leader 2:* Oh, one more thing. If anyone sees me playing favorites, please call me on it, because if I do it in here, I do it outside of here, too, and that's not how I want to conduct myself as a professional.


This confrontation by Leader 2 meets the criteria for appropriateness listed in chapters 6 and 8: it is solicited rather than imposed, descriptive rather than evaluative, properly timed, and so forth. Instead of pointing an accusing finger, Leader 2 confronts Leader 1 with an "I" statement, which makes the confrontation easier for Leader 1 to hear.


### Division of Labor: Substance versus Process

A group leader working alone must monitor both the content and the form of group interaction—not only what is happening but how it is happening—and keep it all in place as it unfolds. With coleadership, there can be a division of responsibilities. When one leader gets caught up in a rapid-fire exchange, the other can make a process statement. Such mutual support and coordination between the leaders need not be limited to spontaneous rescue operations. On the contrary, it is desirable for the leaders to work out a division of responsibilities before each session (perhaps alternating roles from one session to the next). One leader might say:

> "Today I'm going to take care of content. I'll identify issues; I'll confront. As for you, if things become disorganized, with people competing, if no one else does it, you check it out with a process statement such as 'What's going on?' Don't forget to monitor what

I'm doing, too. If you see something you have a question about, you might say, 'Al, you're pressing your point. What's going on?' "

That kind of teamwork gives the leaders, and the group, a major advantage. It is like having a linebacker watching what comes over the line while a defensive back looks out for the long pass. Together, the leaders can monitor more efficiently and cover more ground than one leader can alone.

### Resolution of Differences

If members leave their differences unresolved in group, they probably do so out of group as well. Coleadership allows for modeling of a constructive resolution of differences. The leaders can best serve members' needs not by presenting a united front, but by preserving their separate identities and letting the group see them work out their differences. In the course of the group, the leaders may disagree, learn what compromises work for them, and come to trust each other. They also may make process statements afterward about what went on for them. After soliciting feedback from the group, one of the leaders may explain, "What I was trying to do was to help model a resolution of an issue. This wasn't contrived. There actually were differences between us." This modeling can be highly beneficial to the group members.

## The Pitfalls of Coleadership

A number of problems may occur when two counselors lead a group together. Coleaders with different professional backgrounds may have a misunderstanding about their relative status and the roles they are to play in group; they may present themselves to the group as a monolith or even form an unholy alliance to manipulate group members; or a member may get caught in a cross-fire between them. These potential pitfalls are far outweighed by the benefits of coleadership, but group leaders and supervisors should be alert to them.

### Status and Role Conflicts

When two leaders with different kinds of training work together for the first time, there may be a clash of expectations. In one such case, a social worker with years of experience in leading groups co-led a group with a young, well-intentioned psychiatrist who knew little about group work. As the group got under way, it was clear that the two had different conceptions of their respective roles. Afterward, the psychiatrist told the social worker, "I thought you were there to support me." He seemed hurt when the social worker told him matter-of-factly that *he* viewed coleadership (as it is presented in this chapter) as an equal partnership.

As in this instance, the conflict is typically one of experience versus credentials. Although a particular psychiatrist may not have the understanding of group dynamics that a particular counselor has, he or she may be accustomed to being deferred to as "the doctor." To avoid such misunderstandings, it is important to define the ground rules for the partnership in advance.

## Appearing as a Monolith

It is an error for the coleaders to attempt to speak with one voice to the group. They can accomplish more by retaining their individuality and participating in an open process with each other as well as with group members.

## Forming an Unholy Alliance

The united front becomes destructive when it takes the form of an unholy alliance. Here, instead of simply covering up their differences, the leaders actively conspire to manipulate members, saying, "Okay, now let's have a psychodrama"; "Iris hasn't been participating; let's see what we can do with her"; or "Let's get so-and-so." These are extreme examples, but they do happen, especially with relatively untrained leaders fresh from their own recovery programs. The more checks and balances there are, and the more vigilant the supervision is, the better.

## Cross-firing

In a less sinister way, coleaders who are not adequately prepared regarding their roles may inadvertently ambush a member into a humiliating put-down. This pattern, known as cross-firing, is illustrated by the following exchange:

*Leader 1:* Nate, I see you shaking your head. How are you feeling about what happened with Arthur?

*Nate:* He's obviously acting out. He had a problem; he shouldn't have been in the group in the first place. I really don't know why you let him stay as long as he did. It was inappropriate for him to be here, and I'm glad he's gone.

*Leader 2:* You know, Nate, that's all we hear from you. No matter whom we talk about, you're always giving answers. I'm sure everyone else here has feelings, too, and they'd like to share them with us. Why don't we give them a chance?

This is a textbook case of untrained leadership. One leader asks a member a question, and when the member answers it, the other leader cuts him down. Nate's answer is, of course, inappropriate; he is diagnosing the absent member (described in chapter 7 as playing therapist). That behavior calls for a process statement, not a scolding.

## Matching Counselors for Coleadership

Any two experienced group leaders can colead a group according to the model presented here. Nonetheless, clinical benefits can be optimized (where possible) by deliberate pairings. Heterogeneity in the coleaders' backgrounds is desirable, with as much diversity as possible along several dimensions, including age, gender, experience, and professional discipline. The least desirable combination is two middle-aged male paraprofessionals who are recovering addict/alcoholics steeped in twelve-step jargon. The most desirable combination might be the following: a female psychologist in her forties with extensive and varied clinical experience and a male social worker in his late twenties on his first or second job. Ideally, one would be single, the other married.

Diversity allows for both a breadth of perspective on issues that come up in group and a variety of role models for members. A trained group leader of any age, gender, or professional background can model responsibility and effectiveness in problem solving and decision making. However, a leader with whom a particular member can identify personally may be able to model those traits in a more compelling way.

At the same time, group members can benefit from seeing the same qualities modeled by people with whom they do not identify personally. Coleadership can, for example, bring this added dimension of modeling to groups for women who have been victims of violence. A female counselor can be a focus of personal identification, while a male counselor can present a positive male image so that group members do not form an enduring image of all men as assaultive.

This example reflects a conception of professional group counseling as entirely different from mutual self-help groups brought together by shared experience. Included in this conception of professionalism is the group counselor's responsibility to accept the challenge of working with any suitable candidates (on clinical criteria) for the group in question, regardless of age, race, gender, or past behavior. Client-clinician matching may be used strategically to benefit group members, but not as an exclusionary factor based on either the leader's or member's personal preferences (see Edelwich and Brodsky 1991).

## Procedural Guidelines

Group leaders who work as a team need to keep a few process issues in mind so that they can work together smoothly and effectively.

## Preparation and Review

It is important for coleaders to schedule at least ten to fifteen minutes before each session to prepare for group and the same amount of time after each session to debrief and complete their records. Both meetings should be held in an area where group members' records are available for review. Before each session the leaders assess group members' progress, note any unfinished issues from the previous session, address observed patterns of transference and countertransference, and check out their communications with each other. They also divide responsibilities: Who will follow content? Who will track the process? After the session, they process what occurred and note any issues to be picked up next time. This session-to-session continuity does not come about in an ad hoc, impromptu, or spontaneous manner. Rather, the pregroup and postgroup monitoring is to be planned and carried out systematically, in keeping with an overall professionalism. The greater the care taken with these details, the better the services to group members will be.

## Group Notes

The responsibility for charting the group notes is best shared by the coleaders, with one of them writing the notes after one session and the other doing so after the next. Checking out each other's notes is another safeguard by which leaders make sure they are processing issues with a shared understanding. In addition to written notes, the leaders can review each other's work by audiotape or videotape, discussed in the next section as methods of supervisory observation.

## Questions of Content

In groups dealing with domestic violence or substance abuse and other addictive behaviors (such as compulsive eating or gambling), every group leader and every group member carries mental images of what constitutes recovering behavior, as opposed to continued rationalization and justification. For example, one might regard a person's keeping secrets, becoming overly defensive, or not making a clear value judgment or commitment to a plan as behavior incompatible with recovery. These sometimes conflicting mental images are confronted in group, and the disparities between them are resolved or at least aired. It is important that the coleaders also check out their criteria for recovery (or progress) with each other before they come to group. In that way, even if differences remain, the leaders can address them consciously in group instead of being taken by surprise and can then process group members' issues purposefully and coherently.

*Use of Supervision*

Coleadership by no means obviates the need for regularly scheduled supervision. Indeed, group leaders who work together as a team may have an even greater need to use supervision to avoid the temptation to depend exclusively on each other. Although coleadership adds to the checks and balances that maintain and improve performance standards, all other checks and balances must be kept in place as well. For the group leader, whether working alone or in tandem, the resources of supervision, peer support, and professional consultation are available (as they are for all clinicians) for dealing with any work-related problem (see Edelwich and Brodsky 1991). It is a mark of professionalism to upgrade one's work continually by using all available resources.

## Methods of Supervisory Observation

Counseling groups can be observed for purposes of supervision (as well as for review and discussion by coleaders) in any of four ways, each of which has its own advantages and disadvantages:

1. *Blind Supervision.* Here the supervisor simply asks the leader what happened in group and how it went; the leader also may provide written group notes. Perhaps three-quarters of all supervisory sessions for group leaders are conducted in this manner because it is the least complicated and most convenient method. It is not very satisfactory, however, since the supervisor has no firsthand exposure to what goes on in group and therefore is entirely dependent on the group leader's perspective.

2. *One-Way Mirror.* This method allows for direct visual monitoring and note taking by the supervisor while the group is in progress. Using a one-way mirror, the supervisor can observe not only explicit verbal communication that the group leader might not report but also body language and other nonverbal communication that is lost to blind supervision or audiotape. This method is, however, inconvenient and time-consuming for the supervisor and creates no permanent record.

3. *Audiotape.* The advantages and disadvantages of audiotape are the opposite of those of the one-way mirror. Audiotape cannot pick up nonverbal communication, but it does produce a complete verbal record. Compared to videotape, audiotape is relatively inexpensive and easy to set up. Therefore, it is a good medium for routine use.

4. *Videotape.* Videotape is the ideal medium for supervisory observation. It captures all aspects of group interaction in a permanent record. Using vid-

eotape, the supervisor and group leader can go over an entire group interaction frame by frame. It is not, however, cost-effective for the supervisor to review every one-hour or two-hour group session in its entirety on videotape. Instead, the supervisor might conduct a complete review of one session with each group leader. Once the supervisor is satisfied with the leader's general mastery of group process, further supervision may be done more selectively. That is, the supervisor might ask group leaders to bring some segments of a taped session with which they are pleased and some about which they have questions. This approach, like blind supervision, presupposes that the supervisor accepts the group leader's good faith and judgment about what needs to be reviewed. If the supervisor suspects concealment, negligence, incompetence, or misconduct, a more complete review is, of course, called for.

## Issues in Supervision

The supervision of group counselors involves the techniques and procedures common to all clinical supervision. The content of supervision is, of course, the mastery of group process as presented throughout this book. Both group leaders and supervisors should, however, keep in mind the following issues that may arise in the supervision of counseling groups.

### Client Permission

Although the methods of observation described previously are carried out as a matter of course in counseling agencies, they do require the permission of group members. Whether this permission is granted depends, as a rule, on how the group leader makes the request. If the leader says, "They're making me do this, but you don't have to do it if you don't want to," permission may well be denied. The leader stands a much better chance of success by presenting the request in this way: "Hey, I really need this for me. This is just for me and my supervisor to look at, and I really need your help with this." Group members tend to respond positively to such an appeal.

### Misuse of the Trainer or Supervisor

Trainers and supervisors in group counseling need to be alert to some common pitfalls of their role. One is that of being drawn into a didactic role instead of demonstrating group techniques. Group leaders in training are as likely to go into flight as any other group members. Rather than make the effort to participate, they may ask questions such as "what do you do when a member . . . ?" If the training group is intended to model group process, the trainer does well to resist the invitation to lecture. By maintaining the integrity of the process, the trainer gives trainees a model of integrity to carry into their own work with groups.

When group leaders are having difficulties with their groups, they may ask a supervisor to come in and run a group with their clients. Such requests are unrealistic and ill-advised because a group is no longer the same with an unfamiliar leader. The supervisor, however skilled, does not have the benefit of the trust that develops between leader and members over time. Therefore, group members may be overly resistant to the supervisor. (Indeed, the regular group leaders may be setting the supervisor up for this outcome so as to excuse their own shortcomings.) Alternatively, if the group members prefer the supervisor, the group leaders may find themselves upstaged and will have even more difficulty upon their return.

# 10
# Termination and Postgroup Follow-up

Because process-oriented group counseling does not operate on a psychodynamic model, preparations for termination are not as complex or elaborate as in group psychotherapy. As with all previous stages of group process, the emphasis here remains pragmatic and action oriented. Nonetheless, as the group goes on, attention must be given to emotional as well as practical issues surrounding termination. These issues take on increasing prominence during the last few sessions, as group members plan for follow-up activities individually, with one another, and (as appropriate) through postgroup contacts with the leader. Although the group experience has a definite end, suitable follow-up can renew and extend its strengthening influence.

## Reviewing, Focusing, and Closing the Group Experience

Just as there is a consolidation of learning with each particular issue and with each week's experience, so it is with the group experience as a whole. If the group is to model organization, purpose, and direction, members need an opportunity to consolidate and integrate their experience in group. The final consolidation has a number of facets, some familiar and others new.

### Clarifying That the Group is Ending

Group cohesiveness in a closed-ended group is beneficial in the short run; it supports those who are leading the group and helps produce results. It would be counterproductive, however, to allow an atmosphere of elitism, insularity, or dependency to build up around the group. People need to be able to leave when it is time for the group to end.

In a closed-ended group, clarity about the end point helps members make the transition out of the group. If members wish to form social relationships with one another that survive termination, that is their own business. The group itself, however, cannot be reconvened. The group is not to be a crutch, an addiction, or a substitute for something else. When the scheduled sessions end, the group is over.

## Dealing with Separation Anxiety

Separation anxiety should not be assumed in all members. Indeed, in involuntary groups, members who did not want to be there in the first place may be just as happy to leave. As often as not, such coerced members react to termination with varying degrees of invalidation, from polite compliance ("It's over; thank you") to undisguised relief and distancing ("In a week, I'm out of here!") to bellicose rejection ("What good does this do anyway? All we've been doing is shooting the bull. I don't feel any different; I don't see anybody changing"). Voluntary members, however, may well have derived enough support, nurturance, and insight from the group to carry them through to termination. Still, to the extent that their experience has been a positive one, they may feel its imminent ending as a loss.

Another factor affecting the intensity of feelings of separation is whether the group is open-ended or closed-ended. An open-ended group does not end for everyone at the same time. Members may leave when the sessions they have contracted for have elapsed, when they leave the facility, or when the group experience reaches a natural end point for them and they are ready to move on. Although a person leaving an open-ended group may feel an added sense of loss and deprivation relative to those who will still be there, termination may be made easier when familiar members are replaced by new ones. Moreover, the lack of a termination date for the entire group prevents separation anxiety from dominating the group atmosphere and thereby being magnified for the individual.

In a closed-ended group, where such contagion may occur, the severity of the anxiety depends in part on the cohesiveness of the group. In the absence of climate setting and consolidation, a group may lurch through to termination with no positive movement—nothing except a hardening of alliances of convenience and self-protection to allow members to get through the experience. When an inexperienced leader has allowed this to happen, it is not surprising to find the leader anticipating termination with this sort of dirge:

> "A lot's happening now. I know this hasn't been easy for any of us, and now we're nearing the end of the group. I'm sensing a lot of emotions in the air that aren't being expressed. I know that at moments like this there are a lot of emotions going on, and it's better when we can express them. I'd like to hear a little more about what you're feeling."

Emotions are not being expressed because the leader, for one, is not expressing them. Following a pattern undoubtedly set early in group, he does not own his feelings but throws the responsibility over to the group. "I" don't have feelings; "we" or "you" do. In a group thus led, there is no hope of having members own and process their feelings of loss. In any case, members are not likely to feel much of a loss—just a blankness and numbness as the group comes to a merciful end. When the group climate is one of ownership, accountability, and resolution, however, positive feelings can be expected to develop among group members, and the group experience may well be one that they will miss. By the same token, that experience will have conveyed strengths that can be mobilized for dealing with termination.

Mourning a loss and dealing openly with feelings of grief can be a valuable learning experience, but only if the feelings are there to begin with. Grieving should not be imposed on people, as the leader in the previous quote was doing. Instead, separation anxiety might best be approached in the spirit of "We don't want to give you any problems you don't already have." If someone does find it difficult to leave the group or to see the group end, it is important to let the person know that this loss is just a reflection and extension of other losses that occur in life. Group members have left school, with its friendships and camaraderie. They may have left a family, a neighborhood, a close-knit military unit, a valued work environment. Leaving the group is no different. Some anxiety and conflict are a normal part of the learning experience as the person realizes that it is necessary to let go and move on.

The leader conveys these points not by lecturing or pontificating, but by making "I" statements and encouraging others to do the same. In termination, just as before, the leader models open, truthful self-disclosure. The leader, too, has experienced pain, joy, and conflict in group, and his or her life has been touched by the group's sharing. The leader, too, may have feelings of separation and loss and may anticipate missing the group. If the leader bypasses these feelings, so will the group. If the leader owns these feelings, group members are more likely to own them, too. Like the rest of the group, the leader also knows what it is like to separate from parents, school friends, lovers, and so forth. By making "I" statements about the pain of those separations and how he or she has coped in such stressful moments, the leader once again serves as a model for taking effective control of one's life. As group members follow with their own "I" statements, separation anxiety (like any other issue that comes up in group) is resolved through group process.

### Blocking Doorknob Disclosures

Just as at the end of a session (as described in chapter 7), members may bring up new issues that cannot be resolved in the time left in group. As before, this may be a manipulative, disruptive gesture, or it may be a response to the stress of termination. The group experience may have been so need satisfying that the person is reluctant to let go. The leader blocks this behavior by making clear that not all issues in a person's life can be resolved in group. If the person wishes, there may be ways to work on the issue in postgroup follow-up (as outlined later in this chapter).

### Putting Unfinished Business in Perspective

Group members may feel that they have unresolved issues with the group leader, with one another, or in their own lives. Even the most well-adjusted person has such unfinished business. The question is how much it intrudes on one's life. Being in group may arouse unrealistic expectations of across-the-board resolution, and the disappointment of these expectations as termination approaches may produce anxiety. Nonetheless, as long as group members are moving to take effective control of their lives and have their needs met, dealing with unfinished business (in a psychotherapeutic sense) is a luxury.

Termination is a time to review the theme of resolution versus closure, which was explored in chapters 7 and 8. This form of consolidation of learning, while it has been occurring all along, must be confirmed and reemphasized at the end, when disappointed expectations of closure are bound to arise. As the group nears its conclusion, one may feel that one has not quite resolved an issue when in fact one has resolved it. It is just that one's mental image of resolution is actually one of closure, of tying things up with a ribbon. With some issues, there may never be full closure, only the kind of resolution described earlier: "Okay, the world isn't going to change, but I think enough of myself and my life to go on and not dwell on this misfortune/outrage." Greater healing may come with time and further movement in one's life. The more one fulfills one's needs in other areas, the less energy one should have to put into unfinished business. It is essential that the leader continue to make relevant personal disclosures by giving examples of resolution and closure from his or her own life.

The desire for more complete closure can be a positive force to the extent that it motivates implementation of plans after termination of the group. Areas on which a person wants to work further may be addressed by contracting with the group to do assignments, arranging with other members for mutual support, or going into individual counseling or therapy.

### Sharing Group Journals

Members who have kept a journal may, if they wish, read from it at termination as feedback for the group. For example, an entry might read: "When you first came in, Jim, I felt threatened by you because you're verbal, articulate, and relate well to others. I wrote down how I thought you were dominating, but now I've learned how I can deal with you on equal terms, and so I don't resent you anymore." This sharing, like keeping a journal in the first place, is voluntary. Group members may wish to continue keeping a journal after the group ends as part of, and support for, a plan of action.

### Reinforcing Consolidation of Learning

It is important for members (especially those who heretofore have been relatively inactive) to review and consolidate what they have learned in group. Members speak about what they have learned and how they have learned it, both inside and outside of group. Turning points and crises may be shared, along with moments of joy, sadness, or frustration in group. One might talk in concrete, specific terms about what one did to implement a plan of action, what the outcome was, how one reacted to the changed situation, and how one benefited or did not benefit from taking a risk (one can benefit even if the outcome is negative). After conveying one's changing perception of oneself, one may solicit feedback from the group, which at this late stage must be clear, precise, and focused on practical steps one might take to facilitate positive change. There is not enough time to process feedback that might leave a member feeling awkward or incomplete.

The leader, meanwhile, is looking for a reaffirmation and strengthening of the member's value judgment. If there is resistance to the process at this stage, it means that the member has not made a solid value judgment. Calmly assessing the situation, the leader brings the issue back to group: "So-and-so hasn't made a value judgment. I accept that. There may be a time when he or she will." The leader's mental road map then points back to identifying, clarifying, and consolidating. Once again, the question before the group is "What does the person really want?" Thus, termination provides another measuring point for the member's commitment. Right up to the end, the leader models the group's reaction—that is, the group's understanding of what is and is not a value judgment.

Like the weekly review of learning, termination also gives the leader an opportunity to own and consolidate his or her experience in group. For example, an inexperienced leader whose mastery of group process is still tenuous might have reason to say, "I haven't always owned my feelings here. I've talked a lot about 'we' and 'us' instead of 'I' and 'me.' So I can learn from this, too."

## Applying Learning to Life Outside the Group

By the time termination approaches, the group is thoroughly oriented toward the future, focusing on concrete, detailed planning for behavioral change. Having consolidated what they have learned, members must prepare to implement it outside the group. Here the tone of termination is decidedly upbeat. In line with reality therapy, the group transmits strength while being truthful and without being condescending. The leader is saying, in effect, "If you take what you've learned in group and use it on the outside, I have confidence that your needs are going to be met and that you can be a more fulfilled and actualizing person."

### Developing, Reaffirming, or Fine-tuning the Plan of Action

As members prepare to take what they have learned "on the road," each can draw on the others' support in a final rehearsal of their plans for behavioral change. This is done not with abstractions and generalities, but with nuts and bolts. As explained in chapter 8, "The plan is a practical blueprint, broken down into small, concrete, incremental steps and backed by commitments to specific actions on the part of the member as well as commitments of support on the part of others in the group. The plan is programmed for accountability and designed for success." The leader, while not dictating the details, facilitates the process.

The blueprint consists of what one is committed to doing outside the group, when one is going to do it, who is going to help, what resources one will use, and why it will be to one's benefit to do it. The action planned must be immediate and unequivocal. Good intentions such as the following are not enough: "The next time someone asks me to do something I don't want to do and don't have to do, I'll politely decline to do it." Without a commitment to immediate and definite action, good intentions tend to fall through the cracks and disappear. Therefore, the leader asks instead, "With whom in your life *now* can you be a little more assertive? When will you have your first opportunity to do it?" Similarly, there is no place for the word *try*. Trying anticipates failure. If someone says, "I'll *try* to do such and such," the action proposed is to be broken down to an initial step to which one can commit oneself. What *can* one do unequivocally?

Special attention should be paid in termination to those hitherto silent members who have been learning by "osmosis" rather than by processing their issues out loud. Although group members can learn a great deal just by listening to other members process issues, those who have approached the group in this manner are to be encouraged to work hard in termination to consolidate learning and plan a course of action.

### Exercises

The problem-solving exercise outlined in chapter 8 can be reintroduced now as members develop and refine their plans of action and look forward to implementing them. Similarly, rehearsal and role-playing exercises can be used (as described in chapter 8) to address members' fears concerning anticipated encounters and confrontations. In termination, these exercises can be made available to members who did not do them earlier but who are now emboldened to do so. Not all members develop at the same pace, and it takes some members the duration of the group to learn to take possession of these tools. The aspiration (not always realized) is for everyone to do so by the end of the group.

### Processing Unrealistic Expectations

The cautionary theme of "expectations versus limitations" from the pregroup interview (chapter 2) is taken up again in termination. Now, however, it encompasses not only the group experience, but also what one does to implement it after it is over. Being in group will not transform one's life magically, even if one takes steps to apply what one has learned to one's life outside the group. In the cauldron of life's stresses, even conscientious, enthusiastic group members may not always carry out their plans in an optimally effective manner. In any case, the expectation that change will be swift and permanent can lead to disappointment and discouragement. Typically, change is slow and subtle, and visible results may be slow in coming. Therefore, as members prepare to leave the group, the leader sets a tone of hope and encouragement tempered with realism.

If the leader has modeled this perspective all along, there is no need now for heavy-handed reminders (which, on any issue, would be out of place at the end of a process-oriented group). If the leader finds it advisable to reemphasize these themes, it can be done with "I" statements, such as "This is what happens to me when I become so needy, when I want a transfer or a promotion so badly, that I create expectations for myself that are unrealistic." The statement is followed by an example from the leader's own life. Thus, group process is maintained to the end.

### Written Contracts

A written contract can have both symbolic and practical value in reinforcing a person's commitment to carry out a plan. It is like a souvenir that one takes home from a ball game, except that it is a record not of an event already concluded, but of intentions for the immediate future. As with the group journal, the contract is not a mandatory assignment; the motivation must be from within. No one will be around to enforce the contract, although voluntary, supportive follow-up contacts with other group members may be included in the plan.

The contract, developed by the member with feedback from the group (including the leader), should reflect the realism, specificity, and concreteness of the plan of action: What are you going to do? When are you going to do it? Whose help do you need? What might prevent you from doing it? With whom will you follow up? Again, it is a blueprint, only now it is committed to paper.

### Arranging for Supportive Postgroup Contacts among Members

Members are free to have social contacts with one another after termination, except when they are residents in agencies that restrict such contact. If members have used the group properly, they must be presumed able to make personal choices that, in any case, it is their prerogative to make. If they have not used the group properly, what they do afterward is beside the point. The group leader has no part in these voluntary arrangements, except to suggest ways in which members can support one another in living up to their plans and contracts.

### Confidentiality

A reaffirmation of the group norm regarding confidentiality is advisable to make clear that this is one norm that survives termination. Again, however, preachy reminders are inappropriate. Instead, the leader might make a low-key "I" statement, such as the following: "I've found that sometimes when time passes since I've been in a group and heard the norms stated, I might get a little careless and spill some gossip, and I have to remind myself not to do that because I don't want to be gossiped about, and that's not how I want to meet my commitments to other group members."

### Recommendations or Referrals to Outside Resources

For people who have persistent problems of adaptation and difficulty in getting their needs met, the group can be a valuable conduit to community resources, providing access to professional treatment services (medical or psychological), social-welfare agencies, self-help support groups, and educational opportunities. While the group is going on, however (assuming that the person is capable of participating in group), group process takes precedence over facilitating such outside contacts. Although a person's needs may be apparent at the outset, recommendations or referrals should be deferred at least until consolidation of learning occurs and perhaps until termination. To make recommendations before then would be a form of advice giving, which is to be avoided. It becomes appropriate either when the person has used group process to decide on a course of action or when the group is winding down and soon will no longer be available. Even then, the outside contact should be solicited. The leader might say, "I have a recommendation for you. Would you like to hear it?"

A recommendation is more informal and less specific and it carries less weight or authority than a referral. It is simple and matter-of-fact: "I would recommend that you go to Alcoholics Anonymous"; "I would recommend that you see a physician about your heart problem"; "I would recommend that you call the board of education and start your high-school equivalency tests." A referral is more formal, specific, and directive. The leader may put more emphasis on it at the outset by saying, "What you need is outside the scope of this group." The leader continues: "I'm referring you to a financial adviser, Wanda Winegrad, to consolidate your debts"; "In view of some of the things that have gone on in group, I would like to refer you to Melissa Birchfield for sex therapy for you and your boyfriend"; "I'm referring you to the love addicts' group, and this is the name of the sponsor you can call." Mentioning a specific name, which might not be done with a recommendation, adds force and urgency to the referral. The leader might also ask if the member wants to make a contract to follow through on the referral.

Whether a recommendation or a referral is made depends in part on the degree of perceived need and in part on whether the member has made a value judgment. Usually, if a value judgment has not been made, no more than a recommendation is warranted. If a value judgment has been made, the leader has more leeway to make an outright referral. A referral makes sense when the member has said, in effect, "I really do want to learn to read and write"; "Maybe I do need medication for my blood pressure"; "Hey, I really do need a little more than this. This group was a springboard for me to go on and take control of my life. I think now maybe I do look at the world differently. I do think a sex addicts' group would be good for me."

Having made the recommendation or referral, the leader respects the member's right to decide whether or not to pursue it. The leader's involvement and investment at this point should coincide with that of the person whose interests are at stake. If the member is lukewarm, the leader might just say, "If you want to know anything more about it, please give me a ring."

Are referrals ever to be enforced by sanctions? The question applies only to involuntary groups, and then only in specialized contexts. If a person has met the expectations and agreements of the group—that is, has come on time, has participated appropriately, and has not disrupted the group—then the fact that the person does not do exactly what the leader advises does not justify coercion. The group itself is not a police agency. More than anything, the group experience is intended to be a positive one. What basis does the leader have for using coercion? Whose needs are being met by attempting to direct a member's actions? If a member doesn't feel a need for a particular resource at present ("I don't need financial counseling right now," or "It's not worth it for me to go to the literacy program"), the leader can simply go back to the "what if" clause that is used when a member declines to make a value judgment in favor of change: "What if it then becomes a problem for you?"

A group member may, however, have problems too severe to be overlooked. For example, if a person comes into group appearing placid and impassive, it is then revealed that the person experiences outbursts of anger that he or she finds uncontrollable in the absence of intervention, and there is good evidence of severe discomfort with self and others, then a further referral should be strongly urged. If the leader believes there is a substantial threat of violence (such as arson), it is his or her responsibility to say, "I think you need a little more than this group right now." It is a question of judgment. Even here, though, the group leader does not have any direct coercive authority. If the leader makes an assessment at termination that the person might be dangerous to self or others, that should be indicated in the group notes. The leader is responsible for reporting this assessment to the employing agency, which in turn reports it to the referring agency. This breach of confidentiality is covered by the consent form signed by the member at the beginning of the group (chapter 2).

In the case of members mandated to group counseling by the courts for infractions related to substance abuse (such as driving while intoxicated), the court may require a determination of which group members need further treatment, such as intermediate care or even detoxification. The group leader must, therefore, be knowledgeable about available treatment options and criteria for referral. Professionals in the field should be aware of the constitutional issues involved in mandated referrals to self-help groups with religious implications (Luff 1989). In line with this concern, the agency's referral network should include not only the familiar "anonymous" fellowships for alcoholics, narcotics abusers, overeaters, and so on, but also newer, more purely secular approaches such as that of Rational Recovery (Trimpey 1989).

The variety of examples mentioned in this section suggests the range of resources—medical, therapeutic, educational, and practical—to be included in the leader's and the agency's referral network. They run the gamut from vocational counseling to diagnostic screening (such as AIDS testing). It is the group leader's responsibility to know about such community resources and to know how to find out about those in specialized fields. Clearly, a diverse network of professional contacts can enhance the leader's effectiveness in this aspect of group work.

## Postgroup Follow-up

After the group is over, the real work begins. Continuity of involvement among group members, as well as between members and leader, can be desirable and valuable, provided it reinforces and builds upon what has been done in group. In termination, the leader outlines the types of follow-up contact that are appropriate and feasible, and group members arrange for follow-up with the leader and with one another. Such follow-up is a form of quality assurance for both member and leader, revealing how change is unfolding on an ongoing basis.

## Review Sessions

Ideally, it would be beneficial to have the group meet for a follow-up session three to six months after termination, as recommended by Corey and Corey (1987), to get feedback on members' implementation of their plans, monitor the achievement of goals, and share feelings of accomplishment or frustration. Usually, however, group follow-up sessions are not feasible either for open-ended groups, which have no fixed membership or end point, or for mandated groups, in which the motivation to return tends to be absent. Such sessions may be welcomed, however, by the more highly motivated members of voluntary groups—for example, those concerned with love relationships.

In lieu of follow-up sessions for the whole group, ongoing personal contacts among group members can provide a support network that survives termination. As noted previously, this informal support network can be used to facilitate problem solving. Where possible, the leader can encourage voluntary subgroups of the original group to hold review sessions at their own initiative. These sessions would have an agenda similar to that of the group as a whole: sharing, progress reports, feedback, further planning, and accountability. The agenda is to be set by the participants (with guidance from the leader if requested). It should not be any more rigid and programmed than the group itself was; if anything, there is even more emphasis on spontaneity and creativity. For instance, the numerous termination and postgroup exercises presented by Corey and Corey (1987) might be used (if at all) in a selective, discriminating way and might best serve to stimulate group members to devise their own exercises. Among those exercises, the one that comes closest to continuing group process is one in which members break into smaller groups to review the group experience; they describe what they have learned about themselves, about group process (for example, factors that facilitate or inhibit a group's functioning), and about the rewards gained from taking risks.

## Individual Activities to Reinforce Learning

As one moves from an environmental support system to a self-support system, it is helpful to have tools that one can use on one's own, without having to be in contact with the leader or group. For example, some people whose lives have been disorganized or unmanageable learn to discipline themselves by keeping a journal in which they write down their thoughts, goals, and aspirations. A postgroup journal, which can be treated as a continuation of the group journal described in chapter 3, is more focused than a diary. It marks high and low points in a person's daily life and records how the person goes about meeting the four basic needs identified by reality therapy: (1) relationships and belonging; (2) self-esteem, power, and control; (3) fun and recreation; (4) freedom and choices. (These basic needs are discussed in chapter 5.)

A variation on the journal is the *weekly inventory*, given out by the leader at termination, which consists of questions for the person to answer at the end of each week. The following questions fit easily on an 8½- by 11-inch sheet of paper, with enough space below each question to write in an answer:

1. What was the high point of the week?
2. Whom did you get to know better this week?
3. What was the major thing you learned about yourself this week?
4. Did you institute any major changes in your life this week?
5. How could this week have been better?
6. What did you procrastinate about this week?
7. Identify three choices you made this week.
8. Did you make any plans this week for some future event?
9. What unfinished personal business do you have left from this last week? How long have you been carrying it? How long do you plan to carry it?
10. Open comment:

Different clinicians (see, for instance, Silverstein 1977) have their own versions of the inventory, which can be modified as desired to fit the needs of a particular kind of group. The inventory is a useful adjunct to group process because it "asks relevant here-now questions, highlights the need for plan-making, allows for no excuses, and gives a person something to look forward to" (Silverstein 1977, 92).

Another tool for self-assessment and value clarification is the *life-planning board*, which helps a person identify issues of concern and prioritize goals, either in a particular area of life or in relation to one of the four basic needs. This is how we have presented this exercise to people who are dealing with job-related crises or frustrations:

A person is given a blank piece of 8½ by 11″ paper and asked to tear it into 12 parts. On each of the first 11 sheets the person writes one of the common frustrations in the help-giving fields, as dictated by the person administering the exercise. The 12th sheet is left blank as a "Wild Card." Here the person can call attention to any issue not covered in the standard list. After rearranging the slips of paper so as to rank the 12 items in order of importance, the person then describes how he or she experiences each of the 12 frustrations. (Edelwich and Brodsky 1980, 111)

For job burnout, we have used this list of items (with one removed to leave room for a wild card):

- Not enough money
- Too many hours
- Career dead end
- Can't measure success
- Powerlessness
- No support for important decisions
- Bad office politics
- System not responsive to clients' needs
- Not appreciated by supervisor
- Not appreciated by clients
- Too much paperwork
- Not sufficiently trained for job

The wild card enables people to call attention, in their own words, to issues that matter to them. For example, some items regularly brought up in the job burnout exercise are sexism, administrative dilemmas, bad personal image, lack of community awareness and support, and disappointment with peers (Edelwich and Brodsky 1980).

As a postgroup exercise, the life-planning board is used to identify and clarify issues, perhaps in an area that the person did not process in group or one in which the person has reached a higher level of actualization (thus creating a new set of issues) since the group ended. The leader, tailoring the items to the person's needs, gives the person the exercise to take home at termination or sends it to the person after a follow-up call. For example, for the question "What are you looking for in a permanent love relationship?" the following items might be used:

- Physical attraction
- Intelligence
- Commonality of interests
- Sense of humor

- Sensitivity to needs
- Good sex partner
- Successful career
- Free of addictions
- Good communication
- Same religion and commitment
- Would make good parent

*Postgroup Contacts*

In maintaining postgroup contacts with members, the leader treads a thin line between indulging excessive dependency and missing an opportunity to provide strategic support whose value may far exceed the time invested. Ongoing involvement after termination represents a statement by the leader that "even though you're no longer in the group, we still keep you in mind." Suitable contacts include checking on how the member has followed through on recommendations and referrals, occasional requests for support made by the member on the telephone, and occasional one-to-one follow-up sessions if feasible (that is, if not ruled out by limitations on the leader's time). If a member checks back for support in appropriate ways, the leader might acknowledge a continuing relationship by sending a Christmas or birthday card (but not a Valentine!). The leader might even send each member a card the first Christmas after the group has ended; subsequent contacts would depend on the response to this initiative. (For further discussion of the limits of appropriate contacts between helping professionals and clients, see Edelwich and Brodsky [1991].)

Postgroup contacts are not only for therapeutic benefits, but also to evaluate the effectiveness of the group. A tool that serves both purposes is a brief questionnaire sent to former group members about six months after termination. If it were sent much earlier, the recipients might still feel coerced and, in any case, would not have had sufficient time to consolidate and implement their learning. How would they know immediately after the end of the group how much it had benefited them? They would know better when they had a chance to apply their learning out in the world. In addition, coerced members who believed that their fate was contingent on the group leader's recommendation might be less than completely honest. At no time is a high response rate to be expected from coerced members. However, the leader may glean some useful feedback from the responses that do come back.

The questionnaire, sent as a letter from the group leader, should be limited to one or two pages and may include questions such as the following:

- What were your expectations when you came into the group?
- In what ways were those expectations realistic?
- In what ways were they unrealistic?
- What did you like about the group?
- What didn't you like?
- How did you use the group?
- What have you put into practice that you learned in the group?
- How did the group help you?
- Did the group meet your needs?
    If so, how?
    If not, why not?

This evaluation is not a popularity contest. It is an attempt to get real feedback, an expression of continued caring and connection, and a way of refocusing the former member on the goals of the group. Group counseling is designed to be a positive experience, even if it takes six months or a year for the member to view it as such. Although we do not aim to please the customer at the time and at all costs, we are working in the customer's interest.

While striving to keep some ex-members connected to the group experience, the leader simultaneously may need to help others separate from it. A person's desire for continued attachment—whether by demanding frequent contacts with the leader and other group members or by reenrolling for another group—does not necessarily signify that such attachment is in the person's best interest. Certainly it is a positive development, up to a point, for a coerced member to decide that groups are not so bad after all. It is, however, the leader's responsibility not to be seduced by this flattering outcome, but to be clear about why the person is showing this degree of attachment and whose needs are being met. If the person is avoiding new challenges by socializing with a now familiar and reassuring group of people ("Oh, I really like groups"), that is not the purpose of the group. At that point, the leader ceases to be a facilitator and starts to be a guru. The leader must resist being cast in this role and instead act in the long-term interest of the client.

A person who is looking for intimate bonds would do better with a referral to Parents Without Partners, a church group, or a group that helps its members face the practical and emotional challenges of dating. A person who seeks out frequent group meetings as an alternative to substance abuse should be referred to a mutual-support fellowship organized for that purpose. A person who appears to be looking for ways to fill time might be referred to a volunteer charitable or public-interest organization. By calling upon other social networks or support systems when needed, the group leader maintains the integrity of group counseling and prevents its primary purposes from being obscured.

## Measuring Success

Some people, even in coerced groups, make dramatic changes in their lives; others are untouched by the experience. They comply, pay lip service, and express gratitude, but there is no real acceptance. In any given group, the latter outcome probably is more common. Group leaders must come to terms with these incomplete results, and with any "expectations versus limitations gap" of their own, as part of their termination process. For this as well as other reasons, it is advisable for coleaders to meet after a group ends to put the history of the group in perspective.

As a rule, group leaders are held accountable not for client outcomes (such as recidivism), but for the skill, sensitivity, and ethics with which they conduct the process. This policy accurately reflects the limited influence one group can be expected to have on a member's life. If the leader does nothing more than establish a relationship so that a person who gets in trouble again will at least call back, that is a significant accomplishment, and it is not brought about by being punitive or coming across as an extension of the courts or other referring agency.

To evaluate their own outcomes with the same human understanding they are trained to show toward group members, group leaders can keep in mind the following precepts, which are discussed in more detail in Edelwich and Brodsky (1980) and, in the case of the third item, in chapter 6 of this book:

- *Set realistic goals.* You are bound to be disappointed if you think that your agency's mission is to save the world.
- *Focus on the successes, not the failures.* No one can help everybody. Think about the one case where your efforts have made a difference, not the many that were beyond your control.
- *Focus on the process, not the result.* You are responsible for how you exercise your skills (itself an essential source of satisfaction), not for whether a person responds or circumstances cooperate.
- *Keep a time perspective.* It takes more than a few weeks for significant, long-term personal change to occur.
- *Do not interpret results self-referentially.* It takes many people and events to bring about change. You may not have had much to do with

some of the successes you see, and you may not be around to see some that your intervention made possible.

An experienced group leader tells the people he trains, "If someone asks your profession, you can say you are a farmer. If you plant the seeds well, they may bear fruit in benefits that others down the line will harvest."

# References

The Augustine Fellowship. 1986. *Sex and love addicts anonymous*. Boston: The Augustine Fellowship, Sex and Love Addicts Anonymous.

Beattie, M. 1987. *Codependent no more: How to stop controlling others and start caring for yourself*. New York: Harper/Hazelden.

Berne, E. 1985. *Games people play*. New York: Ballantine.

Carnes, P. 1986. *Counseling the sexual addict*. Minneapolis: CompCare.

Corey, M. S., and G. Corey. 1987. *Groups: Process and practice*. 3d ed. Monterey, CA: Brooks/Cole.

Cox, W. M., ed. 1987. *Treatment and prevention of alcohol problems: A resource manual*. Orlando, FL: Academic Press.

DiClemente, C. C., and J. O. Prochaska. 1985. Processes and stages of self-change: Coping and competence in smoking behavior change. In *Coping and substance use*, ed. S. Shiffman and T.A. Wills, 319–343. Orlando, FL: Academic Press.

Edelwich, J., and A. Brodsky. 1980. *Burnout: Stages of disillusionment in the helping professions*. New York: Human Sciences Press.

———. 1986. *Diabetes: Caring for your emotions as well as your health*. Reading, MA: Addison-Wesley.

———. 1991. *Sexual dilemmas for the helping professional*. Rev. ed. New York: Brunner/Mazel.

Ellis, A., and R. A. Harper. 1975. *A new guide to rational living*. N. Hollywood, CA: Wilshire.

Gelles, R. J., and M. A. Straus. 1988. *Intimate violence: the causes and consequences of abuse in the American family*. New York: Simon & Schuster.

Glasser, W. 1965. *Reality therapy*. New York: Harper & Row.

———. 1985. *Control theory*. Scranton, PA: Harper Collins.

Goleman, D. 1989. New studies finding many myths about mourning. *New York Times*, 8 August, C1, C6.

Hester, R. K., and W. R. Miller, eds. 1989. *Handbook of alcoholism treatment approaches: Effective alternatives*. New York: Pergamon Press.

Ludwig, A. M. 1985. Cognitive processes associated with "spontaneous" recovery from alcoholism. *Journal of Studies on Alcohol* 46:53–58.

Luff, E. 1989. The first amendment and drug/alcohol treatment programs: To what extent may coerced treatment programs attempt to alter beliefs relating to ultimate concerns and self concept? In *Drug policy 1989–1990: A reformer's catalog,* ed. A. S. Trebach and K. B. Zeese, 262–266. Washington: Drug Policy Foundation.

Marlatt, G. A., and J. R. Gordon, eds. 1985. *Relapse prevention: Maintenance strategies in the treatment of addictive behaviors.* New York: Guilford.

Monti, P., D. Abrams, R. Kadden, and N. Cooney. 1989. *Treating alcohol dependence: Treatment manual for practitioners.* New York: Guilford.

Neidigh, L. W., E. L. Gesten, and S. Shiffman. 1988. Coping with the temptation to drink. *Addictive Behaviors* 13:1–9.

Norwood, R. 1985. *Women who love too much.* Los Angeles: J. P. Tarcher.

Peele, S. 1989. *Diseasing of America: Addiction treatment out of control.* Lexington, MA: Lexington Books.

Peele, S., and A. Brodsky. 1976. *Love and addiction.* New York: New American Library.

Peele, S., A. Brodsky, and M. Arnold. 1991. *The truth about addiction and recovery: The Life Process Program for outgrowing destructive habits.* New York: Simon & Schuster.

Prochaska, J. O., and C. C. DiClemente. 1985. Common processes of self-change in smoking, weight control, and psychological distress. In *Coping and substance use,* ed. S. Shiffman and T. A. Wills, 345–363. Orlando, FL: Academic Press.

Sanchez-Craig, M., D. A. Wilkinson, and K. Walker. 1987. Theory and methods for secondary prevention of alcohol problems: A cognitively based approach. In *Treatment and prevention of alcohol problems: a resource manual,* ed. W. M. Cox, 287–331. Orlando, FL: Academic Press.

Schappell, E. 1989. In rehab with the love junkies. *Mademoiselle* October, 217, 252–253.

Seligman, M. E. P. 1975. *Helplessness: On depression, development, and death.* San Francisco: W. H. Freeman.

Shiffman, S. 1985. Coping with temptations to smoke. In *Coping and substance use,* ed. S. Shiffman and T. A. Wills, 223–242. Orlando, FL: Academic Press.

Shiffman, S., and T. A. Wills, eds. 1985. *Coping and substance use.* Orlando, FL: Academic Press.

Shupe, A., W. A. Stacey, and L. R. Hazlewood. 1987. *Violent men, violent couples.* Lexington, MA: Lexington Books.

Silverstein, L. M. 1977. *Consider the alternative.* Minneapolis: CompCare.

Silverstein, L. M., J. Edelwich, D. Flanagan, and A. Brodsky. 1981. *High on life: A story of addiction and recovery.* Middletown, CT: Jerry Edelwich, New England Association of Reality Therapy.

Trimpey, J. 1989. *Rational recovery from alcoholism: The small book.* Lotus, CA: Lotus Press.

Wolf, S. 1974–75. Counseling—for better or worse. *Alcohol Health and Research World* (Winter):27–29.

Yalom, I. D. 1985. *The theory and practice of group psychotherapy.* 3d ed. New York: Basic Books.

# Index

# About the Authors

**Jerry Edelwich,** MSW, CISW, is assistant professor of drug and alcohol rehabilitation counseling at Manchester Community College, Manchester, Connecticut. He is director of the New England Association of Reality Therapy. Together with Archie Brodsky, he has coauthored *Burnout: Stages of Disillusionment in the Helping Professions* (1980), *High on Life: A Story of Addiction and Recovery* (1981), *Diabetes: Caring for Your Emotions as Well as Your Health* (1986), and *Sexual Dilemmas for the Helping Professional* (1991).

Edelwich, who received his MSW degree from the University of Connecticut, has served as a clinical supervisor or consultant for the U.S. Navy, correctional and youth services agencies, and other clinical and training facilities. He presents workshops throughout the world on individual and group counseling skills, staff burnout, client-clinician sexual dynamics, human sexuality, professional ethics, and drug and alcohol rehabilitation. He has conducted training sessions in clinical supervision for the National Association of Alcoholism and Drug Abuse Counselors (NAADAC). He is a member of the New England Association of Specialists in Group Work.

**Archie Brodsky,** a professional writer, is senior research associate at the Program in Psychiatry and the Law, Massachusetts Mental Health Center, Harvard Medical School. In addition to the books he has written with Jerry Edelwich, he is coauthor of *Love and Addiction* (1975), *If This Is Love, Why Do I Feel So Insecure?* (1989), *Medical Choices, Medical Chances* (1990), *The Truth About Addiction and Recovery* (1991), and *Decision Making in Psychiatry and the Law* (1991). He also has coauthored numerous journal articles.